THE PIRANDELLIAN MODE
IN SPANISH LITERATURE

The Pirandellian Mode in Spanish Literature From Cervantes to Sastre

WILMA NEWBERRY

State University of New York Press Albany
1973

The Pirandellian Mode in Spanish Literature from Cervantes to Sastre

First Edition

Published by State University of New York Press
99 Washington Avenue, Albany, New York 12210

Printed in the United States of America

Library of Congress Cataloging in Publication Data

Newberry, Wilma, 1927–
  The Pirandellian mode in Spanish literature from
Cervantes to Sastre

  Bibliography: p.
  1. Spanish literature—History and criticism.
2. Pirandello, Luigi, 1867–1936—Influence. I. Title.
PQ6045.N4   860'.9   77-171181
ISBN 0-87395-089-5

CONTENTS

PREFACE

This study is the result of my admiration for the genius of Luigi Pirandello and an awareness of relevant connections between his ideas and the literature of Spain. My initial idea was to undertake the study of Pirandellian influences on twentieth-century Spanish playwrights; however, from the beginning it was apparent that the differences between Pirandello and the Spaniards who have been attracted to his themes are significant. Many Spanish writers combine such borrowings from abroad with similar ideas already present in the Spanish tradition. My investigation thus led me in ever-widening circles until ultimately my project expanded to include constant themes and techniques, beginning with Cervantes, which can be associated with Pirandello. My hope in writing the present work, then, is to make a contribution to Pirandellian-Spanish studies by examining a corpus of material through Pirandellian "eyes" in order to reveal certain consistent patterns in Spanish literature.

ACKNOWLEDGMENTS

I am extremely grateful to Dr. E. Carole Brown, who helped me rewrite and revise the entire manuscript, and to Mrs. Margaret A. Mirabelli of State University of New York Press for her valuable editorial assistance. I also wish to thank the Research Foundation of State University of New York for two summer grants for research in Italy and Spain. And, finally, I acknowledge with thanks permission to reprint the following chapters which originally appeared in somewhat different forms as articles: "The Influence of Pirandello in Two Plays of Manuel and Antonio Machado," *Hispania,* May 1965, "Echegaray and Pirandello," *PMLA,* 81, 1966 (© 1966 The Modern Language Association of America), "Pirandello and Azorín," *Italica,* March 1967, "Luca de Tena, Pirandello, and the Spanish Tradition," *Hispania,* May 1967, "A Pirandellian Trilogy by Jacinto Grau," *Forum Italicum,* December 1967, "Aesthetic Distance in García Lorca's 'El Público': Pirandello and Ortega," *Hispanic Review,* April 1969, "Cubism and Pre-Pirandellism in Gómez de la Serna," *Comparative Literature,* Winter 1969, and "Pirandellism in the Plays of Pedro Salinas," *Symposium,* Spring 1971.

INTRODUCTION

The great impact Pirandello made on the twentieth-century theater is predicated on the fact that Pirandellian themes need not be limited to a particular genre or epoch; the thematic breadth of the Italian writer's work links him to the literature of all time. Pirandello's thematic impact, however, is inextricably connected to his innovative theatrical techniques. For example, through such devices as the physical transplantation of an actor from the stage into the assembly of spectators, Pirandello obliterated the distinctions between the realms of fiction and life and abolished the traditional distance that existed between the stage and the audience. The physicality of such technical devices complements Pirandello's thematic insights, which reveal the impossibility of separating such opposites as illusion and reality, fiction and life, or madness and sanity. The term *Pirandellian* then, identifies a concept which synthesizes physical and ideational variations on the theme of the interplay of illusion and reality.

Spanish literature has, since Cervantes, been absorbed with themes which later interested Pirandello. Don Quijote, for example, is a hybrid of complexities which intrigued the Italian: he is guided by illusion, is neither clearly mad nor completely sane, is unable to perceive the boundary between fiction and reality, and is constantly confusing the reader and his fellow characters about his real nature. Calderón, Lope de Vega, Ramón de la Cruz, Tamayo y Baus, Echegaray, and Galdós also either use techniques remarkably similar to those of Pirandello or anticipate his philosophy. Probably the most surprising discovery is how Ramón de la Cruz's often neglected *sainetes* come to life when considered in a Pirandellian framework.

Contemporary with Pirandello but independent of him, two

Spaniards reacted to twentieth-century influences in much the same way as did Pirandello. Ramón Gómez de la Serna's *El teatro en soledad,* examined from a cubist point of view, reveals how painting techniques can be translated into theatrical terms and at the same time is a true precursor of *Sei personaggi in cerca d'autore.* It is with Miguel de Unamuno, however, that we find the Spaniard who is most closely attuned to the more profound aspects of Pirandello's art and whose attitudes most nearly approximate those of the Italian.

The Spanish writers who adapted Pirandello's actual techniques and ideas are never servile imitators. They developed his innovations in their own way and actually rejected as much as they accepted from him. These authors generally worked out of a strong national tradition into which Pirandellian themes were easily assimilated. Pirandello's influence is direct and acknowledged in Azorín, the Machados, and Luca de Tena. García Lorca, Grau, Casona, Salinas, and certain contemporary playwrights show similarities in themes and techniques which are partly due to direct influence, but which might also be attributed to what Unamuno called "algo que flota en el ambiente." For the contemporary period in particular, the Pirandellian approach is basic, for it provides a common ground for discussing lesser known plays as well as the more famous works. Very few general studies have been written about the twentieth-century Spanish theater, so the present work not only reveals the Pirandellian aspects of the contemporary period, but it also attempts to examine more fully the productions of twentieth-century playwrights.

❦ Part 1
Pirandellism Without Pirandello

❦ 1 ❦
MIGUEL DE CERVANTES

In Cervantes, the line between fiction and reality is constantly wavering, one situation which reveals the overlapping and confusion of reality and fiction seems to generate another. These effects, unbounded by country or epoch, certainly influenced Pirandello, who was familiar with *El Quijote*. Very soon after Pirandello's plays became popular, Américo Castro noticed certain close resemblances in how Cervantes and Pirandello interpret art and life,[1] and since then comparisons between the two writers have been made frequently.

Don Quijote cannot distinguish between fictional heroes and historical characters, and it soon becomes obvious that in a book both appear to exist on the same plane and both are more truly alive than is any living man whose deeds are unrecorded. This realization seems to tempt the author to secure a special type of immortality by mentioning himself in the work of art and thus placing himself on the same level of reality as his characters. Pirandello does this in *Sei personaggi in cerca d'autore,* and there are several occasions in *El Quijote* when Cervantes introduces himself into his own novel. During the book-burning episode, for example, *La Galatea* is saved, and the priest says that Cervantes is a great friend of his. Later Cervantes alludes to his captivity in Algiers when one of the characters tells about a Spanish soldier named "tal de Saavedra"[2] whose exploits during his attempts to escape will remain in the memory of the people of that region for many years.

In the second part of the novel when Sancho realizes that he is a character in a book, he remarks that people may say whatever they wish about him because it is worth any price to be in books and go from hand to hand. This observation reminds Don Quijote of similar cases, such as when a courtesan complained to a poet be-

cause she had not been included in his malicious satire against
"damas cortesanas" and insisted that he remedy this oversight, after
which she was satisfied "por verse con fama, aunque infame"
(5:152). Don Quijote also gives several examples of people who
have been motivated to commit crimes by the desire to perpetuate
themselves as historical characters.

When the author and other real men take on some fictional traits,
it seems natural for the reverse to take place, for the fictional characters to become more human by becoming at least partly autonomous. In certain episodes, especially in the second part of the novel,
Don Quijote is conscious of his nature as a character in a book. But
even in the first part, it is possible to picture Don Quijote in search
of an author when he imagines how the writer will describe his first
sally and recites the high-flown sentences in the true novel-of-chivalry
style which he hopes the wise man will use. Don Quijote envies the
future epoch in which the stories of his feats will merit remem-
brance, and he exhorts his future chronicler not to forget Rocinante.

There is an interesting moment in which Don Quijote suggests
that the author not only records the action but also influences it.
After Sancho spontaneously calls Don Quijote "El caballero de la
triste figura" for the first time, Don Quijote asks him why he has
done so. Sancho replies that it just occurred to him that his master
had "la más mala figura, de poco acá, que jamás he visto" (2:115).
However, Don Quijote tells him that the true reason is that the wise
man in charge of writing his history must have thought that it
would be well for Don Quijote to take a descriptive appellation as
did all knights in the past and therefore he must have suggested to
Sancho the notion of calling Don Quijote the Knight of the Sad
Countenance.

In the second part of the novel, when Cervantes permits his
characters to be fully conscious of their appearance in a book, Sancho
excitedly reports to his master that Sansón Carrasco says that his
history was published under the title of *El Ingenioso Hidalgo don
Quijote de La Mancha*. Sancho further relates that he himself as
well as Dulcinea appear and that even things which happened when
they were alone are discussed, "que me hice cruces de espantado
cómo las pudo saber el historiador que las escribió" (5:66). Américo
Castro believes that a basic similarity between Cervantes and Pirandello is that both make their characters conscious of their fictional
natures. "Conviene aislar bien este tema del personaje consciente de
su existencia dentro de la obra de arte." [3]

In both *El Quijote* and *Sei personaggi in cerca d'autore* the characters wish to be presented as they really are. Sancho and Don Quijote worry that the author may not tell things as they actually happened, which anticipates the father and stepdaughter's insistence in *Sei personaggi* that events be represented on the stage exactly as they were experienced. Don Quijote fears that if the author is his enemy he may have distorted the facts, mixing truth and falsehood and telling things which have nothing to do with the story. In a manner which suggests the father's complaint in *Six Characters,* Sancho expresses his fear that the author will misinterpret and overemphasize his bad characteristics.

Don Quijote's relationship with his author reveals a facet of his character not usually associated with the unselfish chivalric knight. In his assertion of self before his author, Don Quijote shows himself to be almost more egocentric than are Pirandello's six characters or Unamuno's Augusto Pérez. He complains that the author should not have wasted time with the interpolated stories in the first part of the novel, but rather should have dedicated himself completely to Don Quijote's own feats:

> Y no sé yo qué le movió al autor á valerse de novelas y cuentos ajenos, habiendo tanto que escribir en los míos . . . Pues en verdad que en solo manifestar mis pensamientos, mis sospiros, mis lágrimas, mis buenos deseos y mis acometimientos pudiera hacer un volumen mayor, ó tan grande, que el que pueden hacer todas las obras del Tostado. [5:78]

The lengthy conversation about the first part of the book takes place before anything has happened to furnish material for a continuation of the story. But Don Quijote asks if the writer promises a second part, and Sansón answers that as soon as the author finds the continuation of the story for which he is searching he will deliver it to the printing press. Sancho is concerned about the author's financial motivation, for he realizes that commercial purpose does not often inspire great literary creations. He understands that their future adventures are the material of the story and promises that he and his master will give the author enough adventures to compose one hundred more parts.

In addition to discussing the first part of their adventures, they express great annoyance that Avellaneda has audaciously written a spurious part of *Don Quijote de la Mancha*. Perhaps the appearance of this book accentuated Cervantes' feeling that the characters were part of himself, as it was probably a traumatic experience to read a poor imitation which distorted the personalities of his characters. Besides criticizing the spurious *Quijote* bitterly, Cervantes completed his revenge by causing one of Avellaneda's characters to become autonomous, appear in the second part of his own novel, and turn against his original author. In fact, he is even made to sign a declaration that the Don Quijote who appeared in Avellaneda's novel was not the real one.

The vision of life as an intermingling of illusion and reality can suggest a theatrical metaphor, that life is theater or that theater may be a part of life. From the moment the first innkeeper decides that he is dealing with a madman and humors Don Quijote in order to amuse himself, the knight's fantasies begin to alter reality, and his fellow characters become actors who must improvise in part according to Don Quijote's *scenario*.

Sancho soon learns that when Don Quijote asks him to carry out impossible tasks it is in his best interests to distort reality in order to avoid punishment. Sancho is responsible for Don Quijote's belief that Dulcinea has been changed into a farm girl by the wicked magician who is pursuing him, because he assures Don Quijote that the girl is Dulcinea and is beautiful.

The most persistent provider of chivalric material is Sansón Carrasco, who desires to help his friend and goes forth dressed as a knight determined to defeat Don Quijote and force him to return home in order to be cured. Dorotea, a young lady who is travelling in search of her lover, agrees to play the part of a Doncella Andante in order to lure Don Quijote back to his village. She invents a story in which she is a damsel in distress. She begs Don Quijote to follow her back to her country in order to help her, but before they arrive, his friends decide that it would be simpler to convince him that he is enchanted and carry him back to his village in a cage. So in the course of the novel, Don Quijote actually finds himself in many situations which occurred in books of chivalry.

Eventually the people who are trying to help Don Quijote do irreparable harm to him, a situation which Pirandello later develops in *Enrico IV* where well-meaning persons damage the hero when they try to cure him by their own unscientific methods. Often in the adventures Cervantes created the deceivers themselves are beguiled or confused, showing that it is impossible to control fiction or to isolate it from reality.

The most elaborate conscious alteration of reality occurs in the second part of the novel when the duke and duchess, being acquainted with Don Quijote as a character in the first part of the novel, decide to provide a setting in which Don Quijote's version of reality does not clash with his surroundings. The duke and duchess instruct their courtiers and servants to treat Don Quijote as if he were a knight, and in a *commedia dell'arte* fashion the servants enthusiastically invent scenes that the duke and duchess could not have anticipated. They are successful enough to reinforce Don Quijote's madness: he states that this is the first time he has really believed himself to be a true knight errant and not a fantastic one.

Frequently, as later in Pirandello, the situation gets out of hand and life enters into the farce. When the servants send cats into Don Quijote's room, the animals become uncontrollable and injure him, showing that life cannot be held in check by the intentions of the drama. When Don Quijote is about to fight a duel with a man who will not marry the woman he dishonored, the man runs away. The duke and duchess do not want to cancel the duel, so they send a substitute. However, life intervenes—the substitute falls in love with the lady, wishes to marry her, and thus removes the necessity to fight.

One of the most famous cases where Don Quijote does not recognize the separation between theater and life is in the Maese Pedro episode. Thinking the play is reality, Don Quijote charges the stage to help Melisandra and in doing so destroys all of the puppets. Even later when he partially recognizes his error by paying for the puppets, he will not reimburse Maese Pedro for the doll which represents Melisandra because he believes Melisandra is safe in France. During the puppet show Don Quijote's frequent interruptions underline the fact that he cannot recognize the boundary between art and life which should exist in a well-organized world.

The puppeteer, Maese Pedro, also known as Ginés de Pasamonte, has many roles in the novel. His first appearance is as a prisoner whom Don Quijote frees. He is also an author because he has written his autobiography and intends to continue the project. As the creator of puppet plays, he is a type of director and shares Don Quijote's ability to occupy simultaneously several levels of reality.

Don Quijote himself is a shifting combination of character, actor, and creator. When he begins his adventures he is consciously imitating the actions and words of a legendary chivalric knight. He refuses to do anything which he has not read about in these books.

For example, he does not wish to give Sancho wages because he knows of no knight who ever paid his squire. The best example of Don Quijote as actor occurs in Sierra Morena before he sends Sancho on his mission to speak to Dulcinea. Don Quijote wants Sancho to tell Dulcinea how unhappy her knight is because of the jealousy which he imagines. So before Sancho leaves, Don Quijote performs for him: "Que quiero imitar á Amadís, haciendo aquí del desesperado, del sandio y del furioso, por imitar juntamente al valiente don Roldán cuando halló en una fuente las señales de que Angélica la Bella había cometido vileza con Medoro; de cuya pesadumbre se volvió loco" (2:290). At times it seems that the madman is playing the madman: "Loco soy, loco he de ser hasta tanto que tú vuelvas con la respuesta de una carta que contigo pienso enviar á mi señora Dulcinea" (2:292). He even seems like a stage director for his own performance, saying that it is now necessary for him to tear his clothing, scatter his weapons, and knock his head against the rocks. At the same time he insists that his actions are authentic: "Todas estas cosas que hago no son de burlas, sino muy de veras; porque de otra manera, sería contravenir á las órdenes de caballería, que nos mandan que no digamos mentira alguna, pena de relasos, y el hacer una cosa por otra lo mesmo es que mentir" (2:300).

The ambiguity in Dulcinea's personality is in keeping with the blurring of reality in *El Quijote*. At the beginning of the novel it seems that Dulcinea is merely a girl who serves as the point of departure for Don Quijote's imaginings. However, later Don Quijote clearly becomes Dulcinea's creator when he states that he imagines everything that he says is so and that he paints her in his imagination as he wishes her to be. When the duchess suggests that Dulcinea is a product of Quijote's creative imagination, a "dama fantástica" whom he has painted with all the charm and perfection he wishes, the knight answers that only God knows whether or not there is a Dulcinea in the world, or whether she is a product of fantasy. He further says that matters of this type should not be investigated completely, an attitude we can compare to Pirandello's in *Così è (se vi pare)* when the neighbors' inquiry does not lead to a solution of the mystery.

Although to a lesser extent than other Pirandellian characteristics, there is also a sort of spectator or reader participation. The most interesting example of this is when Cervantes includes the marginal note attributed to Cide Hamete Benengeli which questions the authenticity of the Cave of Montesinos adventure. In this citation Cide Hamete lists all the facts at his disposal but refuses to make a decision about the matter, preferring that the reader decide for himself.

Don Quijote's madness is a fluctuating element of the novel. He is quite reasonable unless chivalry is involved, so the confusion arises from his appearance of sanity until something happens to catapult him into the world of chivalric adventure. Reading novels of chivalry has induced signs of madness even before Quijote goes to the extreme of actually undertaking knightly adventures, but eventually his mania affects everyone around him, and at times Sancho seems even more insane than his master.

As in Pirandello's *Enrico IV,* a very tenuous boundary exists between sanity and insanity as well as between reality and fantasy. The characters are puzzled about Don Quijote whose lucid discussions make them question their judgment that he is insane. At times Don Quijote even talks sanely about his insanity. A gentleman whom he meets on the way to Barcelona, after hearing Don Quijote speak about his adventures, sums up the impression which Don Quijote often makes: "Aquí le tenían por discreto, y allí se les deslizaba por mentecato, sin saber determinarse qué grado le darían entre la discreción y la locura" (8:89).

Just as illusion often appears preferable to reality, so madness is sometimes better than sanity, as Don Antonio realizes when he says that he hopes God may pardon them for the harm they have done to everyone in attempting to return sanity to the most *gracioso* insane man in the world. He asks them if they do not understand that Don Quijote's sanity cannot contribute to the world as much as his insanity.

Pirandello often focuses attention backstage in order to reveal the inner workings of the theater which are usually hidden from public view. Cervantes takes the readers behind the scenes with a similar purpose when Don Quijote visits a printing press and calls attention to the process and material from which books are made. Don Quijote arrives when they are printing the spurious *Quijote,* and translations are discussed.

Américo Castro emphasizes the fundamental innovation of *Sei personaggi in cerca d'autore* when he says that in contrast to traditional writings in which everything was completed, we now watch the formation of artistic materials; we go underground where the roots are. When we are reading a traditional novel, he says, we

are not aware of the scaffolding, but "este Pirandello nos obliga a
estar viendo el cuadro y juntamente la paleta y pinceles con que
se pinta. Y no sabemos qué nos interesa en mayor grado." [4]

The materials of creation and the self-conscious artist are especially important at the end of the *Quijote* when Cide Hamete
Benengeli addresses his pen, but throughout there is a consciousness of the presence of the author and the problems of artistic
creation.

At the beginning of the book Cervantes seems unclear about what
position he will maintain as author in *El Quijote;* this emerges,
however, as he writes. He begins the knight's adventures as a
simple narration, but very soon he mentions that he is using written
records and that the authors who write about Don Quijote do not
agree on some points. In chapter eight, in the middle of an adventure, we learn that the author has broken off writing because he
has not found the document which contains the continuation of
this episode and Don Quijote's other deeds. Then, before he continues the adventure, he tells how he finds the manuscript in Arabic
written by Cide Hamete Benengeli and explains how he arranged
for its translation. He makes the whole foundation of the novel
somewhat unstable because he plants doubt about the honesty of
the Arab, but the author later changes his attitude, saying that Cide
Hamete Benengeli was very exact and was worthy of other historians' emulation.

Of course this ambiguity is compounded when Don Quijote
thinks about his future author, calls him a wise enchanter, and gives
him suggestions about the novel, but in the first part of the book a
clear separation must be made between Don Quijote's idea of his
author and Cervantes's pretense that a series of authors is involved.
There is a significant juxtaposition of Don Quijote's sincere, though
mistaken, impression that a wizard author is hovering over him,
and Cervantes's contrivances to give his novel the aura of reality by
his false assertion that he is merely transmitting information contained in the files of La Mancha. In the second part of the book
after Don Quijote learns that Cide Hamete Benengeli is responsible
for the novel, he must acknowledge the existence of this author who
is also an invention, although a more prosaic one, than is his *sabio
encantador.*

By one method or another throughout the book Cervantes calls
attention to the process of creating a novel. For example, the characters discuss Cide Hamete Benengeli, the translator intervenes to

state that one part of the novel seems apocryphal to him, and Cide Hamete Benengeli himself enters emotionally into his own book, such as when he states that he would like to suppress part of the story because it does not seem believable, but he decides against this. Finally, at one point, Cide Hamete Benengeli even discusses his artistic problems and complains about having embarked on a story with so few characters.

Pirandello's 1908 essay *L'umorismo* attests to a thoughtful reading of Cervantes's great book. Several themes in *El Quijote* which Pirandello analyzes in this essay are similar to those with which he himself was identified after he became famous as a playwright. Foreshadowing attitudes that many of his own characters have who live so completely immersed in their own version of reality that objective truth becomes unimportant, Pirandello states that Don Quijote does not pretend to believe, as does Ariosto, in the marvellous world of chivalric legends, but that he *really* believes in it; he internalizes it and it is his reality, his reason for existence.

Don Quijote, says the future author of *Così è (se vi pare)*, knows that the windmills are windmills, but they are also giants. Cervantes's hero has not changed the giants into windmills; on the contrary, the magician Frestón has changed the windmills into giants. "Ecco la leggenda nella realtà evidente,"[5] remarks Pirandello.

Pirandello would like to know who Don Quijote is and why he is considered mad. He thinks Don Quijote was really born in Alcalá de Henares in 1547 and grew out of Cervantes's own unhappy experience in trying to be a hero. He repeats the Spaniard's statement that he has created someone who resembles him.

In *L'umorismo,* also, Pirandello discusses the autonomous character which later became so important in his own work. He states that when a poet really succeeds in giving life to a character, he lives independently from his author, to the extent that he can be imagined in situations which are different from those in which the author has placed him, and he can be seen acting according to the intimate laws of his own life, laws which not even the author would be able to violate. Pirandello imagines an author-character interview taking place while Cervantes was in prison in which Cervantes witnesses a discussion between the Cid, who was fortunate enough to be born at a time when his heroic talents were appropriate, and Don Quijote, who lived outside of time in a legendary world. This imagined opportunity for the author to communicate with autonomous characters anticipates Pirandello's treatment of the subject in *La tragedia d'un personaggio* and *Colloqui coi personaggi*. Many years later, when Pirandello wrote *Sei personaggi in cerca d'autore*, Cervantes was still on his mind because he mentioned Sancho Panza as one example of a character who will never die, unlike the author who is simply the instrument of creation.

Although *El Quijote* best lends itself to comparison with Pirandello's writings, Cervantes's plays also use techniques not unlike those of the Italian. For example, in *Pedro de Urdemalas*, Pedro, who during his life takes the roles of worker, blind man, gypsy, hermit, and student, in the last act decides that acting will be his permanent profession, because the roles he performs on the stage will give him, in a permanent framework, the variety he needs in his life. Actors in this comedy discuss the rehearsal for the play which they will perform before the king. Pedro explains to the author the characteristics which he thinks a good actor should have and why he believes he is well qualified for the profession. The *Alguacil de las comedias* also appears on the stage. Pedro tells Isabel, the girl brought up with the gypsies and then discovered to be of noble birth, that the difference between their fates is that her dream will be carried out in the real world and his on the stage. Pedro will be king when there is one in the play, but she is a queen both legally and because she deserves to be one.

At the end of *La gran sultana*, Madrigal, a character very similar to Pedro because of his ingenuity in deceiving people throughout the play, states his intention to write a comedy about "La gran sultana" and to give himself the same role he has in life, thereby very cleverly turning life into art and then into life again.

In *El rufián dichoso*, the second act opens with a conversation between Comedia and Curiosidad which Cervantes uses to explain why contemporary theater does not employ classical techniques. Among other things, Comedia explains the new attitude toward unity of time in order to justify the fact that the play's protagonist spends the first act in Sevilla and the second in Mexico.

Los baños de Argel centers on a frequently interrupted *coloquio pastoril* being recited for Christian captives. An improvised introduction, intended to annoy the Moor who is present, precedes the *coloquio*, the *sacristán* breaks the actors' progress, and the entry of a wounded Christian completely disrupts the skit as the hero remarks:

> Acabense nuestras fiestas
> cessen nuestros regozijos

que siempre en tragedia acaban
las comedias de cautiuos.[6]

In *La entretenida* Cardenio pretends to be da Silva, Marcela's cousin and fiancé who comes from Peru to marry her. There is also a play-within-the-play when, during a party, servants perform an *entremés* which they have written. Ocaña and Torrente play themselves in the performance and, after reciting the memorized lines for a while with several interjections by one of the authors to show approval of his handiwork, they draw away from the script and play out their real rivalry for the love of Cristina, much to the consternation of the author who does not recognize his words. Ocaña and Torrente apparently wound each other badly; a real *alguacil* runs in thinking that his services are needed, but is soon informed that he is dealing with a comedy and not a tragedy. The play-within-the-play is particularly interesting in this drama because Cardenio pretends he is Marcela's fiancé, until the arrival of the real fiancé destroys his pretense.

Although the *género chico* later employed many Pirandellian techniques, Cervantes's *entremeses* contain no Pirandellism of this type. While social satire rather than consideration of the nature of illusion is uppermost in Cervantes's mind, one *entremés, El retablo de las maravillas,* does involve the interplay of fiction and reality. In an inversion of a traditional legend which Cervantes probably had read in *El Conde Lucanor* and which the modern reader would know best in the version Andersen told in *The Emperor's New Clothes,* the charlatans are not unmasked when the truth is stated. However, this is only an apparent triumph of illusion over reality because even though the people involved have not seen the show which was described to them, they must continue to pretend that they have witnessed it in order to prove their purity of blood.

Although Cervantes's plays utilize certain theater-within-the-theater techniques, his masterpiece is far more deeply in tune with Pirandello's works. And despite the many Spaniards whose works would anticipate Pirandello or who would later actually be influenced by him, Don Quijote remains the most Pirandellian character in Spanish literature.

FROM LOPE DE VEGA TO GALDÓS

A survey of Spanish literature from the beginning of the seventeenth to the end of the nineteenth century reveals that Spanish writers were often attracted to themes and techniques which Pirandello has made so captivating in the twentieth century. For example, in the Spanish theater of the Golden Age, Lope de Vega's *Lo fingido verdadero* (written sometime between 1604 and 1618) leaves the boundary between art and life unclearly defined. The confusion results from Lope's particular handling of the play-within-the-play technique and perhaps the best way to demonstrate Lope's intent is to contrast *Lo fingido verdadero* with another play, Shakespeare's *Hamlet* (1602), which, while employing the same technique of interior drama, is not characterized by the overlapping of fiction and life. In *Hamlet* the play-within-the-play is based on the life of Hamlet's family and is intended to have an impact on life, but there is no doubt where the play ends and life begins. Ophelia remarks that Hamlet functions as a Greek chorus when he explains the circumstances of the interior play. In *Lo fingido verdadero* the play-within-the-play becomes confused with reality because the actors as real people are involved in the events. The spectators are uncomfortable because they do not know whether they are observing a play or a private conversation between the actors.

Lo fingido verdadero is based on the life of San Ginés, who was martyrized about A.D. 285. The play-within-the-play serves to portray the experience of a pagan actor who was converted to Christianity while reciting the lines of a Christian martyr. In addition to the two inner plays in the second and third acts, the first act reflects the *gran teatro del mundo* idea of life as a play in which a man's salvation depends upon his performance. While he is dying, Carino admits that he has been playing the role of king a very short time, and poorly at that.

In act 2 Ginés, who is actor, director, and author for his company, receives permission from the Emperor Diocletian to present his own play, a work which concerns the rivalry between Octavio and Ginés for Marcela's love. During her performance, the actress Marcela is confused because Ginés has gone beyond the script, she has no lines with which to answer him, and at one point she exclaims that she wishes the play were true. Octavio calls her by her real name, and the emperor and the other spectators are uneasy and suspect that the actors are representing the drama in their own lives. When Marcela and Octavio run away together, both in the play and in life, Ginés asks the emperor to order pursuit of the fleeing lovers, and the emperor, showing a very fine perception of the multiple possibilities involved answers:

> ¿Es esto representar
> y a la invención convenible,
> o quieres mostrar, Ginés,
> que con burlas semejantes
> nos haces representantes? [1]

In the third act, while Ginés is rehearsing, he finds himself going beyond the part that he had written—he asks for baptism although such a request is not in the original script and a voice tells him that he will be saved. Later an angel appears on the stage in place of the boy who was to have played the role, and Ginés asserts that he has learned his part from a book which the angel has shown to him. He says that he is a Christian and that his author is Christ. Furthermore, he states that in the second act the emperor's wrath is written, and in the third his own martyrdom. Diocletian asks: "¿Hablas de veras?" (p. 196) and when answered in the affirmative, says that he will play his own role in the drama and sentence Ginés to death. The play closes with the impalement of Ginés, who maintains that he is now a "cristiano representante," (p. 199) that the human comedy which is all nonsense is over, and that he is going to heaven.

Of course the supernatural machinery gives this play an added dimension in which even heavenly beings participate in the comedy. Fiction and reality overlap considerably, confusion is constant, and improvisation, spectator interventions, discussions of the actors' problems, and appearance of stagehands all contribute to make *Lo fingido verdadero* a true precursor of twentieth-century plays in which one cannot perceive the boundary between illusion and reality.

The religious implications found in comparing life with theater were exploited quite differently by Calderón in *El gran teatro del mundo* (c. 1633), an allegorical *auto sacramental*.[2] In this *auto* God is the *Autor* who assigns roles to men and then rewards or punishes them depending upon their performance. The word *Autor* here has the widest possible meaning, for it signifies Creator as well as manager-director of a theatrical company. The play which God's company will perform is obviously more in the *commedia dell'arte* than a written tradition. In several places Calderón's vocabulary suggests this is exactly his intention, for he uses *Ley* which not only means God's law but also the *scenario* for the *commedia dell'arte*. In addition the test consists of each actor's individual interpretation of his role. While each person has free will and may improvise as he sees fit, there is, as in the *commedia dell'arte,* an accepted way to respond even though the effect is that the actor ad-libs.

The World, who appears personified, is the stage and is also in charge of distributing the proper costume to each actor. Some of the performers are uneasy because they will not be able to rehearse; they will not even know when to appear on the stage (to be born) and when to leave (to die). The *Autor* tells them that they must not know beforehand when these things are to happen, but that they must always be ready to finish their roles. However, they will have a kind of prompter who later appears with a script as the Law personified and delivers the *Loa* which is the introduction to the performance. The Law's prompting is usually only one admonishment: "Obrar bien, que Dios es Dios."[3] When they perform the play-within-the-play the actors are conscious that they are playing roles, and at the end they are summoned one by one to leave the stage: "Al teatro pasad de las verdades, / que este el teatro es de las ficciones" (p. 117). The World takes away their costumes, making them all equal in death, and they then appear before the *Autor* who is at a table with chalice and host and wishes to know which of the ex-actors will dine with him. Those who did not perform well will be dismissed from his company.

Of course Calderón also treated the idea that life is like a play in his most famous drama *La vida es sueño* (1635): man's stay on earth is a brief performance the merits of which must decide his eternal punishment or reward. The matter is further complicated in *La vida es sueño* because Segismundo is not sure at the end of the play whether he is dreaming or awake. But he decides that even though his experience may have been illusory, he must act as if it were real, because he knows that his final destiny depends on his actions during his tenure as king.

Luis Vélez de Guevara also wrote a play with Pirandellian overtones, *El rey en su imaginación* (c. 1620), which deals with a king deprived of his birthright. Brought up as a wealthy farmer's son, Carlos has no reason to suspect that this is not his true social position. He becomes a soldier, and one day he is crowned a mock king in a game with his companions. As soon as they crown him he feels that he is a true king and acts like one. His friends think he has lost his mind and even consider trying to cure him, which is quite reminiscent of *El Quijote*. At the end of the play it is revealed that Carlos's compulsion to believe he is king is based on fact, for he and the woman who is now queen have been switched at birth. The theme of the play, then, that royal blood has a force of its own which cannot be hidden, is not Pirandellian, however, when Carlos pretends he is king while he has no reason whatsoever to think this may be true, he expresses an attitude worthy of certain Pirandellian characters. He realizes that everyone thinks that he is insane but he feels if insanity brings contentment it is justified.

Luis Vélez also achieves certain Pirandellian effects in the first act of his *La Baltasara* (c. 1635), which concerns an actress who feels the compulsion to abandon her career for a life of religious seclusion. The first act takes place in the theater before she has made her final decision. In the first scene a boy fastens to the wall the poster which announces the name of the play. Rodrigo and Alvaro, gentlemen who are fond of the theater and of the actresses, comment about Baltasara and the forthcoming performance. The play will begin soon, and the stage directions indicate that the troupe of actors, in different parts of the *patio* will appear as refreshment vendors. On the stage the spectator-actors converse to create the atmosphere of the theater before the performance begins. But voices are soon heard demanding to know why there is a delay. So the guitar players appear but then Saladino, who is the *autor,* asks the musicians why they have begun before Baltasara has arrived. At that moment the actress does come in and recites on horseback; however she is confused and delivers the lines which belong at the end of the play. Then there is an alternation between her own thoughts, the lines she is reciting from the play, and singing from within which supports Baltasara's new intention. Miguel, the *gracioso* and Baltasara's husband, asks that his wife be prompted. But she answers that it is not necessary to instruct her because she now realizes that the world is deceitful and there is something beyond this. She is determined to abandon the theater, and bids everyone farewell. The spectators do not know what is occurring—Don Alvaro, speaking from the balcony, begs her to reconsider her decision. "Spectators" in the *gradas* and in the *cazuela* comment, then Miguel, the *autor,* and the musicians come out and bemoan Baltasara's departure.

There are technical similarities in *La Baltasara* and *Ciascuno a suo modo* because the total environment of the theater is presented. Spectators talk among themselves, discussing the play and the actors, and then participate from the audience. Baltasara, unable to recite her lines, becomes confused and then apparently turns the play into a recital of her own problems. This agitates the manager-director and at the end of the first act we have the impression that a play isn't being performed at all.

Actors who converted to Christianity seemed to fascinate the playwrights of the Golden Age. Gerónimo Cáncer, Pedro Rosete, and Antonio Martínez collaborated in writing *El mejor representante, San Ginés,* which treats Ginés's conversion quite differently from the way Lope de Vega did.

In this version, which depicts a wider span of Ginés's life, when Ginés and Julio, soldiers in Diocletian's service, are told that the *autor* of a theatrical company needs a leading man and a *gracioso* they become interested, a tryout follows and the *autor* invites Ginés and Julio to join his company. Policarpo, a poet, reads the company his new play, entitled *El cristiano bautizado,* which disgusts Ginés because he despises Christians, but finally he agrees to play the role, and he does so well in rehearsals that word reaches the emperor, who demands to see the play the next day. When Ginés practices his lines he unconsciously begins to add words to his role, realizing only after he has uttered them that they are not in his script. When he is performing in the play-within-the-play he addresses Christ, telling Him that He well knows that the words being spoken come from Ginés's soul. Ginés falls silent and the emperor thinks he is acting: "O que bien aquel silencio / que los Christianos afectan / finge." [4] As in Lope de Vega's play, angels miraculously appear. Ginés changes his lines, saying that he is playing himself and loves Christ. The *autor* states that this is not in the script and asks Policarpo to prompt, but since Policarpo is also a Christian, he encourages Ginés to continue affirming his Christian faith. Ginés tells the emperor that he is really a Christian, that he has chosen a better company than his present one, and describes in theatrical terms certain biblical characters (David, for example, is the poet; Luke is the painter; Peter is the wardrobe master; and, of course, Christ is the *autor*).

Ginés also tells the emperor that the world is a theater and that although Diocletian is now Caesar, after death he will be forced to surrender his royal garments. Diocletian answers that since the world is a theater he will now perform with Ginés the scene of his justice. If Ginés doesn't change his mind, he will be martyred in the same amphitheater in which he was applauded before.

In quite a different way Tirso de Molina (1584–1648) combines fiction and reality in *Quien calla, otorga*. Like Cervantes in the second part of the *Quijote*, Tirso has his characters discuss the play *El castigo del penséque* to which *Quien calla, otorga* is the sequel. Chinchilla tells Rodrigo, who was the hero of the first play, that his reputation is ruined in Spain because of his actions in the previous play, and he is known as the "para poco." Chinchilla goes on to say:

> Hizo un diablo de un poeta
> de tu historia o tu desgracia,
> una comedia en Toledo,
> *El castigo,* intitulada,
> *del penséque,* que ha corrido
> por los teatros de España,
> Ciudades, villas y aldeas.[5]

Chinchilla says that when he saw the play in Guadalajara he became so angry that he almost knifed the actor who represented him. He tells Rodrigo that he will not be able to return to Spain unless he reforms, because he is so irrevocably identified with the character that they now call him Don Rodrigo del penséque. Later Chinchilla tells Rodrigo that there must be a second part of the *Penséque,* again breaking into the illusion of reality created by the play to remind the audience that Rodrigo and Chinchilla are characters in a play.

After the long period which separates Golden Age theater from modern theater Leandro Fernández de Moratín wrote *La comedia nueva* (1792), a play about a play. In this comedy Moratín satirized incompetent playwrights who have not taken the trouble to prepare themselves in the fundamentals of their trade. The action occurs in a café located next to the theater. In the first act Don Antonio and the waiter Pipí discuss the poets and their friends who are noisily celebrating upstairs in anticipation of the successful première that afternoon.

Don Eleuterio, the playwright, begins to compose a new *tonadilla* to be used the next day, illustrating Moratín's criticism that many playwrights do not realize that the production of art requires long, careful labor. Don Serapio, an ardent theater fan who encourages mediocrity, and Don Hermógenes, a ridiculous, pedantic man are partly responsible for Eleuterio's belief in his ability to write for the theater.

In act 2 the author, his family, and friends discuss the disputes between the two theatrical companies in Madrid. Agustina, Eleuterio's wife, tells her sister how her husband has assured his success in the theatrical world by becoming friendly with many of the people involved.

Antonio returns to the café to tell his friends that the theater is sold out and he cannot obtain a seat. The others then realize that because Don Hilario's watch had stopped they are missing the play. Don Pedro returns before long—he left the theater as soon as he realized that the play was worthless. It was also poorly received by the audience which almost demolished the theater in protest. Don Pedro then convinces Eleuterio that he should not continue writing for the stage.

Moratín's *La comedia nueva* led Ventura de la Vega to write a very interesting drama about the theater, *La crítica del sí de las niñas,* which was performed in 1848 on the twentieth anniversary of Moratín's death. It is one of the most entertaining plays which take one behind the scenes of the theatrical world, for Ventura de la Vega adopts characters in Moratín's plays, and the result has much in common with the lobby scene in *Ciascuno a suo modo.* Since Molière's name is often associated with Moratín's, it is quite appropriate for the title of Ventura's play in Moratín's honor to evoke Molière's *La Critique de l'École des Femmes.*

La crítica del sí de las niñas is supposed to be taking place in the lobby of the Teatro de la Cruz during and after the performance of *El sí de las niñas.* The ticket-taker and the servants who are waiting for their masters converse, and when the play is over the spectators come out. The first group of spectators includes Paquita, Don Carlos, and Don Diego from *El sí de las niñas.* Although Diego is somewhat like his namesake in Moratín's play, Paquita is exactly the opposite of Moratín's Paquita. She criticizes the submissiveness of the Paquita in the play she has just seen, and it is obvious that although her own father wants her to marry wealthy old Don Diego (as did Paquita's mother in Moratín's play), this new Paquita will not meekly obey her father's wishes. Carlos is also quite different from his Moratinian equivalent in that he is disloyal to Paquita, who is only one of his many lady friends. Ventura de la Vega, through the inquiry of one of his characters, tells why he has changed the fictional personages:

> ¿Dónde está el Moratín de nuestra época; que así como aquél pintó la tiranía paternal, y la educación monjil y gazmoña de su tiempo, nos enseñe el reverso de la medalla, la relajación de los lazos sociales, con la magia de aquel pincel que nadie después ha sabido manejar como aquel insigne poeta? [6]

The second group of characters is composed of the critics unchanged in character from Moratín's *La comedia nueva*. Hermógenes expresses the opinion that unlike Molière's characters, Moratín's are "retratos de circunstancias que murieron" and are not eternal types:

> "¿Quién es hoy don Eleuterio? ¿Quién es don Serapio? ¿Quién es don Hermógenes?" Don Pedro answers him: "¿Quién es don Eleuterio? El señor que habla mal de la comedia, porque no ponen en escena la suya. ¿Quién es don Serapio? El señor que repite como un eco lo que les oye a ustedes. ¿Quién es don Hermógenes? ¡Usted!" [p. 230]

Eleuterio criticizes his original author, Moratín, although he recognizes that he was "un hombre de alguna chispa" (p. 221). He explains how he would revise *El sí de las niñas* to conform to his own taste, which is for exaggerated romanticism. Another character shows how casual some spectators are about attending plays. That evening the Viscount has paid short visits to each of the theaters which are honoring Moratín, has read the news in the casino, and has mixed everything into a composite play, which is a synthesis of reality and illusion.

Another anniversary celebration inspired Ventura de la Vega to compose *Fantasía dramática para el aniversario de Lope de Vega* (1859). This consists of two parts, to be performed as the prologue and epilogue for Lope de Vega's *El premio del bien hablar*. The prologue takes place in the Corral de la Cruz in 1632 and shows several stagehands putting the finishing touches on a stage prepared for the performance of Lope's play while the *autor* is giving last-minute instructions. Lope de Vega arrives and converses about his plays with the *autor* and the actors, an opportunity Ventura de la Vega takes to praise Lope's work and to speculate about the problems involved in theatrical productions of Lope's time. One actor wonders if Lope could not change the end of the play and emergencies arise which threaten the cancellation of the performance. But Lope de Vega gives the actors their final instructions, the orchestra plays, and Lope's play is performed.

Ventura de la Vega's epilogue, which consists of Lope de Vega's horoscope, follows. Lope learns from a seer that a cloud will cover his star in the eighteenth century, but in the nineteenth his greatness will again be recognized. Lope is then told about the 1859 homage and asked if he would like to see the celebration. Lope falls asleep and is taken from the stage in his chair.

One of the best examples of a nineteenth-century play-within-the-play is Tamayo y Baus's *Un drama nuevo* (1867), which can also be compared to Lope de Vega's *Lo fingido verdadero* in that they are both plays about actors whose life and the play in which they are acting become indistinguishable.[7] Shakespeare appears in *Un drama nuevo* in the capacity of director and adviser to the actors. He shows at the beginning of the play an attitude toward his characters that Pirandello was to share when he explains to Yorick that he is in a hurry because "Aguárdanme en casa muchos altísimos personajes, que por el solo gusto de verme vienen desde el otro á este mundo." [8] Of course he is referring to historical characters and not fictive ones as does Pirandello in *La tragedia d'un personaggio*, but we do have here the idea of the author-character interview.

At the beginning of the play Yorick convinces Shakespeare to give him the role of the deceived husband in the new drama. Yorick is the company's comedian but has suddenly felt the urge to play a tragic role. His own wife, Alicia, will play the part of the unfaithful wife, and Edmundo, a young man with whom Yorick has a father-son relationship, will play the lover. We soon discover that Edmundo and Alicia are to have the roles which reflect their actual lives, because they love each other passionately and for Yorick's sake have been struggling to keep their love secret. They confessed their love for each other while they were playing the parts of Romeo and Juliet: "Animados por la llama de la hermosa ficción . . . Alicia: Unida á la llama de la ficción, la llama abrasadora de la verdad . . ." (p. 207). Shakespeare offers to help the young lovers resist temptation.

The villain of the piece turns out to be Walton, whom Yorick has deprived of the central role in the new play. Yorick, anxious to succeed in his role, practices the lines throughout the latter part of the first act, and when coming in on tiptoe behind his wife, suddenly recites the line "¡Tiemble la esposa infiel; tiemble!" (p. 213). She faints, asking for pardon and thus Yorick begins to suspect the truth. In the second act, which takes place the day of the new play's première, he agonizingly attempts to confirm his suspicion. Alicia faints again when Yorick confronts her with her infidelity, and Yorick suspects that the guilty man is Shakespeare. When the latter leaves with Alicia in order to help her back to her room, Yorick asks: "¿Se ha convertido la realidad de la vida en comedia maravillosa, cuyo desenlace no se puede prever?" (p. 242), but his suspicion of Shakespeare is soon dispelled.

The third act takes place backstage during the performance of the last act of the new play. The author and the *traspunte* are delighted about the audience's reaction, but Walton blanches every time he hears applause, which reinforces his desire to avenge himself. Since the information has fallen into his hands that Alicia and Edmundo intend to run away together after the play, and he has the evidence in a letter, the method of revenge is obvious. When Yorick comes backstage he seems more like Conde Octavio, whose part he is playing, than himself. Walton tells him that he has proof of Alicia's infidelity and Yorick wants to see it immediately, but Alicia won't give it to him and in the struggle Walton obtains it. At the same time the *traspunte*, the author of *El drama nuevo*, and Shakespeare are frantic, because it is time for Yorick to return to the stage and he refuses to go without having obtained the letter first. But Walton tells him he will give it to him later, and the *traspunte*, the author, and Shakespeare finally persuade him to go back on stage—there has even been a break in the play because of this trouble. Shakespeare threatens violence to obtain the letter, so just before going on stage Walton gives him the stage letter.

The second part of the third act is the play-within-the-play, recited in verse. The actors are on the stage and the prompter is in his shell. Soon Walton gives Yorick, instead of the stage letter, the letter which Edmundo has written to Alicia. The play and life coalesce; lines from the script mix with spontaneous exclamations. The prompter frantically tries to correct the actors—he even lifts his head above the shell, taps with the script on the edge of the stage, and prompts in a very loud voice. Yorick soon falls into a chair, unable to go on, but the prompter insists, and Yorick then recites the words of the comedy which express his own feelings. As Tamayo y Baus explains in the stage directions:

> Yorick, cediendo á la fuerza de las circunstancias, y no pudiendo dominar su indignación y cólera, hace suya la situación ficticia de la comedia, y dice á Edmundo como propias las palabras del personaje que representa. Desde este momento, la ficción dramática queda convertida en viva realidad, y, tanto en Yorick como en Alicia y en Edmundo, se verán confundidos en una sola entidad el personaje de invención y la persona verdadera. [pp. 277-78]

Yorick takes down two swords and tells Edmundo to select one. Edmundo is about to kill himself with his sword, but Yorick announces his intention to kill Alicia with the other and, still using the words of the play, Edmundo rushes to defend her, Yorick struggles, and Edmundo falls mortally wounded. When Alicia sees his blood, the play-within-the-play ends, as she calls for help from Shakespeare. The author, the *traspunte,* and all the actors and employees of the theater come onto the stage surrounding Edmundo. Alicia asks Yorick to kill her now. He insists that she be still, but he cannot prevent her from embracing her dead lover.

Shakespeare addresses himself to the public to explain that the play which was being performed cannot be finished because Yorick, carried away by his enthusiasm, has really wounded the actor who plays the part of Manfredo. He also informs the spectators that Walton has just been killed in the street, apparently by his adversary in a duel. He asks the audience to pray for the dead and also for the murderers.

The technique of this play certainly anticipates Pirandello's theater-within-the-theater trilogy. The plot involves the real lives of actors; prompters, the author, and the director (Shakespeare) have very important roles; and at the end stagehands come onto the stage. When Shakespeare speaks to the audience the barrier between art and life disappears.

A change in genre moves the discussion from the drama to a consideration of certain novels by Benito Pérez Galdós. The strange way in which this author has handled certain characters and the manner in which illusion and reality overlap in *El amigo Manso* (1882) and *Misericordia* (1897) certainly suggest Pirandellian tendencies.[9]

The protagonist of *El amigo Manso* aggressively affirms that he does not exist, and that if it is necessary he will call in witnesses to support this assertion. He is a "condensación artística, diabólica hechura del pensamiento humano,"[10] and he explains how he is able to speak even though he does not have a voice, and how he is writing these lines which will become a book, even though he has no hands. He appears to be a man, he says, because someone summoned him and through certain subtle arts makes him seem like a living person.

He explains that he has a novelist friend who has already written thirty volumes and has begged Manso to help him with the next volume. The novelist knows that Manso has an agreeable and easy topic and has offered to buy it from him for words, ideas, emotions, and glue with which to put them all together.

The protagonist is confused about the exact method which the writer has used to turn him into a character: "Creo que me zambulló en una gota de tinta; que dió fuego a un papel; que después fuego, tinta y yo fuimos metidos y bien meneados en una redomita que olía detestablemente a pez, azufre y otras drogas infernales" (p. 1166). A little later he came out of a red flame converted into mortal flesh, and pain told him that he was a man. At the end of the novel he dies, apparently because his story is over. The same perverse friend who brought him into the world takes him out of it with witchcraftlike actions. The peace he feels makes him realize that he is no longer a man.

The rest of the novel seems quite traditional although, as Robert Russell points out, in the case of two of the protagonists, Irene and Manuel, it seems that Manso imagines them to be one way and they turn out another, and thus the author within the novel, Manso, is unable to control his characters.[11]

Máximo Manso certainly may be considered a precursor of Unamuno's Augusto Pérez and Pirandello's six characters in that he is aware of his nature as a fictional personage. He is also reminiscent of Don Quijote whom Galdós mentions several times. Although the unusual presentation of Máximo Manso gives him a place in the family of autonomous characters, unlike most of them he is not committed to his fictional identity, and there is no conflict between creator and character. In fact, the author-character relationship in *El amigo Manso* is quite pleasant. Manso gives the author a subject for the novel as a favor to him, and when his task is over he quietly goes to Limbo, relieved to be out of the world in which men suffer.[12]

One of the most interesting examples of a world in which reality and illusion overlap and often cannot be distinguished is in Galdós's *Misericordia*. The characters live in the most abject poverty, and illusion alone gives them dignity and allows them to hope for a better future. For example, Obdulia at times "da en figurarse cosas buenas. Más vale así. Es de las que se creen todo lo que fabrican ellas mismas en su cabeza. De este modo, son felices cuando debieran ser desgraciadas." [13]

Frasquito Ponte, Obdulia's friend, is even poorer than she but in compensation his imaginative power is greater. Galdós believes that the ability to separate oneself from reality in order to imagine a beautiful and happy existence is an inexhaustible wealth.

Almudena, the blind beggar, claims that he knows a magic process which will make Benina wealthy. She listens to him avidly: "Y si a pie juntillas no le creía, se dejaba ganar y seducir de la ingenua poesía del relato, pensando que si aquello no era verdad, debía serlo. ¡Qué consuelo para los miserables poder creer tan lindos cuentos!" (p. 1910). Benina's greatest adventure in the field of the imagination is that she elaborately lies about the existence of a benefactor, Don Romualdo, to conceal the fact that she must beg in order to put food on her proud mistress's table. But even Benina, always completely conscious that she is prevaricating, almost begins to believe her own falsehood: "Encaminóse a San Sebastián, pensando por el camino en don Romualdo y su familia, pues de tanto hablar de aquellos señores, y de tanto comentarlos y describirlos, había llegado a creer en su existencia." But she soon stops herself in her imaginings: "No hay más don Romualdo que el pordioseo bendito" (p. 1929).

However, Doña Paca, Benina's mistress, even dreams that Don Romualdo announces to her that she has received an inheritance. Benina, somewhat dismayed, nevertheless explains to her: "Los sueños, los sueños, digan lo que quieran, son también de Dios: ¿y quién va a saber lo que es verdad y lo que es mentira?" (p. 1936).

The coalescence of reality and fantasy seemingly becomes complete when Don Romualdo actually appears to announce that an inheritance has been left to Paca. When Benina discovers that Don Romualdo really exists she is completely disoriented: "Lo real y lo imaginario se revolvían y entrelazaban en su cerebro" (p. 1951). To make matters more confusing, Don Romualdo is very similar to the man whom Benina has fabricated. She even feels the impulse to seek him out to tell him, "Señor don Romualdo, perdóneme si *le he inventado*. Yo creí que no había mal en esto" (p. 1960). She would also like to ask him if he is *her* Don Romualdo or another. As it turns out, although the person of Don Romualdo seems to Benina exactly like the man she has invented, certain other details involving his family and life are entirely different. Although Benina is quite confused for a while because her invention seems to have come to life, she finally concludes that this Don Romualdo is not the product of her imagination: "Y ya estoy segura, después de mucho cavilar, que no es el don Romualdo que yo inventé, sino otro que se parece a él como se parecen dos gotas de agua. Inventa una cosas que luego salen verdad, o las verdades, antes de ser verdades, un suponer, han sido mentiras muy gordas" (p. 1991).

Paca even begins to doubt the nature of Benina, because it comes to light that Benina is a beggar, and this does not concur with Paca's idea of her. She asks Don Romualdo to ignore "las *Beninas* figuradas que puedan salir por ahí, y se atenga a la propia y legítima *Nina;* a la que va de asistenta a su casa de usted todas las mañanas, recibiendo allí tantos beneficios, como los he recibido yo por conducto de ella" (p. 1968). So there is an interesting inversion in Paca's mind: the "false" Don Romualdo turns out to be true, but his appearance unmasks Benina, and Paca, seeing only the superficial picture, is incapable of understanding that the Benina thus discovered is a much nobler woman than she could ever have imagined, so she insists upon clinging to the lie.

From the early seventeenth to the late nineteenth century both prominent and obscure Spanish writers employ themes and techniques which we associate with Pirandello in the twentieth century. During almost the same time span the writers of the *género chico* were also cultivating theater-within-the-theater devices. But since these short plays were so abundant and they show such a wide variety of Pirandellian techniques, the *entremeses* and *sainetes* will be the subject of an entire chapter.

RAMÓN DE LA CRUZ AND
THE *GÉNERO CHICO*

It would not be an exaggeration to state that in the Spanish *género chico* there are many examples of Pirandellian plays in embryo. These works fuse theater and life, the separation between actors and spectators disappears, and the process of forming the play becomes much more important than the plot; in fact, in many cases this process *is* the plot. Many of the traits present in Pirandello's most famous plays are found in the *entremeses* and *sainetes:* actors go into the audience, spectators (who are really actors, of course) intervene in the action of the play, and playwrights, manager-directors, actors, prompters, and stagehands are presented as themselves. In addition these short plays show the experiences of the actors in their private lives, the setting is often a rehearsal, and the audience is allowed to share the problems and crises which are part of theatrical life. Emilio Cotarelo remarks that some of Ramón de la Cruz's *sainetes* about theatrical customs seem to be so historically true that they sound like a report of something which really happened in the theater or to the actors rather than the product of the playwright's imagination. The fusion of art and life in several of Cruz's *sainetes* is so complete that they are inextricably bound to life; that is, they cannot be separated from the circumstances under which they were performed. *La cómica inocente* (1780), for example, a piece about an actress who is making her debut, depends for its very existence on the fact that the *sainete* was written expressly for the young actress who was to perform on this important occasion.

The majority of the works of the *género chico* may be classified as comedies or farces, and the destruction of aesthetic distance (see pp. 29–35 for a discussion of this phenomenon) is not so shocking to the audience when it occurs during this type of play as it is in a drama. As Fergusson points out, "comedy in any period assumes the presence of the audience."[1] But since these interludes were performed between the acts of a regular play, we must consider the possibility that the breakdown of distance which occurred in them may have contaminated the drama which they accompanied, especially when we recall that the actors who participated in the *entremeses* and *sainetes* were the same ones who took part in the plays, and in these interludes they often refer to the main play. The *Historia del teatro español* explains the result:

> Al terminar la primera jornada de la comedia se ejecutaba un entremés y luego una tonadilla; después la segunda jornada, seguida de un sainete y de una tonadilla; por último, la tercera jornada y un baile. Semejante falta de unidad destruía el efecto de las obras e imposibilitaba a los actores ponerse en situación. Como el tiempo apremiaba, no era extraño ver salir en el entremés al Alcalde de Polvoranca con montera de paño, guirindola de festón y coturno griego, según refiere Moratín.[2]

Thus the cumulative theatrical result of destroying the barrier between stage and audience may be very similar in Cruz's epoch and in the twentieth century.

Cotarelo traces Spanish plays about the theater from Agustín de Rojas through Quiñones de Benavente to Ramón de la Cruz. "Puede decirse que Rojas fué inventor y señaló el camino que luego habían de seguir Quiñones de Benavente, y en el siglo XVIII D. Ramón de la Cruz."[3]

One untitled *Loa,* published in *El viaje entretenido* in 1604, will serve as an example of Agustín de Rojas's work. It begins with a conversation between Rojas and Gómez in which Rojas criticizes the latter because he has the temerity to offer a performance to the Sevillians even though his company is inferior. Is this the way you thank Sevilla, he inquires, for all the favors she has done for you? Gómez admits that the company is imperfect, but the actors are humble, anxious to please, and novelties are always accepted. He asks Rojas if he would like to see the members of the company, and with this pretext introduces the actors, who each speak a few lines. They praise the city, and Sevilla, personified, welcomes them:

> Representar no temáis
> ni de mí desconfiéis,
> y ruego a Dios que ganéis
> todo cuanto deseáis.
> Yo a mis hijos pediré
> que os amparen y no ofendan.[4]

Asensio discusses the fusion of person and character in two anonymous *entremeses* published in 1609 where the actor Pedro Hernández is the title character:

> La fusión de persona y personaje, sea que el actor continúe su papel fuera del tablado, sea que lleve a las tablas su propia idiosincrasia, era favorecida por la improvisación. Pedro Hernández se ha incorporado al folklore.[5]

But it is Quiñones de Benavente who is a clear precursor of Pirandello within the boundaries of the *género chico*. This early seventeenth-century playwright, in his *jácaras* and *loas,* shows the *autor,* actors, prompter, ticket collector and wardrobe master on the stage in their own capacities. The frame which separates art from life is broken when actors recite from among the spectators in different parts of the theater, thereby making the audience conscious of its ability to intervene in the play. The theatrical people take the playgoers into their confidence and tell them about their problems in presenting the performance; emphasis is placed on the process of putting a play together, and Quiñones de Benavente wrote an *entremés* about a play. There is an effect of spontaneity, interruptions and mistakes have the purpose of convincing the audience that the *jácara* or *loa* has not been written in advance, and often doubt exists about whether the play has actually begun, as later in Cruz's *Soriano loco* and in Pirandello's *Questa sera si recita a soggetto*.

Hannah Bergman draws attention to the lack of theatrical illusion in Quiñones de Benavente's plays:

> Aun más notable es su negación sistemática de la ilusión teatral. El entremés nos recuerda constantemente que lo que vemos en las tablas no es vida sino teatro. El entremés tiene plena consciencia de su forma, de su función, de sus límites, aunque a veces los rechaza.[6]

The most interesting little plays by Quiñones de Benavente in which life and art interpenetrate are the *loas*. Bergman points out that they served the practical purpose of the now familiar printed programs. They describe the entertainment to be offered, introduce the actors, and, by showing informal scenes from the actors' lives, establish a close relationship with the audience. For example, the *Loa con que empezó Tomás Fernández en la corte* (1636) is a lively play which really seems to take the audience behind the scenes. In the first song the actors say how happy they are to be there and how wonderful Madrid and Madrilenians are. The *autor* (manager-director) speaks to the audience, and the actors and actresses identify themselves. Bartolomé Romero, for example, says that when he was *autor* he asked the favor of the audience for his whole company, but now that he is an actor he only asks for himself. Bernardo, the *gracioso,* interrupts his speech to scold his son, Juanico, who is playing on the stage. The *autor* tells about the plays his company is prepared to perform. When the *gracioso* again reprimands his son, the boy rebels and says that his father isn't the only one who can be a *gracioso* and appeals to the *autor* to listen to him. Then follows what may be termed a tryout. The *loa* ends with the other actors telling about themselves and offering to serve the public.

In Quiñones de Benavente's *Loa que representó Antonio de Prado* (1635), the *autor* complains that many of the best actors have left his company, and he pathetically adds that even his dog has run off. He wonders how he can serve the public with his remaining company. Frutos tells him to open the "eyes of his soul," and then there appears a tree on which are perched all the members of the company with guitars and lyres. According to the stage directions the trunk of the tree comes out of Prado's chest. The fact that he had been sleeping at the beginning of the *loa* makes the fantastic scene possible. The actors introduce themselves in a song from the tree. They then discuss the financial problems of the *autor* and it is revealed that he had to sell his wife's dresses in order to compete in Madrid. The musician remarks that Prado should not begin the season without having many *comedias* or his competitor will get ahead of him. The *autor* says that they have three new *comedias* by Calderón, and the *autora* adds that the first one which they will present is *No hay burlas con el amor.*

In the *Loa segunda, con que volvió Roque de Figueroa á empezar en Madrid* (1628) there is an effect of spontaneity. Roque, the *autor,* appears before the traditional opening music is played to tell the audience that he is very glad to be there. Bezón reprimands Roque for having come out before the music has played and even before the actors are ready. Roque protests that his desire to see the public was so strong that he didn't realize what he was doing and tells Bezón that nothing can be done about his untimely entrance and that they must go on from there.

> Pues ¿qué he de hacer?; ¿qué remedio
> pondremos porque no entiendan
> que hacemos lo que está hecho? [7]

They then plan what they will do to correct the error and decide how the program will proceed from there.

Almost all the playwrights wrote *entremeses* for Juan Rana, the most popular comic actor of the time. Certainly the most intriguing example from a Pirandellian point of view is *El triunfo de Juan Rana*,[8] whose author is unknown. After Juan Rana had been retired for many years, the royal family and the theatergoers wished to honor him in a *fiesta* at the Retiro. The actors bring him on in a triumphal chariot, but they say that it is not he but his statue because Juan Rana will not leave his home. Rana answers:

> ¿De suerte que aunque había presumido
> que era yo el que venía con tanto estruendo,
> soy mi estatua y no yo? Ya, ya lo entiendo.[9]

The droll situation, as Cesco Vian remarks, "culminava in questa splendida battuta . . . pirandelliana: 'Si yo estuviera aquí, ¡cuánto me holgara!' "[10]

The tradition established by Quiñones de Benavente and his precursors culminates in Ramón de la Cruz (1731–1794), a *sainetero* whose work includes approximately fifty short plays based on theatrical customs. These *sainetes* are the most completely developed short works which deal with the theater-within-the-theater theme, he wrote many more of them than did any other playwright, they are longer and treat many more aspects of the theme. Therefore, in discussing the *género chico*, Cruz's *sainetes* are the ones which allow for the most convincing use of the term pre-Pirandellian, not only because of technique, but in some cases even in cumulative effect and attitude.

Cruz's reputation as merely a superficial satirizer of his fellow countrymen's customs with emphasis on the popular and picturesque perhaps requires reexamination, because some of the *sainetes* which show the inner workings of the theater provide more than playful interludes. If we examine *Las resultas de las ferias,* one of Cruz's most interesting *sainetes,* we see that in addition to focusing on the playwright's problems and the material from which plays are made, we can also consider it a humoristic play in Pirandellian terms, for in it is expressed the *sentimento del contrario* which is integral to Pirandello's thought and which he analyzed in his essay *L'umorismo.*

Las resultas de las ferias (1773) opens with an animated street scene, in which one of the conversational themes, the tendency of Madrilenians toward prevarication, serves as superficial preparation for the subsequent philosophical dialogue which suggests that casual observation of human behavior does not reveal the essence of its meaning. Eusebio, the *autor* of a theatrical company, appears. As in all the plays Cruz wrote of this type, the *autor* really holds this position in the company which is performing the *sainete*. Eusebio tells his companion Merino that he is concerned because he does not have a new *sainete* with which to open the theatrical season, and his company will be in trouble if they use an old one: "Salga usted con cosa vieja, / y verá lo que le aguarda." [11] Merino and Eusebio ask a poet to write a *sainete* for them, but he replies that he is no longer writing for the theater "Por falta de ideas; pues no hay alguna / que hoy al público complazca" (2:393). Merino wonders how it is possible that as long as there is a world inhabited by men and women, their strange actions could fail to give material to the theater. The poet answers that he used to think the same thing, but now he sees the world in a different way, and he praises the prudence, modesty, and order with which people live. Merino thinks that the poet is being ironical, but when he says, "Cuidado, que a usted es preciso / entenderle a la contraria" (2:393), the poet denies that he is being insincere: "Lo digo como lo siento, / no hay ironía que valga" (2:393), and invites them to go with him to the plazuela de la Cebada where they will see all the virtues enthroned. Then, although they observe a number of people acting in ways which usually provide subjects for *sainetes,* the poet still refuses to recognize that these actions are reprehensible or hilarious. Merino pleads with him to observe a while longer, and the poet agrees but tells his friend that as soon as he reflects he will see that he is mistaken. After they have inquired into the true motives for the apparently unusual or ridiculous actions, the spectators change their initial impression of a situation. Everything, upon deeper inquiry and thought, turns out to be reasonable. Even an old man who spends his time and money courting young girls although he will not give his wife enough for household necessities is rejected by the poet as an object of ridicule. He explains that entertainment is necessary for man and each person has his own way of obtaining that enjoyment.

After another lively scene involving country girls and the men who are trying to gain their attention, Merino and Eusebio insist that the poet has ample themes for the *sainete,* but he is adamant in his refusal to write for the theater:

> Que todo esto es divertido
> natural; y mientras haya

ferias, modas y cortejos,
ha de haber extravagancias;
y no ha de haber quien las diga,
aunque hay tantos que las hagan.
Y está muy puesto en razón
que petimetres y damas
vivan, inventen y triunfen,
hasta ver en lo que acaba. [2:397]

Eusebio and Merino admit defeat and decide that during the following day's rehearsal they will see what can be done.

Las resultas de las ferias shares the quality of ambiguity with
other literature in which art and life overlap. Moreover, two additional facts must have further disoriented the eighteenth-century
spectator. In the first place, the part of the poet is played by Chinita,
who was the greatest *gracioso* of his time. His appearance on the
stage was enough to cause laughter even before he began to speak,
so it is quite possible that he may not have been believed in a serious
role. The other fact is that the *sainete* contains autobiographical
elements, for Cruz decided to retire as a playwright precisely because he was harshly criticized for mocking many types of people
in his popular, satirical plays. *El poeta aburrido,* which Cruz wrote
in the same year as the play under discussion, was intended to be
his farewell to the stage. Although the constant abuse and criticism
to which he was subjected may actually have caused Cruz to consider the deeper meaning of actions which appear to deserve
mockery, it is also possible that in *Las resultas de las ferias* he may
have been experimenting with a method of writing which would
permit him to criticize freely while maintaining that no criticism is
intended. In *Las resultas de las ferias* there are both situations which
upon close examination turn out to be inappropriate subjects for a
sainete, and others which could be used. The play shows scenes
from life about which the spectators must come to their own conclusions, and the last speech by the poet seems to suggest this approach. In any case, the play must have confused the spectators in
the same way as do other writings in which art and life coalesce.

The cumulative result certainly foreshadows Pirandello's "senti-
ment of the contrary." In his essay *L'umorismo,* Pirandello uses the
example of an old woman grotesquely painted and dressed in clothing appropriate for a much younger woman. She causes the casual
observer to laugh because her appearance is incongruous with her

age. But when the humorist reflects on the possible reasons why she
has adorned herself in this way, such as the desire to keep the affection of a husband who is younger than she, he arrives at the *sentimento del contrario,* which distinguishes a humorist from a comic
writer. As Oscar Büdel explains:

> Here now is the turning point for Pirandello: his reflective state
> of mind prohibits him from laughing any longer, because it has
> made him pass beyond this first notion of the contrary and
> penetrate more deeply into the issue. From a mere realization of
> the contrary (*avvertimento del contrario*), he has arrived at a
> sentiment, a feeling of the deeper issues involved (*sentimento
> del contrario*), and the result is a conflict of emotions.[12]

Before proceeding, we should consider certain conditions prevalent
in the Spanish theater which contributed to the production of those
plays where art and life interweave. In the first place, there were
many outstanding comic actors in Madrid at this time. In one of
Cruz's *sainetes* (*Todo el año es carnaval*) he tells how important one
such actor is.

> ¿Con que Chinita está malo?
> Pues sainete sin Chinita
> es hacer migas sin ajos;
> puches sin miel, y chorizos,
> sin pimiento colorado.[13]

The fans, who were aptly called *apasionados,* also idolized many
other actors. These actors provided a fine subject for the *sainetes,*
and Cruz wrote with specific actors in mind. In the *sainetes* which
belong to this group, the actors are indicated in the script by name,
whether they appear as themselves, as in the case of Eusebio in *Las
resultas de las ferias,* or when they were to play another part, as
when Chinita is addressed as Don Hilario in the same play.

Of course even when an actor appeared on the stage in the guise
of a character, the spectators probably still thought of him as himself.
In several cases this creates a comic effect. In *La comedia de
Valmojado,* for example, Espejo plays the part of a village official in
a town where the actors have gone to assist the villagers in the
performance of a play. Soriano, an actor from Madrid who plays
himself, remarks that he is sorry Espejo was unable to make the
trip to Valmojado. Espejo answers: "Es un grande majadero;/ pero
a mí me hace reir" (2:192). He is then asked to imitate Espejo, but

excuses himself, saying that he must dress for his part in the play.

The theatergoers attended often and did not appreciate reruns any more than present-day television addicts do. Thus there was pressure on the *saineteros*—and Cruz was by far the best among them—for a steady stream of new *sainetes*. The playwright's desperate activity has been documented, for he added a few words to the last page of one of his *sainetes*, "Sainete escrito en 7 horas para apestar en media." [14] After another he wrote, "Fin a las cuatro y diez minutos de esta mañana, 14 de febrero." [15] Thus themes which were close at hand must have been attractive to Cruz.

The actual *autor* frequently appears in the plays under discussion. This was possible because it seems that the manager-director came from the actors' ranks. In fact, one *sainete*, the *Loa* of 1772, begins with the violent dispute six actors have for the position.

The artistic impression Pirandello creates in many of his plays that the audience has begun to participate was much more within the realm of actuality in eighteenth-century Spanish theaters. The behavior of the audience was often shocking and seemed to fluctuate depending upon the amount of control exercised and the atmosphere set by the reigning monarch and his ministers. There were often disturbances in the theater, there were cases of spectators who became the center of attention, and the most enthusiastic theatergoers formed groups called *bandos* which actually had the power to participate in decisions about the programs which would be offered. [16]

Under the circumstances, then, a *sainete* such as *El pueblo quejoso* (1765), which contains many elements like those of *Ciascuno a suo modo*, for example, was not as surprising in the eighteenth century as it is in the twentieth. However, it is intriguing to observe many of Pirandello's techniques in miniature in Ramón de la Cruz, and the result produced is effectively the same as that of the Italian playwright. Considerable detail in summarizing *El pueblo quejoso* is necessary in order to transmit the flavor of this amusing little play. [17] As in most *sainetes*, the actors enter singing and dancing. Ramón de la Cruz whimsically remarks in the stage directions that they enter in this way because they are happy people and because the directions tell them to do so. Ayala appears, still only half-dressed for his role as a Moor, interrupting to complain because his companions are singing a song about him which he does not understand.

Ayala inquires about the roles of the others. Guzmana tells him that she has three, one of which she does in the *corral* dressed in her street clothing. Her other parts and those of her companion take place all over the world, in a true reaction against neoclassical drama. The *autora* comes out and angrily inquires why they are conversing on the stage. She tells the plot of the *sainete,* which involves the search for Ayala who, when he is finally found as a renegade in the Ottoman Empire, is tortured, and she says the *sainete* ends with a song. Ayala suggests that since it has ended they should go on with the third act of the *comedia,* but the other actors tell him they wish to continue with the *sainete.* He then delivers a long tirade in criticism of plays and asks the *autora* to look for better playwrights. She answers that she has searched and has consulted with well-known writers who tell her that the people only appreciate jokes and nonsense and that ideas bore them.

Ayala then turns to the spectators, asking how they feel about this. Spectators, really actors, of course, from different parts of the auditorium answer that this is not true, and one adds that if the actors will wait for them a moment this offense will be answered in public. Almost immediately the *autora* announces that two gentlemen from the *luneta* (the first rows of the theater) are in the dressing room

> con la rara
> pretensión de que en el teatro
> han de desmentir su infamia.[18]

They enter and subsequently two representatives each from four other sections of the theater appear on the stage to discuss the theater. The spectators occupy sections of the theater which correspond to their social class and sex, and when they appear on the stage the class distinctions are preserved by giving them chairs fitting their station in life, from gilded ones for the gentlemen to an overturned water bucket for the mason's helper.

The laborers express their opinions in music. In the *tonadilla* which Coronado (who plays one of the laborers) sings, he praises some of the actors, saying that people will attend the theater regardless of the program as long as Mariana, Guzmana, and Coronado sing certain favorite songs. At the end of the play the *autora* thanks the people and concludes that since there is no consensus among the spectators she will continue to offer a variety of entertainment.

El pueblo quejoso presents in embryonic form many Pirandellian elements—spectator participation, discussion of the play, disclosure of the inner mechanics of the theater, actors who appear as themselves, the manager-director in a central role which is particularly like that of Dr. Hinkfuss in *Questa sera si recita a soggetto,* and complaint about and criticism of everything connected with the theater.

Spectator interventions, both from the auditorium and on the stage, occur in other *sainetes* also, and an example can be seen in *El sainete para la comedia de las señoras* in which the actors, who are angry because the actresses are putting on a play without them, mock them from various parts of the theater. In the introduction to *La bella madre* the spectator-actor appearance seems to involve the real audience more completely than in any other case. The *autora* explains to the audience, using prose to give the effect of spontaneity, that the actors neglected their responsibility of providing a new *sainete.* She will ask the company to come out and "el patio les dará una corrección para que se enmienden" (1:138). When they appear, Nicolás says it was Chinita's fault, therefore he is the one who should be executed, but they cannot find him because he ran away as soon as he was threatened. "¡Qué muera!" they shout, and Chinita answers from the *tertulia,* where he is hidden, "Ya lo oigo" (1:138). They don't see him yet and wonder if he is in the *cazuela,* the section of the theater reserved for the women. Chinita then stands up in the *tertulia* where he had gone to look for a confessor after they threatened to kill him. This is the part of the theater where the priests customarily sat, so here there is something akin to real involvement of certain members of the audience. The actors solve the problem of not having a play, and Chinita, still in the *tertulia,* says he will come down to play his part.

La cómica inocente is another *sainete* which reverses the conventional viewer-actor relationship in order to draw the attention of the players toward the audience. Juanita, the new actress, says she has come on the stage to find peace because it is too noisy, dirty, and crowded backstage. She knits and sings to herself, and then, according to the stage directions, she may sing a *seguidilla* if she wishes in order to warm up for the *tonadilla* which she will sing later. Coronado, the *gracioso,* asks her why she is on the stage and inquires if she is not intimidated by all the men in the audience. Juanita's answer is that the men are far away and as long as Coronado and his companions do not cause laughter or anger, everyone is quiet. When she asks Coronado about different parts of the theater, he gives her a very interesting description of the seating arrangements, with pertinent remarks about the type of spectator who occupies each section.

In several cases Ramón de la Cruz obtains an effect similar to the one that would be found in Pirandello's trilogy, which causes the audience to have serious doubts about where the play begins and life ends. The stage directions for *Soriano loco* (1772) state that the actors should enter speaking in a natural way, uttering phrases of regret. An actress, pretending to be confused, protests that this is not the way today's *sainete* begins. But they continue their lamentations, and another actress inquires: "¿Es esto sainete, o qué es?" (2:271). An actor tells her that it is unlikely that they will be able to perform a *sainete* today or even the third act of the play unless Callejo is able to substitute. One actor suggests that at least the new actress could sing the *tonadilla,* but Polonia, who would ordinarily be the one to sing, objects. The *autor* comes out and two actresses request his permission to leave the company to return to their homes. Merino says that the actresses and the audience must be told what has happened, because, after all, the actors had begun the *sainete* without knowing about the misfortune, which is that Soriano has lost his mind, apparently because he has too many roles in too many plays and worries that a failure might reap him the "reward" of having eggplants or cucumbers thrown at him. Soriano appears and acts as if he really is insane, and Mariano inquires if it is the custom in Madrid to permit a rascal to ruin *sainetes* and delay the action of the plays. Soriano eventually regains his senses, and everything works out well, but the confusion about where life ends and the play begins is similar to that found in *Questa sera si recita a soggetto.*

El sainete interrumpido produces a similar impression, but in this case a regular *sainete* seems to be proceeding normally until, without warning, life jolts the play to a halt. Eusebio, in the company of others, rushes in and bemoans the disappearance of his child, who happens to be his real-life daughter, Mariquita. He wonders if she could have fallen asleep or fainted behind one of the flats. The actors who had been performing ask him what he is looking for and why he has interrupted their *sainete.* Eusebio explains, and the actors also become concerned over the girl's whereabouts. Other actors who had been searching in different parts of the auditorium report that she is not in the *cazuela,* nor in the *patio,* and certainly not in the *tertulia.* The *sainete* has been ruined by the interruption, and Mariquita won't be there to sing the *tonadilla* which was to have ended the interlude. Aldovera thinks he hears Mariquita under the stage, so they go out to continue the search. The result is the same as in Pirandello's *Ciascuno a suo modo,* where interruptions make it impossible to finish the play.

As has been pointed out in the discussion of *El Quijote,* the attempt to introduce life into the work of art may very easily suggest its opposite, that the whole world is a theater. In *Las damas finas* (1762) there is an excellent illustration of this possibility. Ladvenant asks Plasencia why he is putting on his cape, as it is six o'clock and the *sainete* is about to begin. Plasencia answers that the *sainete* should be rescheduled for four o'clock. They ask him what the *apasionados* will say if he doesn't go on, and Plasencia answers that when they know where he is going they will be the first to approve, for he is going to the Prado, where many *majos* are taking their afternoon strolls. Ponce says that because the *comedias* are being performed there won't be many people on the Prado, but Plasencia replies:

> Harán mal, porque allí, amigos,
> se ofrecen mejores lances
> que aquí, siendo cada uno
> del suyo representante. [1:68]

Ladvenant is of the opinion that the episodes from real life which might seem like theatrical scenes would be accidental and not formal *comedias.* Plasencia disagrees and in a picturesque passage describes in theatrical terms the action which takes place on the Prado.[19]

Ironically, Plasencia's point of view is shown to be correct in his own life, because the scene switches and it is revealed that the seven young ladies who have made Plasencia believe that he is the only man in their lives really have a number of suitors. First they are shown with their visitors, supposedly during the play when they think that Plasencia will not be visiting them, and then after the play when Plasencia arrives.

It is already obvious from the *sainetes* which have been described that there is considerable focus on the actors, the *autores,* and the playwrights. The prompter, who will be present in Pirandello's plays, is also given attention, especially in one *sainete, La comedia de maravillas.* This involves a play given in a home by an amateur group and, as in many other *sainetes,* the process of arranging for the production of the play is much more important than the plot of the play. Chinita takes the part of the prompter and in his first appearance comes out and asks the audience (within the play in this case and on the stage) if someone has a hat which the character actor may borrow. Later he asks to borrow a sword belt from a soldier. Finally the stage lights go on, the music starts, and Chinita "se pone a apuntar de modo que le vean" (1:302). Espejo, in an aside to Chinita, tells him to prompt louder. In the middle of one of Espejo's speeches Chinita swears because he has been burned by the candle he was holding. He drops the script and the candle, and by this time everyone is laughing. Espejo tells him to behave and a dispute develops. In this *sainete,* then, the prompter does not remain hidden as in a conventional play, but rather becomes the center of attention.

Even Pirandello's most impressive contribution, character autonomy, has its equivalent in the *sainetes.* In *La crítica,* which takes place in the rehearsal room in the *autor*'s home before all of the actors have arrived for rehearsal, a notary, a doctor, and a *petimetre* pay a visit to the *autor* Martínez. The notary says that his companions have sent them as their representatives to ask the *autor* not to portray them on the stage any longer. The doctor and the *petimetre* are also dissatisfied with the way the members of their groups have been treated on the stage, and their words show that their idea of what they are is far different from the satirist's impression. These people stand for types which have been criticized in the theater, and thus are not exactly comparable to Pirandello's six characters who are completely engrossed in their own intimate life. However, the concern Cruz's characters show about being misinterpreted on the stage is like the concern shown by Pirandello's characters.

In the next scene of *La crítica* four *majas* from four different sections of Madrid enter. They have been sent by their companions to demand that the *autor* stop representing *majos* and *majas* on the stage as low-class scamps. And they threaten reprisal: they will form four groups, and armed with cucumbers they will surround the theater, then:

> Sitiarán el tablado,
> y que á la triste *fegura*
> que remede maja ó majo
> sin mucha honra, le echarán
> de la escena á pepinazos. [2:83]

This resembles the Delia Morena episode in *Ciascuno a suo modo* when Delia goes backstage and slaps the face of the leading lady because obviously the play is based on Delia's life and she cannot endure to see her love experience acted out. Although the two plays are far apart in many ways, they both present people who rebel when they see themselves represented on the stage.

In *El poeta aburrido,* which is similar to *La crítica,* there are two unusual confrontations between characters and author. The poet, Don Justo, has come to the *autor*'s home to give him some new parts that he has written. Each of the actors asks if there is a part for him, but the poet answers that he doesn't know whether there is or not because,

> La idea sólo [lo sabe]; porque ella
> ha de elegir los actores
> más propios a sus escenas,
> alternando en el trabajo
> todos, según las ideas. [2:388]

The first part he has written is for an abbot who, without vocation or education, takes what belongs to another cleric, who is more useful to the church. At this point, Ponce suddenly appears, dressed as an abbot, and Granadina remarks that without a doubt it must have been the devil who told him to appear at such an opportune moment. The appearance of Madame Pace in *Sei personaggi in cerca d'autore,* which occurs after the stage has been carefully set so that she will be lured there to play her part, shares something with Ponce's entrance in *El poeta aburrido.*

Basically, almost all the *sainetes* which belong to this group derive their tension from and base their conflict on the very real problems which constantly faced Ramón de la Cruz and the companies of actors with which he worked. Probably there were situations very similar to those depicted in *La batida* and *La hostería de Ayala* in which an actor who has run away is pursued and brought back by the other members of his company. Also, when the *autor* and actors are depicted in *La feria de los poetas* as unsuccessfully trying to find a good play to purchase from a group of poets, we sense their real frustration. Another view of the problem is presented in *El casero burlado* where the *autor* is looking through reams of paper and books for a *sainete* which he may use. At the same time, Granadina is composing music and Chinita is writing poetry. The *autor* says he doubts if he can find a play which will satisfy the public. They ask Chinita what he is writing, and he answers that he is working on a *sainete,* and it may not turn out too badly, for he has stolen the idea.

The *autor* says that it is more difficult to write a *sainete* than it is to write a *comedia*. Chinita's *sainete* is short enough so that everyone will be able to endure it, the actors say. The foregoing is the brief introduction to an old *sainete* which was supposed to make this eighteenth-century rerun more palatable to the audience. Very frequently the substance of the *sainete* is that there is no new *sainete* for the day's performance and a way must be found to remedy the situation.

Cruz's most original description of the very difficult task which confronted theatrical companies appears in *El diablo autor aburrido*. In this *sainete* Chinita arrives on the stage mounted on a dragon. He is supposed to represent the devil, who is disconcerted because he has heard that Eusebio Rivera's company is in trouble. If the company disbands and the actors take up other ways of life as they plan to do, he'll lose business, because people of the theater often go to hell. So he appears at the theater in the form of Chinita who is absent that day because of illness. He takes with him four assistant devils who have adopted the forms of other actors who are also away. Eusebio Rivera gladly relinquishes the manager-directorship to him, but the devil soon discovers that the job is not as easy as he had anticipated, for there are far too many problems. The devil is exposed when a message arrives saying that Chinita will not be able to appear at the theater that day. The devil confesses and is relieved to escape from such an impossible situation. But his appearance has given the company their *sainete* for the day, as they will be able to turn their experience with the devil into a performance.

Even the *sainete* form has its equivalent in Pirandello's plays. The *intermezzi* which were part of the *commedia dell'arte* repertory are the Italian equivalent of *sainetes,* also known in different periods in Spain as *pasos* and *entremeses.* Pirandello's *intermezzi,* which appear between the acts of *Questa sera si recita a soggetto* and *Ciascuno a suo modo,* are more closely related to the main play than Cruz's are, but they have much in common with the *sainetes* in that they are a step closer to life than is the main play, and they are performed during the intermission.

After Ramón de la Cruz, one of his followers, Juan Ignacio González del Castillo (1763–1800), who worked in Cádiz as a prompter, wrote a *sainete* which deserves discussion as a curious manifestation of the interplay between auditorium and stage. At the beginning of *El desafío de la Vicenta,* Tiburcio appears on stage partly costumed for his role and is seen looking for a sword which he needs to complete his outfit. He leaves the stage and Vicenta comes out. She is angry because she does not have a part in the play and, seeing the script next to the prompter's shell, she tears it up and stamps on it. When the actors find the pieces of the script they say that there will be no comedy that day. They try to decide what to do and explain to the audience what has happened. The spectators in various parts of the auditorium insist that they be entertained: "Comedia ó morir." [20] There is an uproar, and Fermín, an actor dressed as an old lady, speaks from the *cazuela* saying that there is a pregnant woman there and she must see the play. Ortega answers from the stage that this is impossible and Fermín responds superstitiously:

> Pues es preciso: no nazca
> el inocente muchacho
> con la comedia estampada
> en medio de la barriga.[21]

Vicenta appears in the *patio* on a horse and complains about their treatment of her. Don't they know that a play is worthless without a *graciosa*? They all promise not to neglect her in the future, but there is still the problem of what to do—should they send the audience home or will they be able to perform? The "spectators" who have been shouting to Ortega then inform him that if there is a play they'll be right down, causing the actors on the stage to realize that the spectators are really their companions. Tiburcio then goes to the stage with another script. An *apasionado* who was in the theater has gone home to bring back a copy, so the performance of the play can proceed.

Although the most interesting manifestations of theater-within-the-theater techniques in the *género chico* occur in the early seventeenth century and culminate in Ramón de la Cruz's *sainetes* in the latter part of the eighteenth century, the Alvarez Quintero brothers wrote several short plays in the twentieth cenury which cannot be overlooked. Although they restore the barrier between audience and stage, the plays call attention to the theater as such, and there are interesting juxtapositions of art and life. For example, *El último papel* is a "paso de comedia" about an actress who is giving up the stage for marriage. While this plot is unrelated to the situation of the real woman who is playing the role, the main interest in the play comes from the fact that the actress in her last performance takes the part of a man-hater. Because she must express sentiments entirely opposite to her real feelings, she has difficulty in interpreting the part. But during the visit of a well-wisher she suddenly recites the words of the script to him. He does not realize she is acting and thinks she is out of her mind. However in contrast to the works previously discussed, the overlapping of life and art occurs only within the play and the audience does not share the disorientation.

Los meritorios is a *pasillo* in which actors, actresses, prompters, the director, and other people associated with the stage appear. It opens during a rehearsal and two untalented *meritorios* present themselves to try out for the new play. The scene which they are to recite represents a brief encounter between two secret lovers. They perform very badly before the director, but he is called away and when they are alone they do very well since the words reflect what they are beginning to feel for each other. The director, returning quietly, observes how beautifully they are handling the scene, but when they repeat it for him it lacks the life which had entered before.

The Alvarez Quintero brothers also used a play to expose certain problems of the theater. *Las benditas máscaras* (1922), a "paso de comedia," takes place when Edmundo, a young actor, is studying his part for a new play. Alejandrina arrives with the mission of persuading him to appear at a benefit performance. She convinces him that he should cooperate, even though the actors have made a pact among themselves not to do any more work of this type because people are abusing the privilege of requesting charity performances. Then he remembers that Alejandrina's uncle is the new secretary of the treasury, so he asks her to intervene to prevent further taxes from being imposed on the theater. The attitude is set forth that if the Spanish government does not subsidize the theater as other governments do, at least it should avoid destroying the theatrical institution with taxes.

Perhaps the most interesting theater-within-the-theater play the brothers wrote is *Pepita y Don Juan* (1925), in which characters are treated autonomously. This *loa* was written for the function whose purpose was to raise money to make a statue of Juan Valera for a park named in his honor. Pepita Jiménez appears with Antoñona and they are visited by feminine characters from nineteenth-century novels: señá Frasquita, Marianela, Marta and María, Sotileza, and Fortunata who bring Pepita flowers. Suddenly Cervantes's Gitanilla appears as if by magic. She says that she is going to take

Pepita to the *alto imperio* where she resides. Then the actress who plays the part of Pepita Jiménez walks toward the front of the stage, saying that she is no longer playing the role, "Ahora no soy Pepita Jiménez, ni siquiera la actriz que ha encarnado su figura en este acto; no soy sino una mujer española que conoció y amó a Don Juan Valera, y a quien fascinó la lectura de sus preciados libros." [22] She praises Valera in a sincere tribute from herself as a woman, then recites some of Valera's own verses which are appropriate for the occasion. [23]

Within the *género chico* there are many examples of Pirandellism in a minor key. Over a three-hundred-year span the playwrights of Spain demonstrated a conscious awareness of the infinite number of fascinating situations encountered in day-to-day contact with the theater and the fecundity of material these experiences provide when they are transformed into short plays. We see that once the decision has been made to write plays about theatrical experiences, and the stage is expanded to include the auditorium and metaphorically the whole world, certain characteristics can occur despite epoch or country. Since all people involved with the theater in all centuries share certain experiences, it is not unusual to find in these short plays almost all the technical devices associated with Pirandello. However, most of the plays discussed in this chapter have sunk into oblivion, and the techniques which Cruz so boldly used in the eighteenth century fell into disuse, so it is a pleasurable experience to brush off the cobwebs and examine these *sainetes, entremeses, pasos,* and *loas* through Pirandellian eyes.

JOSÉ ECHEGARAY

General critical evaluation of José Echegaray's contribution to the Spanish stage has for many years been unfavorable, although the public, unimpressed by the other playwrights of his time, joyfully accepted Echegaray's more appealing variety of drama. Critics have variously classified Echegaray as a neoromantic, have accused him of being overly melodramatic, and have attacked the so-called anachronism of his works. While it is true that some of Echegaray's techniques, the passionate emotions his heroes express, the violent situations, and the general atmosphere many of his plays have are strongly reminiscent of the most exaggerated romanticism of the 1830s, there are other aspects of his work which may be interpreted in Pirandellian terms. What might be called the Pirandellian current in Echegaray's plays flows at a deeper ideational level than the more superficial currents of exaggerated romanticism, and a discussion of the Spaniard's thematic comradeship with Pirandello will reveal that the general tide of Echegaray criticism is somewhat unwarranted.

Some of the ideas which Echegaray and Pirandello employ developed out of the Spaniard's legacy from Cervantes and Calderón (a legacy which Pirandello shared), others were products of his time, and many were based on his own intellectual and artistic life. Indeed, certain situations and a number of details in Echegaray's plays later appear in Pirandello's work, which forces one seriously to consider the possibility that Pirandello may have been familiar with the Spaniard's plays and perhaps drew inspiration from them. However, the main purpose of this chapter is not to prove a direct influence of Echegaray on Pirandello. Rather, thematic similarities will be emphasized to show that Echegaray looks forward in many essential ways to the twentieth century and at the same time draws inspiration from the great literature of the past.

Echegaray and Pirandello arrive at similar conclusions when they consider honesty for its own sake in a modern corrupt society. The brutal devotion to honesty illustrated by Echegaray in *O locura o santidad* (1877) and by Pirandello in *Il piacere dell'onestà* shows the isolation of a man who will not compromise with his own standards in order to conform to what society expects of him.[1]

A psychological theme both authors employ in many variations is the escape into madness from a problem which would otherwise have no solution. Both Echegaray and Pirandello portray characters who are sent to an asylum in order to avoid ruining their lives and those of all around them because of their attempt to be completely honest. Both playwrights also study characters who lucidly decide to be insane rather than face life as it is. Interestingly, in both dramatists the themes of honesty and madness often overlap, as they do in Cervantes's great novel.

Both dramatic authors question the nature of reality, have written plays-within-plays, use the problems connected with theatrical productions as conflict in drama, and have attempted to describe the creative process. Both Echegaray and Pirandello satirize romanticism, and they anticipate or answer the criticism they know they will receive or have received for the romantic characteristics of their own work.

Very similar and unusual plots based on dueling episodes are found in Echegaray's *El gran galeoto* (1881) and in Pirandello's *Il giuoco delle parti*. The similarity is especially interesting because it involves the problem of identity which is such an essential part of Pirandello's theater. Another problem of identity is found in the two plays *Un crítico incipiente* (1891) by Echegaray and *Quando si è qualcuno* by Pirandello. Both treat the desire of a well-known writer to present a work without eliciting the preconceived opinions which public knowledge of their authorship would cause, or without changing the image which their followers already treasure.

As stated above, both Echegaray and Pirandello have created characters who are quixotically devoted to honesty. When the curtain goes up in the first act of Echegaray's *O locura o santidad,* the hero of the play, Lorenzo de Avendaño, is absorbed in *El Quijote,* and while he reads he makes such judgments of Don Quijote as:

¡Extraño libro, libro sublime! ¡Cuántos problemas puso Cervantes en ti, quizá sin saberlo! ¡Loco tu héroe! Loco, sí; loco.

El que no oyera más que la voz del deber al marchar por la vida; el que en cada instante, dominando sus pasiones, acallando sus afectos, sin más norte que la justicia ni más norma que la verdad, a la verdad y a la justicia acomódase en todos sus actos, y con sacrílega ambición quisiera ser perfecto como el Dios de los cielos . . . , ése, ¡qué ser tan extraño sería en toda la sociedad humana! [2]

Following in the footsteps of his hero, Lorenzo later has the opportunity to emulate him when he discovers that he was born the son of a humble servant who gave him to a childless woman so that he would inherit a fortune. After his real mother tells him the truth, he ruthlessly insists that name and fortune must be restored to their rightful heirs. But Lorenzo must reckon with his relatives, who are not made of quixotic clay. This selfless devotion to honesty would ruin them completely and perhaps cause the death of his daughter, who has a nervous temperament and who could not marry the nobleman to whom she is engaged if her father insisted upon renouncing his fortune. Fortunately for them, the humble mother sees what her revelation will do to the family and subsequently denies that Lorenzo is her son. She destroys the evidence, which only Lorenzo has seen. So Lorenzo is the only one who is convinced of the truth of his origin and at the end of the play he is led away to an asylum. Unrelenting devotion to justice has no more place in Lorenzo's nineteenth-century society than it did in Quijote's seventeenth century.

Pirandello has created a character very much like Lorenzo in Angelo Baldovino of *Il piacere dell'onestà*. Domenico Vittorini has observed the quixotic quality of this character: "Here is the drama. We are at its very portals where we meet Baldovino, a strange individual who, with his quixotic temperament, dwarfs everyone around him." [3] Vittorini also believes that Pirandello himself has shown in this play how quixotic he is:

Pirandello is here a brilliant and ironical asserter of the power of honesty. As a genial and quixotic knight of Lady Honesty, he breaks his lance against those who preach of her in hollow voices and with solemn faces, while he attacks those who are inclined to think that honesty is just a prejudice of narrow-minded people.[4]

Unlike Lorenzo, whose predicament is no fault of his own, Angelo Baldovino knowingly enters into a morally doubtful situation when he marries a woman who is soon to give birth to a married man's child. But he is an impoverished nobleman who needs the financial security he will thus obtain and who has a well-developed sense of the absurd which preserves his personal integrity in this undignified situation. After the marriage ceremony he comports himself with all the rigorous logical morality of the hero of *O locura o santidad* and even senses the saintlike quality his life thus takes on: "Sospeso nell'aria, mi sono come adagiato su una nuvola: è il piacere dei Santi negli affreschi delle chiese!" [5] Baldovino is so completely dedicated to his role as an abstract concept that when he begins to love Agata, his legal wife, he decides to leave the household. However, Agata has grown to love him and will not permit him to do so.

In both plays friends and relatives react in the same way as in *El Quijote:* such a brutally honest man in search of justice cannot be sane; therefore the only possible explanation is that he is a lunatic. In *O locura o santidad* this supposition leads the relatives to place Lorenzo in an asylum. In *Il piacere dell'onestà* Angelo's whole outlook on life is compared to that of a madman and the possibility that he is truly mad is mentioned.

Madness, of course, is a leitmotif in Pirandello's work; his personal life led him to be emotionally involved with this theme, which he carried to the extreme in *Come tu mi vuoi* by presenting a completely demented person on the stage. Echegaray, under the influence of Ibsen, often treated hereditary insanity. Of course madness is a common topic and does not belong exclusively to any generation or playwright. However, the most significant aspect of this theme which Echegaray and Pirandello share is the use of false madness to suggest the tenuous difference between sanity and lunacy and between reality and appearances.

When Lorenzo is carried away at the end of *O locura o santidad,* he has been driven to show all the characteristics of a madman and even calls himself mad: "Adiós, Angela . . . , mi tierna esposa . . . ¡Veinte años hace que te di, loco de amor, el primer beso! ¡Hoy, también loco, te envío el último!" (p. 443). Then, with a horrible shout of desperation, he sends his wife a kiss and to all appearances attempts to strangle his daughter (although he is really just trying to keep her with him), which convinces all observers that they are justified in sending him to an asylum.

Another Pirandello drama that can be compared to *O locura o santidad* is *Il berretto a sonagli,* one of his Sicilian plays. The plot

centers around adultery. Ciampa, the deceived husband, takes elaborate precautions to prove he knows nothing of the affair. His wife's
lover is also his employer, and he is thus saving position and home.
The injured wife, driven by jealousy, is not so prudent. She plots
successfully to have the lovers caught together, but the evidence
turns out to be inconclusive, and it is still possible to conceal the
affair if Beatrice will only desist in her efforts to convict her husband of adultery. Now everyone unites to convince Beatrice that it
would be disastrous to make the truth public. She would be a
married woman without a home, if her husband did not kill her
first. Also, Ciampa would lose employment and respectability, and
he would not be able to continue living with his culpable wife, to
say nothing of the catastrophe brought down on the guilty couple
whom the Sicilian social code would require Ciampa to kill. Beatrice
thus finds that the path of absolute honesty has led her to the same
position in which Lorenzo of *O locura o santidad* found himself:
the destruction wrought by honesty can only be repaired by a retreat into madness. Ciampa explains to her that it has been decided
that she is mad and must go to the asylum:

> Ha dato di volta a lei il cervello, signora mia! Scusi, l'ha ricono-
> sciuto suo fratello Fifì; lo riconosce il Delegato; la sua mamma;
> lo riconosciamo tutti: e dunque lei è pazza! Pazza, e se ne va
> al manicomio! È semplicissimo! [6]

Ciampa also takes it on himself to explain to Beatrice how she
must act in order to be considered mad. It is very simple; all she
must do is shout the truth:

> Niente ci vuole a far la pazza, creda a me! Gliel'insegno io
> come si fa. Basta che lei si metta a gridare in faccia a tutti la
> verità. Nessuno ci crede, e tutti la prendono per pazza! [7]

Pirandello's *Il berretto a sonagli,* like Echegaray's *O locura o santidad,* is thus a play in which honesty leads to the asylum, a solution
forced on the protagonist by a disturbed society to repair the damage caused by truth.

Both playwrights have also created characters who voluntarily
and against the wishes of others seek madness as a refuge. In
Echegaray's *La realidad y el delirio* (1887) Gonzalo sees clearly that
either he is demented and happy or sane and unhappy and decides
that he prefers the former state. He also finds that the power which
only a madman possesses is enjoyable:

Se asustan cuando me ven enojado y huyen: pero yo no siento esos enojos que aparento: los finjo para que obedezcan: porque todos son cobardes y obedecen cuando se les manda con imperio.[8]

The origin of Gonzalo's madness was a blow received when he jumped from a moving train during a trip he was making with his wife, Angela, and a friend, Enrique. His jump was prompted by the shock of seeing Angela and Enrique draw close together while he was watching their shadows reflected on the wall of a railroad tunnel from a neighboring compartment:

Fue delirio . . . lo que yo vi, mientras el tren volaba: ¡no fue verdad! Como la noche era sombría y los celos son cortantes . . . yo, en la masa de negrura, iba recortando fantasmas, como en la masa de la cantera se esbozan estatuas; y esos fantasmas se me filtraban por los ojos y se me acurrucaban en el pecho; pero ya los arrojaré de aquí.[9]

As in many of Pirandello's plays, the spectators here are at times in doubt about the reliability of a character's perception. In Echegaray's play, however, the spectators' doubt is cleared up before the end of the play, and they know that although Angela was innocent, Enrique was not, and Gonzalo had reason to be jealous. After Enrique has been killed by Gonzalo's father in a duel and just before the last curtain falls, Gonzalo decides that he will continue to live the life of a madman: "Razón humana, nido de pequeñeces . . . renuncio a tí y vuelvo a mi locura."[10]

Pirandello's *Enrico IV* contains many elements similar to those in *La realidad y el delirio*. The original cause of Enrico's madness is also a blow on the head and jealousy (a rival for the love of Matilda had caused his horse to buck) caused his injury. He enjoys the power which a madman possesses to make others obey. During the play he is not mad but pretends to be so, and at the end of the play, because he has killed a man, he finds it necessary to take permanent refuge in madness.

Echegaray's *La realidad y el delirio* also contains the Spaniard's most frequent remarks suggestive of Pirandello's typical obsessions: the problem of truth and illusion, being and seeming. Paulina tells Anselmo: "A veces las apariencias engañan." Anselmo answers: "Pero tales apariencias como estas se parecen mucho a realidades."[11] They compare theater with life and introduce the life-dream theme of Calderón.

Pirandello's *Sei personaggi in cerca d'autore, Questa sera si recita a soggetto* and *Ciascuno a suo modo* carry to an unprecedented extreme the intermingling of theater and life, which, of course, was already a part of world theater tradition. Echegaray, in two of his plays, *El gran galeoto* and *Un crítico incipiente,* also presents the juxtaposition of life and art. In the Dialogue which precedes act 1 of *El gran galeoto,* Ernesto is attempting to write a play. He is struggling to put his idea on paper when Julián, his friend and protector, enters, converses with him, and discusses the idea he is trying to express. They mention Teodora, Julián's wife. When Julián leaves, inspiration finally comes to Ernesto, and he begins to write "febrilmente." Immediately the first act of the play begins; Teodora and Don Julián are seen speaking—it is soon apparent that the author and those who on one level of reality are supposedly friends of the author are now transferred to another level of reality, that of artistic creation. Later, Ernesto himself turns out to be the principal character in the play:

> Tu amiguito, el de los dramas,
> el poeta, el soñador. . . ,
> ¡el infame!, fué la causa
> de todo. [p. 742]

In the second act the play Ernesto had been writing in the Dialogue is discussed, again confusing levels of reality as Julián states:

> el cuidado
> de preparar desenlace
> para este drama está a cargo
> del mundo que lo engendró. [p. 702]

Echegaray's *Un crítico incipiente* combines theater and life in a much different way. Don Antonio has written a play anonymously, he prizes it highly, and he is extremely concerned about its success. Most of the drama takes place during the actual performance of Don Antonio's play—in a rather amusing way the characters run back and forth between the theater and Don Antonio's home to present their reactions. Don Antonio himself has left the theater because of a fainting spell brought on by emotion.

Echegaray does not employ Pirandello's extreme measures in his theater-within-the-theater work, nor do his plays contain the element of improvisation which is so important in this type of Pirandellian play. Still, in the *commedia dell'arte* tradition, it is apparent that

Echegaray has carried the play-within-the-play beyond Calderón, Shakespeare, Moratín, and Tamayo y Baus toward Pirandello's theater, especially in his treatment of the author's role and his attempt to describe the difficult struggle involved in the creative process. Furthermore, both authors show the difficulty, if not the impossibility, of recreating life situations on the stage. They use the word "fantasma" in referring to a character and think of him as an entity independent of the author. This idea is carried to its limit by Luigi Pirandello when a character appears before the playwright and demands to be allowed to live and by Unamuno when Augusto Pérez visits the novelist to discuss his fate.

In Echegaray's *Un crítico incipiente* the author tells what his character means to him, and what has happened to the role on the stage:

> ¡Mi conde Ulrico! La primera vez que lo vislumbré como fantasma de la luz en las sombras de la noche, evocado por la fiebre del desvelo, ¡qué noble, qué grandioso era! Y hoy, ¿qué es? Yo mismo lo ignoro; de tal modo me lo van poniendo. Desde aquel instante sublime de la concepción, hasta el momento presente, ¡qué pobre drama! Y yo, ¡qué angustias, qué sudores, qué dudas, qué desalientos, qué iras, qué apasionadas ansias! Este ser que yo arranqué de la nada, ¿qué es? ¿Una divina creación; un monstruo grotesco, o un ser vulgar, como tantos otros? ¿Qué es? Ya no lo sé: en su primera aparición era sublime; lo era, yo lo veía como si brotase del seno centellante de nube tempestuosa. ¡Hoy lo veo contrahecho, degradado, convertido en arlequín! [12]

A far more familiar passage in which Echegaray attempts to explain the difficulty of staging an idea appears in the preface of *El gran galeoto,* in which the playwright, Ernesto, is attempting to write a drama: "al imaginarlo, yo creí que la idea del drama era fecunda; y al darle forma, y al vestirla con el ropaje propio de la escena, resulta una cosa extraña, difícil, antidramática, imposible" (pp. 646–47). This is a "commedia da fare," just as is the play-within-the-play in *Sei personaggi in cerca d'autore.*

In Echegaray's plays the author's complaints that his creation was sublime and now is vulgar and that the idea cannot be expressed on the stage remind one strongly of the situation in *Sei personaggi in cerca d'autore,* where the characters, when represented by the actors, realize that the interpretation is a complete failure. In the preface to this play, which unlike Echegaray's preface to *El gran galeoto* is not acted out on the stage, Pirandello states: "Il fatto è che la commedia fu veramente concepita in un'illuminazione spontanea della fantasia, quando, per prodigio, tutti gli elementi dello spirito si rispondono e lavorano in un divino accordo," [13] which is reminiscent of the passage in which Echegaray describes how Conde Ulrico first struck his imagination.

Echegaray and Pirandello deliberately satirized romanticism because they were aware that they might be criticized for the romantic characteristics of their work. Echegaray's most complete satire of romanticism appears in *Un crítico incipiente,* where the following remark about the playwright Antonio's dream exemplifies this satiric bent: "¿Si es fuerte? ¡A quién se lo cuentas! Algo así como un terremoto que se pasea por un cementerio a la cárdena luz de la luna y al borde de un volcán (con exageración trágica)." [14] This play rivals the work of Mesonero Romanos and Joaquín Francisco Pacheco in the satire of romanticism. Echegaray also indicates his awareness of the criticism directed against him, as is obvious from such remarks as "Don Anselmo es un poeta rezagado del romanticismo: un vate melenudo." [15]

Pirandello, on the other hand, is more subtle in his satire of romanticism, as he himself explains in the preface to *Sei personaggi in cerca d'autore:*

> Che qualcuno ora mi dica che essa non ha tutto il valore che potrebbe avere perché la sua espressione non è composta ma caotica, perché pecca di romanticismo, mi fa sorridere.
>
> Capisco perché questa osservazione mi sia stata fatta. Perché nel mio lavoro la rappresentazione del dramma in cui sono involti i sei personaggi appare tumultuosa e non procede mai ordinata: non c'è sviluppo logico, non c'è concatenazione negli avvenimenti. È verissimo. Neanche a cercarlo col lumicino avrei potuto trovare un modo piú disordinato, piú strambo, piú arbitrario e complicato, cioè piú romantico, di rappresentare 'il drama in cui sono involti i sei personaggi'. È verissimo, ma io non ho affatto rappresentato quel dramma: ne ho rappresentato un altro— e non starò a ripetere quale!—in cui, fra le altre belle cose che ognuno secondo i suoi gusti ci può ritrovare, c'è proprio una discreta satira dei procedimenti romantici; in quei miei personaggi cosí tutti incaloriti a sopraffarsi nelle parti che ognun d'essi ha in un certo dramma mentre io li presento come personaggi

di un'altra commedia che essi non sanno e non sospettano, così
che quella loro esagitazione passionale, propria dei procedimenti
romantici, è umoristicamente posta, campata sul vuoto.[16]

The comparison which most seriously presents the possibility that
Pirandello may have been directly inspired by Echegaray is that
of Echegaray's *El gran galeoto* and Pirandello's *Il giuoco delle parti*.
Briefly, the situations are as follows: In *El gran galeoto* gossips
erroneously suppose Ernesto to be Teodora's lover. However, when
he overhears Teodora insulted by a stranger he challenges the
stranger to a duel, which Teodora's husband actually fights, because
it is his place to do so. Teodora's husband is wounded and later dies.
In *Il giuoco delle parti* Silia, who is married to but separated from
Leone Gala, has a lover, Guido, and she would like to remove the
"complication" of Leone's presence. She therefore persuades Leone
to challenge a stranger who has insulted her to a duel. Leone agrees,
because this is his formal duty as a husband, but just as Guido has
taken his place for all practical purposes, it is also Guido's duty to
fight the duel, and in doing so he dies.

The similarities of plot are striking: in both plays a stranger's
insult causes a duel in which one person challenges and another
actually fights and is killed. In *El gran galeoto* the supposed lover
challenges and the husband fights, and in *Il giuoco delle parti* the
husband challenges and the lover, who has been acting as husband,
fights. The insistence that each person play his proper part is more
diabolical in Pirandello's play because Leone Gala causes the lover
to fight a duel for which he has no desire. In *El gran galeoto* Ernesto
seriously intends to fight the duel, but he is prevented from doing
so by the timely arrival of the husband. Ernesto does subsequently
kill the stranger after the husband is seriously wounded in the duel.
In both cases, however, the proper person fights; the true legal and
moral husband in *El gran galeoto* and the lover who has been playing the husband's role for many years in *El giuoco delle parti*.
Finally, the circumstances in *El gran galeoto* have a Pirandellian
twist because a falsehood becomes true through the influence of
gossip.

Another revealing example of the kinship between these two
authors is found in Echegaray's *Un crítico incipiente* and Pirandello's *Quando si è Qualcuno*. Both are autobiographical and express
the desire of an older man, well known in the world of literature,
to write sincerely, unburdened by the preconceived opinions which

his name evokes. Echegaray's Antonio writes a play anonymously, but includes passages in the style of another playwright to add to the deceit. Pirandello's *** has written a collection of poems under the pen name of Délago, and he prefaces the collection with a drawing of a young man, who is supposed to be Délago.

*** is much more eloquent than Antonio about his reasons for doing this: he feels imprisoned within the marble statue which is the image the public has of him. He feels that this public image no longer represents his true nature, but the public will not allow him to change. He has become the statue of himself and can only escape by publishing under another name.

The motives of Antonio, Echegaray's playwright, for writing anonymously are at first not clear, since he needs the money, and his name, already well known in the theatrical world, would seemingly help him toward this goal. Subsequently, however, it is obvious that Antonio's financial motive is secondary. This play means more to him than the work he has published under his own name. He loves and defends it passionately, just as *** loves and defends his poems written under the name of Délago, and he too has obtained artistic freedom by the anonymous device. It is possible that Echegaray used this autobiographical play as his vehicle for denying the general assumption that he wrote for the theater chiefly for financial reasons.

The theme of an individual whose personality has made such a strong impression that it is no longer possible to alter the opinion which people have of him is presented in Echegaray's play in another way. A young critic who thinks the play has been written by Don Pablo is firmly convinced of his ability to judge it without attending the première, after attending a rehearsal and by drawing on what he knows about Don Pablo's previous productions.

In both of these plays there are subthemes which again stress the thematic similarities between Echegaray and Pirandello. Perhaps the most important is the contrast between youth and age. In *Un crítico incipiente* the romantic captivations, enthusiasms, and optimism of young people are represented by Antonio's son and daughter, Luisa and Pepe, and Luisa's *novio,* Enrique. Three young people also represent these qualities in Pirandello's play: Pietro, Natascia, and Veroccia.

Both Pirandello and Echegaray acknowledge their debt to the past in these plays. The settings call for busts of Lope, Calderón, and Shakespeare in Echegaray's play, and portraits of Dante, Ariosto,

Foscolo, and Leopardi in Pirandello's, perhaps to contrast the fixed images of past poets with those of the present which are still being formed.

Thus, in shifting the emphasis away from the obvious characteristics of Echegaray's theater in order to view his thematic affiliation with Pirandello, we can see a playwright emerge who is not exclusively a late romantic, but also a forerunner of the twentieth century.

Unfortunately Echegaray criticism has usually only taken into account the five or six most popular plays of the sixty he wrote, and one of the neglected plays, *Un crítico incipiente,* was preferred by the playwright himself and is most revealing.[17] While not easily obtainable, this particular play, in spite of its subtitle "capricho cómico" and its often exaggerated emotions and situations, does reveal that Echegaray did attempt to include a certain intellectual content in his plays, which would make his relationship to Pirandello and the twentieth century more obvious. It is in this play, too, that Echegaray makes a penetrating, prophetic statement about the effects of dramatic efforts to produce something new, personal, and original. Antonio tells his friend Telesforo, "He puesto en esa obra mi alma entera," and Telesforo answers, "Ya lo creo que ha gustado: pero como gustan las obras muy atrevidas. Abren el horizonte a grandes esperanzas; pero una vez abierto el horizonte, por ciertos rumbos pueden venir furiosas tempestades." [18] These storms have not subsided much in the years since Echegaray's death, but perhaps now a reassessment will reveal a playwright who is a link between his literary ancestors and the twentieth century, especially because of his thematic comradeship with Luigi Pirandello.

RAMÓN GÓMEZ DE LA SERNA

El teatro en soledad, written in 1911 by Ramón Gómez de la Serna, and Pirandello's *Sei personaggi in cerca d'autore,* written about ten years later, are strikingly similar in many significant ways. Coincidence cannot be the explanation, and it is extremely unlikely that Pirandello knew about Ramón's play,[1] which was published in an obscure Spanish journal.[2] The key to the explanation of this phenomenon may be found by turning to Paris during the "Banquet Years"[3] and especially to the cubist school of painting.

A number of Ramón's commentators have called attention to the resemblance between *El teatro en soledad* and *Sei personaggi in cerca d'autore.*[4] They usually limit themselves to associating the two plays; however, Gaspar Gómez de la Serna has said more than most:

> Baste con aludir al juego escénico de *Teatro en soledad* como antecedente de *Seis personajes en busca de autor,* dando ya esta transposición de planos que tanta fama dio por los años veinte a Pirandello, en la que se barajan ficción y realidad, los [sic.] *dramatis personae* con los personajes reales, rompiendo todas las convenciones y unidades teatrales.[5]

Ramón himself seems self-satisfied about his anticipation of Pirandello. He commented in his autobiography, *Automoribundia:*

> Así se fraguaron *La Utopía, La corona de hierro, La casa nueva,* etc., y ese *Teatro en Soledad* que cuando muchos años después apareció el drama de Pirandello *Seis personajes en busca de autor,* yo me sonreí satisfecho de haber destripado con anticipación esa sombra del teatro con el telón levantado y que yo no hice para el público, pues suponía un público de sombras inexistentes.[6]

Ramón also considers this accomplishment important enough to be mentioned in the short preface to his *Obras completas,* in which he explains why almost all of his plays were excluded from these volumes:

> Quedan también fuera: 'Morbideces,' 'Muestrario,' 'El libro nuevo,' 'Tapices'—que fué el único que publiqué con el seudónimo de 'Tristán'—, y casi todo mi teatro, pues 'El Teatro en Soledad,' que habría podido salvar, ya que los amigos creyeron ver en él un antecedente de los 'Seis personajes en busca de autor,' es algo inconcuso y excesivamente balbuciente.[7]

Despite these numerous references and the fact that several critics have discussed pre-Pirandellism in Spain,[8] this play is not mentioned among the important pre-Pirandellian manifestations. Recently Torrente Ballester compared Ramón's plays to hidden oil deposits which will never enrich anyone because they are so difficult to find. "Me atrevo incluso a asegurar que su búsqueda requiere el mismo espíritu aventurero de los que se lanzan a la prospección de anticlinales, si bien el instrumental sea menos complicado."[9]

This "hidden oil deposit," *El teatro en soledad,* is a very important document in the history of pre-Pirandellism in Spain. The first twenty of the eighty pages are devoted to the "Depuración preliminar" in which Ramón describes his state of mind ("Siento mi cabeza llena de locuras pintorescas, más largas y más vastas que toda cordura . . ."[10]) and his purpose in writing the play ("La labor presente sólo debe dar fuerza de belleza, de variedad, y de *carnalidad* al *leit motiv* de la desesperación bajo la crueldad," p. 3). He also speculates about literature in general, rejects almost all manifestations of the Generation of '98, meditates about artistic creation, and gives his opinions about the future of literature ("La obra literaria tiene que dejar de ser obra literaria, porque así no se justifica de ningún modo," p. 13). In short, this part of the manuscript is a type of literary manifesto.

The play itself opens in a darkened theater with the curtain down while a stagehand replaces the burned-out bulbs. Another stagehand tries to come through the side of the curtain and is angrily warned that he will tear it and is told to enter through the prompter's shell. The last spectator left an hour ago and it is time for the curtain to be up anyway. There is conversation about the spectators, the curtain goes up, the bulb is replaced, the footlights are turned out, and Ramón describes in considerable detail the way the stage and the actors look. For example, "El espectáculo en el escenario es anguloso y grotesco por sus luces, sus maderas, sus hombres y sus mujeres de la calle, sin distinción ninguna, todos arropados y como con chepa" (p. 23). The stagehands continue to rearrange the stage properties while the actors discuss the problems of the stage, the plays, an author, and each other. "El de las gafas," apparently the director, criticizes the stagehands and the actors.

After the actors and stagehands leave for the night, Ramón describes the empty stage, and then the characters appear. They immediately begin to criticize the actors, the play, the author, and the audience. Their most constant criticism of theater itself seems to be the lack of novelty, but this does not matter because they are going to perform their own play. They prepare themselves, the women receiving instructions from the men about how to improve their appearance.

The characters' play (the play-within-the-play-within-the-play) begins in the second act. "La de la frente lunar," the heroine, ("La mujer de todos los dramas") is mourning the death of the old hero of drama ("de cartón y tedio"), but is comforted and encouraged not to mind his death too much by "el descarnado," because, after all, she has been rescued from the same fate. "El descarnado" seems to desire a new type of drama which will be more natural, will be based on true and intimate emotions, and will express the essence of life. "El descarnado's" people, who are pairs of lovers, offer to teach and help her. She calls this the hour of salvation.

In the third act "La de la frente lunar" and "El descarnado" discuss the problem of drama in general and their own drama, which they feel must develop soon, but which they cannot define. There is no conflict: "El drama de amor es imposible porque no hay enemigo" (p. 77). The search for drama itself becomes the plot of the play. They finally reach a definition and a solution:

> Rotos todos los motivos de todos los dramas, llegó el drama absoluto, franco de fuerza y de extensión . . . El drama que no está en el conflicto de la hiprocresía con la inmoralidad, sino en no poder sobrepasar la inmoralidad . . . El drama, en fin, nada más que 'el drama,' sin ningún argumento pequeño ni grande . . . Sin ningún tercero entre nosotros, y sin ningún tercer pensamiento, sólo hecho para nosotros dos, que lo hemos asumido con nobleza. [p. 78]

They conclude that the drama has renewed them, and that they have triumphed over the drama. It is obvious, even from this brief outline, that in form, technique, and even emotion and atmosphere this play is parallel to *Sei personaggi in cerca d'autore*.

Like *Sei personaggi, El teatro en soledad* is a play which serves to dissect the theater and the techniques employed destroy theatrical illusion by showing people and elements which should remain behind the scenes. There are several levels of reality; in fact, in the list of characters the participants are separated into two groups in both plays: characters and actors. In addition, the author and the spectators, who were to become so important in Pirandello's theater-within-the-theater trilogy, are discussed. The characters are even more important in Ramón's play than in Pirandello's, since the stage belongs to them completely during most of the play. The actors and characters do not occupy the stage simultaneously as they do in Pirandello's play, and the actors are unaware that the characters exist; however, the characters have a critical attitude toward the actors very similar to that shown in *Sei personaggi*.

The actors in Ramón's play are presented as a rather sorry lot: poorly dressed, unattractive, and disagreeable. They converse about several problems associated with the mixture of levels of reality, such as when they criticize Enrique, an actor, for playing only himself instead of his role. After the director has left, the actors complain about his control of them: "Este hombre no nos quiere dejar sobresalir y nos prohibe todos los efectos" (p. 29), a complaint rather similar to that found in *Questa sera si recita a soggetto*.

After most of the actors have left, "El guapo" and "La de la gran boa" remain on stage, and a short scene from their private life is played to an empty auditorium. However, they are rudely reminded that they are not performing in a play when their kiss is abruptly interrupted by the hammer blows of the stagehands, who are still working in the rafters, and by the girl's mother who comes to take her home.

A further example of the unhappy result obtained by mixing reality and fiction occurs, according to the actors, when authors are called upon to take a bow although they have not rehearsed nor used makeup.

> Ya ves tú hoy al salir el autor, su nariz resultaba feísima y como un garabato y por su descuido se parecía al personaje más desfavorable de su obra. [p. 26]

Thus, when the author presents himself as a real person in the realm of the actors, he places himself at a great disadvantage.

The director, who is also so important in Pirandello's trilogy, appears briefly to comment on the performance. He sarcastically asks one stagehand who has misplaced some lights if he is going to need a prompter. He criticizes the actors; one has smoked cigars on the stage, although his role is that of a young man, another has called unnecessary attention to himself in a crowd scene. Many are not properly dressed; no one cares about the total effect, but only about the impression he himself is making.

Although spectators do not actually appear, they are discussed, and this shows that Ramón is sensitive to the possibility of spectator participation. The stagehands realize that the spectators also provide dramatic entertainment and they tell how the last ones leave the theater, mentioning "ese espectador como paralítico que sale siempre el último . . ." (p. 23), one who is unable to find the other sleeve of his coat, and the one who forgot something. But the most comical spectator, according to the stagehands, is the one who returns to pick up the opera glasses which he had not brought to the theater with him in the first place.

The characters who arrive after the actors and stagehands have left for the night constitute the core of the play. They are autonomous characters, just as Pirandello's *Sei personaggi* are, and they are also searching, because they are characters without a drama. But unlike Pirandello's characters, they do not even have a story; indeed, they are self-sufficient and do not want an author. They appear to be searching for an absolute expression of true drama.

In both plays the stage itself, stripped of illusion, occupies an important position. Although many details are reversed, the first stage directions of the two plays give similar impressions. From *Sei personaggi* comes the following:

> Troveranno gli spettatori, entrando nella sala del teatro, alzato il sipario, e il palcoscenico com'è di giorno, senza quinte né scena, quasi al bujo e vuoto, perché abbiano fin da principio l'impressione d'uno spettacolo non preparato . . . Sul palcoscenico, il cupolino del suggeritore, messo da parte, accanto alla buca.[11]

And from *El teatro en soledad*:

> El teatro obscuro y visojo . . . Las candilejas apagadas, y de las luces de las dos lámparas de la embocadura sólo encendida una y esa asordecida . . . Esta nota desigual y descompuesta de la luz,

ya pone obsceno, mugriento y desarrapado el ambiente . . . La concha del apuntador se tira hacia atrás, como sobre su nuca, y aparece por ella una cabeza desgreñada y canalla de tramoyista. [p. 22]

In *Sei personaggi in cerca d'autore* the main desire of the characters is to represent their drama on the stage. They suffer when the actors try to play a scene from their life because it lacks authenticity. Vittorini emphasized this important element of the play when he entitled his chapter on *Sei personaggi* "Art Does But Dwarf a Tragic Life." [12] The characters of *El teatro en soledad,* even though they are also actors, have a similar problem: "¡Cada vez sé imitar menos en los dramas la pasión que te tengo!" (p. 42). Later they further discuss the difficulty of representing true emotions on the stage: "Los grandes techos aplastan y desmienten vuestro ardor privado y voluptuoso, mujeres" (p. 43).

The theater-within-the-theater techniques used by Pirandello, which even include such extreme devices as participation by spectator-actors, interruptions, and scenes in the lobby, have led to the decrease or destruction of aesthetic distance. That is, the observer is no longer separated from the art form he is contemplating—he becomes a part of it and is thus unable to view it with the necessary detachment.[13] It is interesting to note that Ramón, who foreshadows Pirandello in so many ways, also touches on this problem. For example, the director tells the actors that their untidy appearance upsets the audience. After he has left, one of the actors observes that when their collars become detached during a performance, it distracts some spectators who involuntarily look at their own collars to make sure that they are in place. Similarly, a young actress remarks that she was afraid the director would mention that during the performance she was smiling at her *novio* who was in the audience. In both cases the audience has overidentified with the actors and thus cannot contemplate the work of art as such. However, there is also a reverse side to this phenomenon—a strong audience-actor *rapport* which enhances the actors' performance. The characters discuss an ideal spectator, who merely by his presence helps them to interpret their roles better:

Cuando veo lucir su sortija sobre el rojo terciopelo del barandal de su palco, me doy más al ambiente, no sé por qué, y me impone ella un gran entusiasmo como si fuera un ideal. [p. 41]

In addition to the technical innovations in these two plays, the moods in them are extremely similar. After Pirandello's death, Ramón wrote an article about him in which he translated the following passage written by the Italian:

> El teatro nuevo tiene un carácter distinto del teatro viejo, que tenía por fundamento la pasión, en tanto que el moderno es expresión de la inteligencia. Una de las novedades que he aportado al teatro moderno es convertir la inteligencia en pasión, haciendo que el público, que sólo se apasionaba en las obras de pasión, se apasionase en las de inteligencia. De ahí que el público se apasione por mi teatro cerebral.[14]

In *El teatro en soledad* the intellectual dialogue almost always has an undercurrent of passion, which yields a tone remarkably similar to that of Pirandello's plays.[15]

Since most of the innovations found in Ramón's play can be explained by applying cubist aesthetic theories, it will be necessary to show his close involvement with the artistic environment of the time. Ramón made his first trip to Paris in 1906, the year in which Pablo Picasso began "Les Demoiselles d'Avignon." In 1909 Ramón described the great impact Picasso was making: "Picasso está en España durante el verano. Todos queremos estallar."[16] Much more important, however, was Ramón's residence in Paris from 1910 through 1911, the most significant period for the development of analytical cubism. He frequented the Bateau-Lavoir, the birthplace of cubism, and became acquainted with many of the leading artists of the day. Ramón himself enjoyed drawing and illustrated many of his writings.[17] He was greatly interested in the artistic innovations of the epoch, and his 1931 book *Ismos* bears witness to this.

In the prologue of *Ismos,* Ramón describes how he reacted to the August 1910 Exposition des Indépendants as one would to sighting the coast of a new continent. "Si algo entre las sensaciones que llenan nuestra alma se puede llamar puro sentido del descubrimiento, fué aquello lo que gocé" (p. 958). He enthusiastically reveals that this was a turning point in his interest in art: "Desde entonces entré en el caos febriciente de la pintura moderna y su interés (p. 958).

In *Ismos* Ramón gives evidence of his commitment to the new attitudes. Of course twenty years had passed since he wrote *El teatro en soledad,* however, certain evidence in the play itself indicates that when he was writing it he was experiencing the same emotions that he more maturely described in *Ismos* which is a very personal study of the epoch then ending. There are twenty-seven "Ismos," ranging from well-established ones (cubism and surrealism) to "Ismos" of his own invention. He explains his attitude:

A través de todo este libro se me verá en mi interminable posición de rebeldía, pero rebeldía con un fondo dramático y emocionado, apasionado de la construcción noviestructurada, lírico del soborno humano que sufre en la plena deshumanización, las vísceras palpitantes, sacando la mano por entre lo diversificante, desfoliando lo virgíneo con verdadera pasión. [p. 959]

Ramón states that he has always been a "vanguardista" and that he is especially a "porvenirista." In a discussion reminiscent of Lessing's *Laocoön* he ponders the relationship between literature and art. He believes that literature is even more capable than art of capturing the new aesthetics: "La posibilidad y sugerencia literarias, su prolificación de materias y temas, su superposición de imágenes es incomparable con la del arte de la pintura" (p. 959), and goes on to explain the limitations of painting as compared to the wide possibilities of verbal expression.

He tells how painters' techniques can also be applied to literature:

El misterio de que una cosa literaria resulte es que estén bien hallados los ángulos . . . Todo estriba en saber apreciar qué ángulo es el interesante . . . Hay que enfocar las cosas en ángulo, no demasiado de frente o demasiado a todo lo ancho, y ¡de ninguna manera! en panorama. En cada asunto o escena hay que hallar el ángulo intencionado, lo que basta para el resto, lo que da a cala la novedad de cada episodio. [p. 960]

He believes that it is necessary to devour innovations, use them, and continue on to new things, for repetition is monstrous in art.

The chapter entitled "Picassismo"[18] is a formal study of Picasso's life and work, where Ramón examines at length the theory of cubism, including the influence of Negro art, the triumph of intelligence,[19] and collages. He thinks cubism is one of the most beautiful rebellions of men against appearance and that it has at its disposal more means of expression than ordinary perspective gives. He also discusses the problem cubists face of animating flat surfaces.

Perhaps his comment which most suggests that playwrights could benefit from the avant-garde painters' attitudes is the following:

"El pintor no quiere engañar con la imitación de las tres dimensiones cuando la pintura puede disponer únicamente de dos. Quiere ser sincero por primera vez y sólo desdoblar la realidad sobre una superficie plana" (p. 990). Since the stage has at its disposal areas which have been considered out-of-bounds for action in most plays, dramatists have a problem opposite to that of painters, but the basic concept they have in common is sincerity in showing the medium for what it is in all its dimensions and with its limitations.

Ramón explains the paradox of cubist art—the desire to express the widest possible vision while limiting oneself to the actual two-dimensional area of the canvas.

> Como se ve en toda la conceptuosidad cubista, reunida por mí con todo trabajo y dificultad, por un lado era estrecha la regla, y por el otro aspiraba a conseguir la mayor visión, inmovilizando el máximo de espacio, representando actos sucesivos en el espacio. Por un lado sólo dos dimensiones interesaban al artista, y por otro aprovechaba el bautismo casual que había llamado cubista a la escuela y quería cubicar las cosas expresando las tres dimensiones del espacio desglosado, sin expresar la profundidad con una dimensión ficticia, como hace la vieja perspectiva. [p. 994]

In the *Historia de las literaturas de vanguardia* Guillermo de Torre points out that the term *cubism* is always used hesitatingly by literary critics: "La referencia del cubismo a las letras siempre ha sido hecha de un modo aproximado, lateral, cuando no con un aire de incertidumbre o de perplejidad." [20] However, the present analysis of *El teatro en soledad* shows that with almost mathematical certainty, cubist aesthetic theory applied to the theater would produce techniques such as those found in Ramón's play and later in Pirandello's. For example, the cubists' abolition of the single viewpoint, their showing the object from a multiplicity of angles, would correspond to the different angles from which the stage is viewed. At one moment we are in the rafters with the stagehands, looking toward the stage, at another we contemplate the empty auditorium with the electrician; we see the author from the actors' point of view and then the actors from the characters' viewpoint, and so on. Also, the cubists broke up volumes. A cubist playwright dissects theater, almost destroying the very medium he is using to convey his art.[21] The collage, which involves the attachment to paintings of "real" items such as newspapers or cigarette packs, would, of course, correspond chiefly to the "life" brought into cubist-oriented drama in the form of spectators, ushers, or stagehands. The superimposed planes so important in cubist paintings become the many planes of reality manifested in the theater by various forms of theater-within-the-theater technique. In essence, both cubism and Pirandellism are intellectual arts, both strive for maximum possibilities of expression and a new confrontation with the materials at their disposal, and both participate in the "art-about-art" trend.[22]

El teatro en soledad, besides being a cubist play in technique, contains imagery of cubist origin, and there are many interesting details in the play which prove that Ramón actually had pictorial representation very much in mind when he was writing it. In the "Depuración preliminar" there are numerous references to painting. These pages, although obviously a literary manifesto, are unintelligible in parts if one does not consider the artistic background of the time.

Ramón confesses that he feels like painting, but instead he will write: "Se sienten ganas de pintar . . . Pero en vez de hacer en un extremo de la cuartilla el *mono* antiguo, antipático y duro con que se resuelve la cargazón de estos ratos, acogemos la palabra revuelta y comprometida." (p. 4).

He stresses the fact that his play is a departure from tradition, and is contemporary:

¿Que esta obra prescindirá del dibujo sereno, directo, tradicional y hasta revolucionario de las cosas? Es natural y es oportuno. Goces en la desesperada, palabras á la desesperada, amores en la desesperada, todo así más apasionado y más vertiginoso, todo así desenlazado del único modo contemporáneo. . . . [p. 4]

Ramón speaks about perspective in a manner which suggests painting rather than literature:

Siento una extensión que contradice la idea de la extensión y de la perspectiva, una extensión demasiado cercana y demasiado visible, llena de cosas y de ámbito que sólo un sentimiento pánico y antiguo hace que no se vean ni se sospechen. [p. 5]

He realizes that he is adapting artistic theory to literature, and finally he actually formulates a literary theory based on these concepts:

Todo lo que se escribe debe descomponerse, fracturarse y posarse al fin sin extravagancia, sin dureza y con un agotamiento que estilizará y situará todo en su perspectiva según un arte decorativo comprensible y seductor . . . Hay que solucionar esa literatura que en vez de desviar los objetos en una refracción visionaria, en vez de proyectarlos, los solidifica, los anticúa, los prorroga sin facultarlos de sus influencias privadas y sin concederles su sexo contrario. [pp. 18–19]

In the play itself there are also numerous details which suggest cubism. The names of the characters sound like the titles of cubist paintings: "La vieja amarilla," "El de la nariz vinosa," "El de chistera," "La de la frente lunar," "La de los aretes," "La de la boca violeta," and "El recio de pómulos." (Some of Picasso's titles are "Mujer en verde," "Señora del sombrero negro," "Mujer con abanico," "La señora del manguito," "La mujer del moño.")

Some of Ramón's character descriptions are verbal sketches of cubist paintings. For example, "La de la frente lunar" is pictured as follows:

Negra y morada en todo lo que no es su frente, aunque su rostro tenga hendida y herida su expresión y su boca, y el resto de su cuerpo esté dibujado con formón desde los pezones al empeine, y apretado del traje de estas mujeres, pegadizo y caído, con una gran fuerza plástica, mojado de sombra, trajes vivos de actualidad después de rechupados y deformados por los desnudos y conteniendo las hemorragias como un tafetán. [p. 36]

and "El alto": armado de una silueta en bloque, más larga pero tan empinada en la cabeza y tan demostrativa y tan férvida en el pecho y tan dura en el rostro" (p. 36).

Negro art and sculpture, as has been pointed out by art historians and by Ramón himself, influenced Picasso in the development of cubism. In *El teatro en soledad* one of the characters declares:

Mira, se me ocurre que estaría bien yo negra, con un negro de ébano . . . Algo que me hiciera más fulminante en esta hora, para sobreponernos más aún a esa decepción del cadáver . . . Y no de un modo artificial sino porque me transformara desde dentro mi voluntad de ser negra, sin variar de formas, y ofrecértelas así más visibles y más cuajadas . . .

Her friend answers, among other things: "Así, negra mía, toda del color del ébano, tan plástico y tan terso y tan iluminado en tus muslos" (p. 59).

There are many other characteristics which clearly indicate Ramón's debt to cubism, for example, pictorial details such as: "todo tu cuerpo lleno de perfiles" (p. 59) and "ha provocado en mí no sé qué materia caliente y broncínea que ha renovado mi plástica" (p. 62). A scorn for beauty similar to that attributed to Picasso [23] can be found in the play when "El descarnado" tells "La de la frente lunar": "Porque soy el que quiere ver tus blancas vacunas, no tu belleza.—¡¡Tu belleza!! como te decía flacamente este cadáver" (p. 46).

In discussing Ramón's relationship to the arts, Rodolfo Cardona shows his relation to the avant-garde:

> Perhaps more sensitive than many of his European contemporaries, Ramón was able to capture, before most of them, certain attitudes that later were to crystallize into movements such as Ultraism, Cubism, Dadaism, Surrealism. To be sure, he is not the only precursor of these movements. His merit lies in the fact that without ever being in close contact with any of them, without ever identifying himself with any literary movement—in Spain or abroad—he has reflected all these movements in his own work. Like Picasso, always imaginative, always creative, always in search of something, Ramón has also touched upon these main artistic "isms" without really taking part in them.[24]

Cardona also discusses pictorial cubist aspects of Ramón's novels, such as simultaneity of planes, juxtaposition of sensations and visions, and especially the "technique of elimination, reducing the subject to the play and byplay of form and colors, with allusions to reality kept to a bare minimum" [25] found in common in Ramón's *Azorín* and Picasso's "The Clarinet Player" (1911–12).

Ramón has also been associated with French literary cubism. In "Apollinerismo," a chapter of *Ismos,* he tells how Delaunay somewhat sarcastically called him "el Apollinaire español" (p. 964). He goes on to say: "De algún modo resultábamos gemelos que no hubiesen estado nunca en el mismo vientre. (Después me había de pasar lo mismo con Max Jacob, que siempre ha de ser para mí el mejillón desconocido.)" (p. 964). Cardona reports that Ramón specifically denied working under Max Jacob's influence when Picasso himself noticed similarity in the work of the two authors.[26]

Several critics have suggested that Pirandello transposed cubist inspiration into theatrical terms. MacClintock comments on Pirandello's changed point of view and compares it to contemporary painting and poetic techniques. He explains that art does not necessarily resemble reality as most know it. Picasso "takes the elements of a form as he sees it and jumbles them into a pattern which has nothing to do with what we see." [27] He believes that Pirandello's philosophy of drama is the same:

> So to Pirandello the drama is also a self-contained medium of expression with conventions of its own and its own justification; the action need not be based upon facts (which are illusory), it need not contain a thesis or teach a lesson, it need not even be probable if only it is psychologically and philosophically true. [28]

Giudice sees another point of comparison which he thinks is made clear by examining Picasso's "Les trois musiciens" and "Sei personaggi":

> *Les trois musiciens* di Picasso sono anch'essi del 1921 e sono, in ultima analisi, una rappresentazione molto vicina a quella del Pirandello, dei *Sei personaggi*. Picasso, molto più raffinato e dotato di un'ironia, in quest'opera stravinskiana, spettrale e festosa, e Pirandello, provinciale e solitario, erano due presenze nella medesima internazionale dell'epoca cubista (della quale facevano parte per altri versi scrittori come Joyce): si creavano, ad opera dei più geniali artisti europei le equivoche *silhouettes* di una umanità autorinnegantesi. Si scioglievano le leggi tridimensionali, la realtà appariva in un'amorale moltiplicazione di piani. La nevrosi pirandelliana e l'altoforno dell'intellettualismo di Picasso erano sullo stesso piano mentale. [29]

Wylie Sypher, in "Cubist Drama," specifically explains many elements of *Sei personaggi* in terms of cubist painting. "Just as the cubist broke up the object into various planes, or as photomontage gave its own sort of polyphonic vision by means of combined shorts, so Pirandello offers a compound image in drama." [30] He further states: "In 'Six Characters' the action . . . improvises upon certain dramatic situations as being reality and upon certain events in life as being art" (p. 290).

Sypher clearly demonstrates how Pirandello employs collage and calls the Boy's suicide a shocking example of this art. He explains the mixture of levels of reality resulting from these techniques, "We cannot say that these persons exist off the stage; and we cannot say they live on the stage. Above all, what is the stage?" (p. 291). He mentions the problem of artistic interpretation, which was indeed in the mind of everyone at this time—is it possible for drama really to interpret life at all? "Pirandello invites us to examine the texture of his drama exactly as the cubist invites us to examine the contrasting textures in his painting, the very invitation raising doubt about holding the mirror up to nature" (p. 293). He discusses the scene where Madame Pace and the step-daughter speak softly, which of course shows the truth of life that would be impossible to communicate on the stage. Sypher examines the multidimensional theater with which Pirandello was experimenting, and points out that there are no clear boundaries between life and art in Pirandello's play, corresponding to the lack of these boundaries in the painting of the time.[31]

The fact that Ramón's play, which was directly inspired by the cubist school of painting, contains many of the same elements which later appear in *Sei personaggi* certainly supports these critics' contention that Pirandello was also influenced by the new philosophy of art. Pirandello was strongly inspired by the parallel philosophical and psychological currents of the epoch, while Ramón shows more concrete influence of cubist painters. Ramón wrote his rather tentative practice piece at the beginning of an epoch during one of the most exciting years of discovery and development of cubism. Luigi Pirandello wrote his masterpiece several years later at the end of the cubist epoch; although art would never be the same, the official denotation of cubism would no longer be applied to subsequent paintings. Ramón was young and greatly inspired by the new movement when he wrote *El teatro en soledad,* while Pirandello was a mature and experienced writer when he wrote his play. Ramón's drama has been forgotten except by a few scholars, while *Sei personaggi in cerca d'autore* is recognized as one of the most significant plays of the twentieth century. Both plays, however, directly reflect the spirit of their age as it appeared in the plastic and literary arts.

MIGUEL DE UNAMUNO

Unamuno is the Spaniard most often associated with Pirandello because *Niebla* (1914) occupies a position in the history of the Spanish novel comparable to that of *Sei personaggi in cerca d'autore* in the theater. In both cases the frame which had isolated fiction from reality is irreparably shattered, revealing new possibilities of literary expression which half a century later have not yet been fully exploited.

Since the late twenties a steady stream of commentary has called attention to the similarities in thought and technique involving the interplay of fantasy and reality in the two writers' works.[1] Special attention has been given to their creation of autonomous characters who claim for themselves as much or more reality than the author. This similarity is all the more interesting because there seems to have been no mutual direct influence. Unamuno's *Niebla* appeared before *Sei personaggi*, but after Pirandello published *La tragedia d'un personaggio*, which contains a character-author interview. Unamuno, in an article published in *La Nación* in 1923, denies that Pirandello influenced him. Both writers certainly learned something from Cervantes and Calderón and from the combined philosophical, psychological, and artistic manifestations which Unamuno so aptly called "algo que flota en el ambiente."[2] However, their literary innovations, which reveal so many common bonds, go beyond all previous treatments of the art-life theme.

Niebla is certainly the most Pirandellian of Unamuno's novels. The often-discussed confrontation between Unamuno and Augusto Pérez in the last part of *Niebla* is only the culmination of a process which begins on the first page of the novel and includes such themes as multiplicity of personality and spectator or reader participation, which Pirandello developed more completely in plays other than *Sei personaggi*.

The most salient feature of *Niebla* is that plot is always subordinate to the process of self-conscious creation.[3] At the beginning Augusto Pérez appears to be a character who lacks awareness of his status as a character, without a "plot" into which to fit his actions in a novel-in-the-making. On the first page of the *nivola* when he appears at the door of his home, he has no mission. Even the direction in which to turn is a decision he finds impossible to make. So, trusting to chance, which seems to be the guiding force of his life, he decides to follow the first dog which passes. Chance fails to provide the dog, and instead, "as if dragged by a magnet," he follows a girl who turns out to be Eugenia, the woman with whom he becomes involved. Throughout the book his actions continue to lack clear direction. At one point he finds himself about to make a trip without knowing why or even where he is going.

> Ya lo había anunciado, primero a Rosarito, sin saber bien lo que se decía, por decir algo, o más bien como un pretexto para preguntarle si le acompañaría en él, y luego a doña Ermelinda, para probarle . . . ¿qué? [4]

The Calderonian concept of life as theater in which all are playing parts exemplifies the multiple relationships of life and theater which saturate the novel. Augusto often acts because he realizes he is being observed and is expected to act in a certain way: "Ve aquí cómo he quedado comprometido con esta buena mujer" (p. 29) he says after he speaks to the *portera* at Eugenia's house.[5] Life is a game; "¿Es o no es un juego la vida?—Hombre, de jugar, jugar bien" (p. 35). And Augusto says to his dog:

> No hacemos más que mentir y darnos importancia. La palabra se hizo para exagerar nuestras sensaciones e impresiones todas . . . , acaso para creerlas. La palabra y todo género de expresión convencional, como el beso y el abrazo . . . No hacemos sino representar cada uno su papel. ¡Todos personas, todos caretas, todos cómicos! Nadie sufre ni goza lo que dice y expresa, y acaso cree que goza y sufre; si no, no se podría vivir. En el fondo estamos tan tranquilos. Como yo ahora aquí, representando a solas mi comedia, hecho actor y espectador a la vez. No mata más que el dolor físico. La única verdad es el hombre fisiológico, el que no habla, el que no miente." [p. 96]

Even insects have roles to play in this novel. Their actions do not seem authentic to Augusto, who senses, although he does not consciously realize, his own unreality and purposelessness: "¡La hormiga, ¡bah!, uno de los animales más hipócritas! Apenas hace sino pasearse y hacernos creer que trabaja" (p. 28).[6] Ermelinda, Eugenia's aunt, thinks that love is also part of the game of fiction invented by poets; in her opinion love is poetic nonsense.

In *Niebla* the characters are simultaneously actors and spectators, with the typical resulting confusion. Victor tells Augusto that they are acting in a play on the stage of consciousness, and that they themselves are also the spectators. Eventually Augusto begins to feel that he is a character and asks Victor what he should do. But Victor explains that he is not a character in a drama or novel and should be content to be a character in a *nivola*—the implication is obviously that in this type of literary creation a character is under no obligation to do anything.

On a more distant level of reality, the reader must participate in the creation of the novel. Victor suggests that if a *nivolista* were hidden behind the wardrobe taking notes of all he and Augusto were saying it would seem to the readers that nothing was happening. Augusto answers that they would say no such thing if they could only see within him. Victor inquires: "¿Por dentro de quién? ¿De ti? ¿De mí? Nosotros no tenemos dentro. Cuando no dirían que aquí no pasa nada es cuando pudiesen verse por dentro de sí mismos, de ellos, de los que leen" (p. 146). The soul of a character, he says, has no more "interior" than that which the reader provides. Thus, in the new art the spectator or reader does not receive a self-contained work with all problems settled and mysteries clarified. He must actively intervene in the formation of the novel and add something of himself to it; there must be a definite reciprocity between spectator and play, between reader and novel. Novels and plays of this type are not static, but are forever changing in the uncertain dimension the reader or spectator supplies.[7]

The impact of theater on life is also shown. Domingo, Augusto's servant, thinks that among members of his social class crimes of passion are unnatural. He does not believe in jealousy, provided that the injured partner does not suffer materially. But Augusto reminds Domingo that his peers do commit many crimes of passion. Domingo retorts that those are the people who have gone to the theater and read novels. He believes that everyone likes to play a part and that no one is really himself, but performs the social role which is imposed on him by others.

Confusion seems to be a necessary part of the scheme of life envisioned by authors who choose to shuffle fiction and reality—it is often difficult to discover where one ends and the other begins. Victor explains that it is necessary to create confusion, to confuse sleep with wakefulness, fiction with reality, and truth with falsehood in an all-enveloping mist.

The play-within-the play, although far from new in the twentieth century, has become one of the important components of Pirandellism. Translated into novelistic terms, several novels-within-the-novel or "novelitas intercaladas" are found in *Niebla*.[8] An additional dimenson comes into the novel with the appearance of Don Avito Carrascal, a character from Unamuno's earlier novel *Amor y pedagogía*. Unamuno carefully explains who Avito Carrascal is in a footnote, so that the illusion of autonomy, which enables a character to pass from one novel to another, will not be lost to those who have not read the previous novel.

The novelist-within-the-novel, corresponding to the playwright-within-the-play, is represented by Victor Goti and later by Unamuno himself. But Victor's role is further complicated by his autonomy as a character which is established through the prologue he writes to *Niebla*. This prologue Unamuno disputes in a post-prologue. On the other hand, as the novelist-within-the-novel he appears to be Unamuno's stand-in, until Unamuno himself enters in the latter part of the work. Victor is also writing a *nivola,* and his description of his technique also describes Unamuno's method of writing *Niebla*. For example, Victor's novel has no plot: "O, mejor dicho, será el que vaya saliendo. El argumento se hace él solo. Mis personajes se irán haciendo según obren y hablen, sobre todo según hablen" (p. 91).

The idea that the novelist himself may not be in full control of the situation and that a character may be autonomous to the point of controlling his author is suggested early in the novel when Victor states confidently that his characters only say what he wishes. This leads Augusto to foreshadow his own confrontation with Unamuno. He tells Victor that at the beginning he will believe that he is controlling his characters, but in the end he may be convinced that the opposite is true, for the characters may really control him. Frequently, he adds, an author becomes the plaything of his fictional personages.

Although Augusto Pérez is not writing a book, his invention of Eugenia definitely parallels the authorial process of creation. He is quite conscious of the fact that he is forming Eugenia: "¡Mi Eugenia, sí, la mía . . . ésta que me estoy forjando a solas" (p. 31), and while he is thinking about "his" Eugenia, he crosses paths with the real girl several times without seeing her. Already Augusto Pérez's fictional creation is more important than the real woman whom he is incapable of describing. Her very materialistic first remark about him, "¡No tiene mal porte y parece bien acomodado!" (p. 33), shows how different the real-life girl is from Augusto's idealized version of her. She uses art for material gains only; the piano, for example, is merely a way of making a living. A more unworthy object of platonic adoration could not be imagined.

Unamuno treats the multiplicity of personality in a somewhat more exaggerated fashion than Pirandello does. Augusto realizes that the *portera*'s idea of Eugenia is different from his own:

¡Oh Eugenia, mi Eugenia, has de ser mía! ¡Por lo menos, mi Eugenia, ésta que me he forjado sobre la visión fugitiva de aquellos ojos, de aquella yunta de estrellas en mi nebulosa; esta Eugenia sí que ha de ser mía; sea la otra, la de la portera, de quien fuera! [p. 34]

She is almost totally his creation, whereas in Pirandello the observer attempts to discover the truth about another, however much he may be hampered by his own preconceived opinions. Augusto is not interested in other points of view and avoids conversation with acquaintances who insinuate that they know Eugenia. He even considers giving her a different name from the one others use because he suspects that there may be more than one Eugenia: "¿Hay una sola Eugenia, o son dos, una la mía y otra la de su novio?" (p. 60).[9] The impossibility of knowing another person is unequivocally put forth when it is suggested that the word *conocer* should be limited to its Biblical meaning: "El único conocimiento eficaz es el conocimiento *post nuptias*. Ya me has oído, esposa mía, lo que en lenguaje bíblico significa conocer" (p. 51).

What one believes is demonstrated to be more important than the actual truth in the "novelita intercalada" about the fireworks manufacturer whose beautiful wife is his main source of pride. After an explosion which blinds him and destroys his wife's beauty, he continues to imagine her as she was before the accident, and the sheer force of the thought causes it to become truth for him: "¿No seguía siendo hermosa para él?" (p. 114).

The lack of a definite boundary between truth and fiction achieves fullest expression in the last pages when Augusto visits Unamuno in Salamanca to consult with him about his decision to commit suicide. At the beginning of the interview Unamuno thinks he has full control of the situation, but after Augusto's initial shock at learning he does not really exist, he recovers and tries to turn the tables on Unamuno, telling him that perhaps he is the fictional personage, the one who does not really exist in life or in death. Augusto even suggests that Unamuno is simply the medium for communicating Augusto's story to the world. Becoming impatient, Unamuno decides that Augusto cannot commit suicide, for he doesn't really exist, but Unamuno can and will kill him. Augusto objects strongly to this fate, but Unamuno implacably informs him it is already written and there is nothing to be done about it.

The manner in which Augusto dies illustrates the confusion which results when fiction and reality intermingle. A telegram from Augusto sent after his death tells Unamuno that the author has had his way. However, three observers disagree about the cause of death: the doctor thinks it was a heart attack, Domingo suggests it was indigestion, and Liduvina believes it was mental disturbance. Domingo seems to have the last word when he affirms "Lo de mi señorito ha sido un suicidio y nada más que un suicidio. ¡Se salió con la suya!" (p. 160). The choice of the method of death is clever because there is no possible way to ascertain whether the heavy meal, which Augusto compares to the last meal of a condemned man, is cause or effect. The decision to overeat, like all of his "decisions" in the book, appears to be made without intention, because the desire to gorge himself comes upon him while he is eating a normal amount. He orders more and more and the act of eating even affirms his existence, *edo ergo sum*. In the prologue of the book Victor Goti assures the reader that his friend did commit suicide, something which Unamuno denies in the post-prologue.

When Unamuno receives the telegram, he repents of his actions and considers resurrecting Augusto, but Augusto appears to him in a dream and tells him that resurrection is impossible. So, in actuality, the fictional character does have the last word.

A comparison of *Sei personaggi in cerca d'autore* and *Niebla* reveals that these two masterpieces do indeed have much in common. *Niebla* is a novel-in-the-making, and Pirandello's play deals with a "commedia da fare." The focus is on the creative process, and both authors have purposely chosen characters and situations which are quite ordinary, and which could not possibly distract the readers from the *raison d'être* of the works.

The concept which Augusto Pérez has of his own being is very similar to the father's in *Sei personaggi*. Augusto protests that he should not have to submit himself to his author's whim because even fictional characters have their internal logic. He cannot do what a reader would not expect him to do. Unamuno believes that a *nivolistic* being is different, but Augusto is not convinced. The father in *Sei personaggi* states that the reality of a character cannot change:

> Non cangia, non può cangiare, né esser altra, mai, perché già fissata—cosí—"questa"—per sempre—(è terribile, signore!) realtà immutabile, che dovrebbe dar loro un brivido nell'accostarsi a noi! [p. 127]

When a character is born, he immediately becomes independent, even of his own author. This enables everyone to imagine the character in situations which the author has not conceived for him, and it also allows the character to acquire a significance the author never dreamed of giving him.

Both the father and Augusto are in this difficult positon. As a character each is at the author's or director's mercy, for this figure must provide the vehicle to express his reality, his existence. At the same time he feels superior to the author because, as the father explains in *Sei personaggi,* he who is a "live" character can laugh even in the face of death. The writer will die, but the character will continue to live even though, as in the cases of Sancho Panza and Don Abbondio, he is not particularly talented nor accomplished miracles. "Eppure vivono eterni, perché—vivi germi—ebbero la ventura di trovare una matrice feconda, una fantasia che li seppe allevare e nutrire, far vivere per l'eternità!"[10] Augusto Pérez has a similar idea of his immortality:

> ¡Yo no puedo morirme; sólo se muere el que está vivo, el que existe, y yo, como no existo, no puedo morirme . . . , soy inmortal! No hay inmortalidad como la de aquello que, cual yo, no ha nacido y no existe. Un ente de ficción es una idea, y una idea es siempre inmortal. [p. 156]

Augusto reminds Unamuno that he has said many times that Don Quijote and Sancho are not only as real but more real than Cervantes.

The author in *Niebla* and the director in *Sei personaggi* are surprised and somewhat resentful at the characters' action. The device of using the director in *Sei personaggi* instead of the author is similar to Unamuno's expedient of allowing Victor Goti to represent him before he himself appears. Both Unamuno and Pirandello mention themselves, and both introduce earlier writings into the work: when *Sei personaggi* opens, the actors are rehearsing *Il giuoco delle parti,* and in *Niebla* Avito Carrascal, a character from *Amor y pedagogía* appears. At the end of the novel Unamuno has a more important part than Pirandello gives himself in any of his plays, but in *La tragedia d'un personaggio* the character-author confrontation is very similar to the Augusto-Unamuno interview. The active participation of the reader in *Niebla* anticipates the importance the spectator would have in *Questa sera si recita a soggetto* and *Ciascuno a suo modo.*

One concern basic to both authors is the impossibility of completely knowing another person. This arises from the twofold complication that each person plays a role and each sees others through the filter of his own personality. Other shared traits emerge from details in the works of Unamuno and Pirandello: both refer to their literary creatures as *fantasmi,* and both employ the mirror as an important element. Both create situations where the character pleads with the implacable author but at the same time is conscious of his value and thinks he is really better or at least more real than the author. The impossibility of discovering the truth in an atmosphere of conflicting opinions and contradictory evidence finds illustration in the doubt about the cause of Augusto's death in *Niebla* and the lack of a final explanation in *Così è (se vi pare).*

In the preface to *Sei personaggi,* Pirandello compares artistic creation to giving birth to a child. No matter how much a woman wants to be a mother, the desire is not enough. One day "ella si troverà a esser madre, senza un preciso avvertimento di quando sia stato" (p. 58). The artist, too, while living collects within himself many germs of life; he can never say how and why at a certain moment one of these vital germs inserts itself into his fantasy in order to become a living creature on a plane of life superior to changeable daily existence. Thus, the six characters appeared before him waiting for him to put them in a novel, drama, or short story. "Nati vivi, volevano vivere" (p. 58).

Unamuno explains literary creation in similar terms in his essay *A lo que salga.* He characterizes as *vivíparos* those writers who when writing a novel meditate about the plot; they think and reconsider their thoughts, whether asleep or awake; in other words, they gestate. And when they feel labor pains and the urgent necessity to exteriorize the obsession which has haunted them so long, they take their pens and give birth.[11]

While the similarities between *Sei personaggi* and *Niebla* are striking, the differences between the two works are equally significant. Considered as companion pieces, they present many of the possible relationships between art and fiction and the process of literary creation in two different genres. Pirandello concentrates on the problems of the stage and the impossibility of satisfactorily translating life into stage material, whereas Unamuno does not find any such obstacles in the wider range provided by the novel.

Niebla seems to have form without content; that is, Augusto, the chief character, although born "alive," has neither strong personality nor desires. This cerebral character moves through a novel without plot. Conversely, Pirandello's six characters are full of passion and have a story, but lack the form which will give their experience the artistic expression that will permit them to live forever as characters.

Augusto does not struggle with his author for his existence as a character. In fact, he does not know for sure that he is a character until the last pages of the novel, when his most important desire seems to be to assert free will, to kill himself rather than be killed by the author. His impulse is to escape from the author, although he realizes this wish cannot be fulfilled. Augusto is never rejected by Unamuno, who feels a strong sense of possession toward his character.

Throughout Pirandello's play each of the six characters is in a different stage of incomplete formation, and the father and stepdaughter are fully aware of their nature. They realize that they need an author to bring them into full being as characters, and their efforts (with the aid of the director and actors) to give dramatic form to their story provide the action of the play.

In both works an injustice has been done to the protagonists. The six characters are created and then rejected, which causes them great frustration. Augusto has been led to think that he is a man and is naturally resentful at discovering he all along has been "un ente de ficción," apparently lacking the free will necessary to decide his own destiny. The religious implications of *Niebla* can never be forgotten; the relationship between author and character is clearly an allegory of that between God and man.

Pirandellism in Spain is intimately related to the Spanish tradition of combining fiction and reality, a tradition represented chiefly by

Cervantes and Calderón, and Unamuno's awareness of this tradition is often noticed.[12] Victor Goti in his prologue repeats Unamuno's opinion that Cervantes is the only Spanish humorist and emphasizes the fact that both authors are named Miguel. Pirandello was also interested in the humoristic aspect of El Quijote and uses scenes from it in his essay L'umorismo to illustrate his ideas.

In a short essay entitled "Historia de Niebla" written in 1932 to be published with the subsequent editions of Niebla, Unamuno re-examines the desire he conceived in the last pages of the nivola to resurrect Augusto, which he did not do because in a dream Augusto told him it would be impossible. Unamuno mentions his own resurrection of the knight in Vida de Don Quijote y Sancho and concludes that the recreation of fictional characters is always possible. Of course Unamuno's Don Quijote is not the same as Cervantes's, but that is not really of prime importance.

Victor Goti specifically explains that the "novelitas intercaladas" are in the tradition of Cervantes. Most important of all, Dulcinea is certainly Eugenia's ancestress, an idea which Unamuno suggests by frequent use of the word "dulce" to describe Eugenia. In fact, the word is used three times in Augusto's first short letter to her. Like Dulcinea, Eugenia is an ordinary person who has been idealized by her admirer, and the invented woman is the guiding force in the novel. The comparison is significant because Augusto is a typical abúlico of the Generation of '98. Dulcinea inspired Don Quixote to strive actively against evil, whereas her twentieth-century counterpart does no more than accentuate the hero's purely cerebral nature.

It is also quite possible that Galdós left his imprint on Niebla, for we know that Unamuno reacted enthusiastically to El amigo Manso.[13] Also the name Máximo Manso (heroic first name plus humble last name) seems to be a clue to the origin of Unamuno's inspiration for the name Augusto Pérez, especially in view of the many other similarities between the two characters.

Although Unamuno's Niebla is the work which best lends itself to direct comparison with Pirandello's plays, the combination of fiction and reality is one of the main characteristics in many of his other writings. Cómo se hace una novela, for instance, is the best example imaginable of the art-about-art trend associated with twentieth-century avant-garde writers and painters. When he wrote this book in 1925, Unamuno was so obsessed with his exile from Spain as a politically dangerous figure that it almost prevented his doing any real creative activity. However, he decided to write a novel about how to write a novel; he would be a character in his book as he was a character in life.[14]

Although he originally wrote *Cómo se hace una novela* in Spanish, Unamuno asked Jean Cassou to translate it into French, to avoid Spanish censorship. Two years later Unamuno retranslated it from French into Spanish, at the same time adding numerous comments.[15]

In the "Comentario" which precedes his Spanish translation Unamuno states:

> Con esto de los comentarios encorchetados y con los tres relatos enchufados, unos en otros que constituyen el escrito va a parecerle éste a algún lector algo así como esas cajitas de laca japonesas que encierran otra cajita y ésta otra y luego otra más, cada una cincelada y ordenada como mejor el artista pudo, y al último una final cajita . . . vacía. Pero así es el mundo, y la vida." [16]

And, effectively, the book contains many levels of reality: novels within novels, truth and fiction, truth that is altered by fiction, and fiction that is confused with truth. Unamuno writes first of all about himself in exile. His own life is a novel and he has created his life. At times he admits to playing a role: "Hago el papel de proscrito" (p. 100).

Cómo se hace una novela is the "novela de la novela, la creación de la creación" (p. 117). The name of the protagonist, U. Jugo de la Raza, is a combination of Unamuno's ancestral names. U. Jugo de la Raza, in addition to being the character and novelist, is also a reader. He is reading a book which tells him that when he finishes, the reader will die with the protagonist; so the "plot" of this "novel," until almost the end of Unamuno's conclusion, which he added in 1927, consists of J. de la Raza's efforts to avoid finishing the book. Unamuno's eventual solution is that J. de la Raza changes from a passive reader who, without thinking for himself, thoroughly identifies himself with the protagonist to an active reader, as Unamuno always wants his own to be, who participates in the formation of the novel. In so doing J. de la Raza is saved and becomes the novelist of his own life.

When he adds his comments in 1927, Unamuno becomes the reader of his own novel, and his comments illustrate how an ideal reader should react to a novel by always adding something of his own. At the same time the other readers of *Cómo se hace una novela* are directly and indirectly forced to participate in the novel:

Nuestra obra es nuestro espíritu y mi obra soy yo mismo que me estoy haciendo día a día y siglo a siglo, como tu obra eres tú mismo, lector que te estás haciendo momento a momento, ahora oyéndome como yo hablándote. Porque quiero creer que me oyes más que me lees como yo te hablo más que te escribo. Somos nuestra propia obra." [p. 139]

The summary at the end of the book leaves no doubt about what Unamuno has been doing:

Cómo se hace una novela, bien! Pero, para qué se hace? Y el para qué es el porqué. Porqué o sea para qué se hace una novela? Para hacerse el novelista. Y para qué se hace el novelista? Para hacer al lector, para hacerse uno con el lector. Y sólo haciéndose uno el novelador y el lector de la novela se salvan ambos de su soledad radical. En cuanto se hacen uno se actualizan y actualizándose se eternizan. [p. 157. This edition often lacks inverted punctuation.]

Thus in *Cómo se hace una novela* there are a number of characteristics which can be associated with Pirandello: the many levels of reality, reader participation, the novelist-within-the-novel, the novel in the making, the novel about the novel. All these features reveal that this essay enters fully into the literary current shared by Pirandello, but beyond this, *Cómo se hace una novela* is one of the few places in which Unamuno actually mentions Pirandello. Jean Cassou, in his "retrato de Unamuno," which precedes his translation, remarks that Pirandello "a cuyo idealismo irónico se le han reprochado amenudo ciertos juegos unamunianos" (p. 27) has kept his mad mother [sic., it was his wife] with him for a long time. This adventure, he remarks, is comparable to Unamuno's life, which has been lived in the company of a divine madman: Don Quijote. And in his commentary on Cassou's remarks, Unamuno characterizes living with a mad person as the "rasgo más íntimo, más entrañado, más humano de la novela dramática que es la vida de Pirandello" (p. 50). He amends Cassou's remarks, however, saying that although he has also lived with a mad person, it is not only Don Quijote but Spain.

Unamuno was sixty-one years old when he wrote *Cómo se hace una novela*. At about the same age (sixty-three) Pirandello conceived the idea of *Quando si è qualcuno,* which treats the problem of a famous poet who is no longer master of his actions, because the image which the public has formed of him is now thoroughly fixed by his past actions—he is the statue of himself.

The same problem is certainly one of the subthemes of *Cómo se hace una novela:* "Mi novela! Mi leyenda! El Unamuno de mi leyenda, de mi novela, el que hemos hecho juntos mi yo amigo y mi yo enemigo y los demás, mis amigos y mis enemigos, este Unamuno me da vida y muerte, me crea y me destruye, me sostiene y me ahoga. Es mi agonía. ¿Seré como me creo o como se me cree?" (p. 71).

The process of literary creation continued to be important to Unamuno, and in *La novela de don Sandalio, jugador de ajedrez* (1930), he rejects reality in favor of fiction even more aggressively than he had before. The narrator is Unamuno, although he makes a weak attempt to hide the fact by using the time-honored device of letters addressed to a friend which he says a reader has sent to him.[17] In this novel without a plot the narrator plays chess with Don Sandalio in almost complete silence while he "invents" Don Sandalio, in the same way that Augusto invented Eugenia, but here the real man is much less important than was Eugenia in *Niebla*. The novelist stops casino members who are eager to inform him about his companion and he would even have avoided knowing the minimum facts about Don Sandalio if that had been possible. At the same time it is apparent that Don Sandalio is "inventing" the narrator. After Sandalio's death in prison, his son-in-law tells the narrator that his father-in-law had often spoken of him. This is a complete surprise because the narrator thought that Sandalio didn't even know his name.

In the epilogue Unamuno pretends to speculate about the true origin of the letters, inquiring if Felipe, the person to whom they were supposedly addressed, actually wrote the letters himself in order to write his own autobiography anonymously. "¿Será todo ello una autobiografía novelada del Felipe destinatario de las cartas y al parecer mi desconocido lector mismo? ¡El autor de las cartas! ¡Felipe! ¡Don Sandalio el ajedrecista! ¡Figuras todas de una galería de espejos empañados!"[18]

Even more than in the case of the other novels which have been discussed, the reader is encouraged to participate actively in this work because Unamuno explains that he has decided to write a novel about a novel, "algo así como sombra de una sombra" (p. 95). He emphasizes that he is not writing the novel of a novelist but the novel of a novel, and that he is writing it for his readers, for the readers that he has formed at the same time as they have formed him. And he says that he is certain that his readers will prefer his system of giving them novels to which they must add the plots.

Although the three novels analyzed above seem to have the most in common with Pirandello's work, other works by Unamuno also contain elements which could be associated with the Italian playwright. In *San Manuel Bueno, mártir* (1933) the protagonist has converted his life into nothing more than the role of a village priest. He wants the people to remain happy in their innocent beliefs, and he does everything possible to perpetuate the farce in an unsuccessful attempt to convert the fiction of belief into reality. He identifies himself with a clown who passes through town, because while the clown is making people laugh his wife is dying. "El santo eres tú, honrado payaso; te vi trabajar y comprendí que no sólo lo haces para dar pan a tus hijos, sino también para dar alegría a los de los otros." [19]

In an entirely different way, *Nada menos que todo un hombre* (1920) may be compared with Pirandello's early Sicilian play, *Il berretto a sonagli*. In both the Italian and Spanish works the heroines are sent to an asylum for a while in order to negate the consequences of their telling the truth about illicit affairs, thus allowing society to believe the fictional situation which is more acceptable.

Unamuno's plays also enter fully into the literary current associated with Pirandello. *Soledad* (1921) is hardly a surprising sequel to *Niebla*. The hero, Agustín, is a playwright-within-the-play who later becomes a politician.[20] There is mention of the idea that all life is fiction, and when Agustín creates a character he goes through something very much like labor pains:

> Es menester que [los demás] sientan mis torturas, que mis criaturas palpiten de vida . . . , de vida y de goce y de dolor . . . ; que pesen sobre las tablas . . . ¡No! ¡Sobre las almas!, que hinchan de pasión el escenario. Y éste es mi drama, el drama del dramaturgo, el drama del parto . . . ¡Le tengo aquí, le siento; me pesa, hasta me cocea dentro de la cabeza y no logro . . . parirlo!" [21]

Life becomes confused with fiction in the mind of Soledad, Agustín's wife. In a concept of parenthood similar to that found in some of Pirandello's plays, Soledad calls Gloria, the actress who interprets the feminine roles in Agustín's plays, Agar, from the Biblical story in which Sara, who couldn't have a child of her own, encourages her

The fictional character triumphs over the real man, as Manuel García Blanco remarks in the prologue of Unamuno's *Teatro completo:* "Se enfrentan y luchan un hombre de carne y hueso con un ser de ficción, y, pirandelianamente, acaba por vencer éste, mientras que aquél, el que pudo y no quiso ser tirano, sucumbe ahora víctima de la tiranía del personaje" (p. 130).

The play echoes a strain which is often found in Pirandello's works. The action is similar to the unsuccessful attempt of Mattia Pascal to pretend to be dead and begin a new existence. It is also reminiscent of *Quando si è qualcuno,* written after Unamuno's play, in which a famous poet unsuccessfully attempts to escape from the fixed image which has been given to him by the public.

The identity theme continues to occupy Unamuno in *El otro* (1926), a work which posits the identity problem within the characters of Cosme and Damián who were identical twins. When the play opens, only one twin remains because he has killed his brother. He refuses to reveal his identity and will only say that he is "el otro." He has covered all the mirrors in the house as he cannot bear to see "el otro." Since childhood he has suffered upon seeing himself outside of himself.[22]

The play centers around the problem of the remaining twin's identity, and "el otro" seems to be more confused than anyone else: "¿Yo? ¿Asesino yo? Pero ¿quién soy yo? ¿Quién es el asesino? ¿Quién el asesinado? ¿Quién el verdugo? ¿Quién la víctima? ¿Quién Caín? ¿Quién Abel? ¿Quién soy yo, Cosme o Damián? Sí, estalló el misterio, se ha puesto a razón la locura, se ha dado a luz la sombra" (p. 816).

The epilogue is especially reminiscent of Pirandello's *Così è (se vi pare)* because Don Juan wants to know the truth, "la solución pública." The *Ama,* who seems to be speaking for Unamuno, thinks it is not necessary to know the truth: "¿La solución pública? Es la que menos debe importarnos. ¡Quédese cada cual con la suya y . . . en paz!" (p. 853).

But Unamuno more clearly makes the comparison between the situation and the fate of man than does Pirandello, although Pirandello may have had something very similar in mind.[23] The importance of the religious overtones in Unamuno's play is made clear when in the last important speech of the play the *Ama,* rising solemnly, utters the following:

¡El misterio! Yo no sé quién soy, vosotros no sabéis quiénes sois, el historiador no sabe quién es (Donde dice: "El historiador no sabe quién es", puede decirse: "Unamuno no sabe quién es."), no sabe quién es ninguno de los que nos oyen. Todo hombre se muere, cuando el Destino le traza la muerte, sin haberse conocido, y toda muerte es un suicidio, el de Caín. ¡Perdonémonos los unos a los otros para que Dios nos perdone a todos!" [pp. 853–54]

Unamuno subtitles *El hermano Juan* (1929), the last play he wrote which is pertinent to our topic, *El mundo es teatro,* a phrase descriptive of all his theater. As he explains in the prologue Unamuno approaches the subject from Don Juan's point of view, because Don Juan is the most eminently theatrical character and he is always representing himself. Of all the plays discussed, this is most directly based on the tradition represented by Calderón's *auto, El gran teatro del mundo,* which Unamuno clearly had in mind: "En este teatro del mundo, cada cual nace condenado a un papel, y hay que llenarlo so pena de vida" (p. 879). The other characters know that Don Juan is an actor, and that he is only the shade of a man playing a part. Antonio remarks that the good actor is the one who conducts himself on the stage just as if he were in his home, but Juan thinks it is the opposite: the good actor is he who conducts himself in his home as if he were on the stage. Both are equally fictional.

As in most of his other writings of this type, Unamuno brings himself into the picture, creating a striking juxtaposition of art and life, when Don Juan inquires:

¿Existo yo? ¿Existes tú, Inés? ¿Existes fuera del teatro? ¿No te has preguntado nunca esto? ¿Existes fuera de este teatro del mundo en que representas tu papel como yo el mío? ¿Existís, pobres palomillas? ¿Existe don Miguel de Unamuno? ¿No es todo esto un sueño de niebla? Sí, hermana, sí, no hay que preguntar si un personaje de leyenda existió, sino si existe, si obra. Y existen Don Juan y Don Quijote y don Miguel y Segismundo y Don Alvaro, y vosotras existís, y hasta existo yo . . . es decir, lo sueño . . . Y existen todos los que nos están aquí viendo y oyendo mientras lo estén, mientras nos sueñen. . . . [p. 972]

El hermano Juan is the play in which Unamuno most aggressively calls attention to the material existence of the stage. Juan often shouts that they are in the theater, "Lo que no olvido es que piso tablado" (p. 918), and the frequent use of theatrical terminology underlines this condition: *bastidores, tramoya, tablas, apuntadores, comediantes.* And by extension, life is fiction, and men are no more than the parts they play.

In these four theatrical pieces, Unamuno treats different aspects of intermixed fiction and reality. In *Soledad* he approaches the topic from the point of view of a man who in his role as author honestly creates fictional situations and then as politician superimposes fiction on life. In *Sombras de sueño* life is theater, for the role which has been given to a human being is more important than the essence of his personality which is completely stifled by the image superimposed upon it. *El otro* is also concerned with the mystery of identity and the nature of personality; as in *Sombras de sueño* the hero can no longer bear to live with the personality which had been established for him. Even in Unamuno's early play *La esfinge* the hero says: "No hago más que representar un papel, Felipe; me paso la vida contemplándome, hecho teatro de mí mismo" (p. 215).

In almost all of Unamuno's work which can be associated with Pirandello, there is also a full awareness of the Spanish tradition regarding fantasy and reality. Unamuno mentioned in an interview in 1928 that he was planning to write a play called *Maese Pedro,* which judging by the following description, would be a definite link between Cervantes and twentieth-century dramatic techniques as found in Pirandello's plays:

> Tengo apuntes de un drama que se llamará *Maese Pedro.* Maese Pedro estará en escena, y sobre ella se levantará un segundo escenario, donde sus muñecos realizarán el drama. Pero Maese Pedro no será un personaje pasivo. Interrumpirá a sus muñecos, discutirá con ellos, hará aclaraciones sobre los motivos que mueven a los personajes.[24]

Critics have suggested that Unamuno was actually influenced in his later work by his Italian colleague. Certainly, when in *El otro* the Ama says that the public solution is the least important of all and "¡Quédese cada cual con la suya y . . . en paz!" (p. 853), the language employed suggests one of Pirandello's titles, *Ciascuno a suo modo,* and the outcome is exactly the same as in *Così è (se vi pare)* in which the bystanders never do learn who Signora Ponza is. And Unamuno's plan for the staging of *Maese Pedro* certainly sounds Pirandellian, especially if the term evokes not only the Italian's plays, but also Spanish plays such as *El señor de Pigmalión* by Jacinto Grau.

But these possibilities of direct influence are of minor importance and Unamuno's writings would probably have been basically the same even if Pirandello had not existed. Unamuno's work has great unity from beginning to end, and statements which sound Pirandellian can be found just as easily in his early work, such as *Amor y Pedagogía,* as in his last plays. The uncanny similarities in their writings, however, will probably continue to interest critics for quite some time, because even the possibility of a sort of negative influence should be taken into account. As Zubizarreta explains: "Don Miguel, que había roto el marco de la ficción en su novela *Niebla,* quizá limitado por la producción de Pirandello, no se atrevió a romperlo en el teatro." [25] Of course it is possible to answer to this that Unamuno simply did not approve of completely tearing down the fourth wall in the theater. The remark quoted above that it is horrible for the horses to come galloping down upon the spectators suggests that he preferred to maintain separation of audience and stage. Also, in the prologue of *El hermano Juan* he seems repelled by the idea of trying to go to the same lengths in the theater which he reached with delight in *Niebla.* He says that Julio de Hoyos wanted to stage *Niebla,* but he firmly rejected the idea because he believed the scene in which Augusto Pérez confronts him would be impossible:

> No cabe en escenario de tablas un personaje de los que llamamos de ficción representado allí por un actor de carne y hueso, y que afirme que él, el representado, es el real y no quien lo representa, y menos el autor de la pieza, que puede estar hasta materialmente muerto. ¿Y cuando presumí después que acaso se propusiera proyectarme a mí, el autor, cinematográficamente, y acaso hacerme hablar por fonógrafo? ¡Antes muerto! Sólo se vive por la palabra viva, hablada o escrita, no de máquina." [p. 857]

In the previous chapter which discussed Pirandello's relationship to cubism, we noted that both Picasso and Pirandello were destructive and playful, that Picasso even drove nails through the back of his paintings, letting the points protrude through the surface. Although cubist tendencies in Unamuno are much more subtle, he does often share the love of whimsy and prank found in the artists of his time. In Victor Goti's prologue to *Niebla* there is the exact equivalent in literature to Picasso's action:

> Y menos mal que ese ingenuo público no parece haberse dado cuenta de alguna otra de las diabluras de don Miguel, a quien a

menudo le pasa lo de pasarse de listo, como es aquello de escribir un artículo y luego subrayar al azar unas palabras cualesquiera de él, invirtiendo las cuartillas para no poder fijarse en cuáles lo hacía. Cuando me lo contó, le pregunté por qué había hecho eso y me dijo: "¡Qué sé yo . . . por buen humor! ¡Por hacer una pirueta!" [p. 10]

There is ample evidence that a great community of interests existed between these two original writers and thinkers of the twentieth century, that they reacted in a strikingly similar manner to the pulse of the age. Yet behind this there is still another parallel: both Pirandello and Unamuno were capable of synthesizing their own personal attitudes toward life with the traditional "life-is-a-stage" concept found in great writers of the past such as Calderón, Shakespeare, and Cervantes.

❧ Part 2
Pirandellism
and the Influence of Pirandello

AZORÍN

Azorín has shown more enthusiastic admiration for Pirandello and the new tendencies associated with him than has any other Spanish writer. For example, in the *Prólogo sintomático* he imagines that the audience exclaims: "¡Bravo! ¡Bravo! . . . ¡El autor! ¡El autor! ¡Originalísimo desenlace! . . . ¡Pirandélico! ¡Cubístico! ¡Es una maravillosa alteración de planos! ¡El autor, el autor! ¡Tendencias nuevas! ¡Completamente nuevas! ¡Así se renueva el teatro! ¡Ya hacía falta un golpe de audacia!" [1]

Apart from his direct references to the Italian playwright, the themes and techniques of Azorín's plays, written soon after Pirandello's first productions given in Spain in 1923, demonstrate that Azorín was inspired by Pirandello to a considerable extent. Critics have limited themselves to pointing out that this influence exists, but have not discussed its implications. [2] Azorín's very enlightening newspaper articles written over a span of more than twenty years on the subject of Pirandello's theater and innovations associated with him have not been studied in this connection, perhaps because they have not all been readily available until recently. [3]

As early as 1925 Azorín realized the far-reaching effects that Pirandello's innovations would have in the theater. His essay, "El arte del actor" is divided into two parts. The first of these, "Neblina en 1590" treats the changes caused by the new theater of Lope de Vega; the second, "Neblina en 1925," discusses Pirandello's contribution. Both trends are compared to a developing and eventually all-enveloping mist: "Hay algo en el mundo que antes no existía. El teatro de Luis Pirandello—teatro del ensueño, de lo inexistente— representa el comienzo de una nueva neblina de la estética. Poco a poco va extendiéndose" (8:925). The mist has extended to France in the theater of Bernstein, Lenormand, and Sarment. Azorín wonders whether within six to ten years all theater will be enveloped in this mist which is forming now. He explains that because of the war, man is repelled by reality and consequently attracted by an inconcrete, spiritual region of psychological phantoms, "una región, en donde lo que predomine no sea el hombre, sino la imagen múltiple, contradictoria e impalpable del hombre. Y ese es el teatro de Pirandello" (8:925).

In one of Azorín's most interesting articles on the subject, "El teatro de Pirandello," (1925) he indicates that he has read two articles which Pirandello wrote about his own techniques. He describes his reaction to one of Pirandello's plays, summarizing three stages in Pirandello's attitude toward reality, three stages which suggest the threefold discipline of the mystic. In the first stage daily reality detaches itself—the concentration is on the personality. "¿Llegamos a creer que nuestra personalidad lo es todo y que la materia circundante no es nada?" (9:145). Doubt begins to enter the spirit:

> Nos tambaleamos, como si estuviéramos un poco inebriados; percibimos que el suelo en que se asientan nuestros pies oscila y se mueve como un frágil e inestable navío. La realidad acaso no exista; tal vez sea una creación nuestra; atraviesa rápidamente por nuestro cerebro el recuerdo de concepciones metafísicas, atrevidas, alucinantes. [9:145]

Once this state of mind becomes customary, the pilgrimage may continue to the second stage where the real world no longer matters because a reality exists which is superior to daily reality. The personality, which is everything, is nothing in itself. Individual identity and the reality of existence are called into question: time makes the personality elusive and one feels like the victim of an agonizing drama:

> ¿Cómo podremos alcanzar, tocar, percibir, aprisionar nuestra propia personalidad? ¿Dónde, dónde, queridos amigos, queridos deudos, está nuestra personalidad? ¿Es la de ayer, es la de hoy, será la de mañana? Nuestras manos se extienden angustiadas en el vacío; no pueden aprehender. Nuestra propia realidad escapa a nosotros mismos. [9:146]

In the third stage, besides escaping from self, the personality escapes from others. "Los seres que nos rodean no ven en nosotros la realidad verdadera, ven otra realidad" (9:146), and what others see in an individual cannot be discovered.[4]

Azorín seems to delight in these meditations based on Pirandello's treatment of the multiplicity of personality and the relativity of truth. He was no less fascinated by Pirandello's technical innovations, which, of course, often reflect and parallel the personality problem and lead to the conclusion that art is more real than life whose reality has been questioned. The theater-within-the-theater (involving several levels of reality and the author as character as well as the play-within-the-play), the autonomous character, and a confrontation with the traditional dimensions of the stage (involving audience participation and scenes played away from the stage) are all treated by Azorín. His meditations are based not only on a knowledge of Pirandello's theater, but also on his familiarity with French theater and French criticism. He knows that things are changing and tries to discover the eventual results of the revolution in the theater. He is aware of the systematic disintegration of form which could eventually lead to the destruction of theater or to an antitheater.

Azorín devotes an entire article to the opinions of Gaston Baty, and summarizes for his readers the French director's concept:

> ¡Adiós, pues, a las obras bien construídas! ¡Adiós al concepto de lo teatral y de lo no teatral, tan dilecto a la crítica! . . . Y que caminamos hacia ese ideal—hacia el teatro espectáculo—lo dice, de modo indubitable, la decadencia, el agotamiento, la caducidad, la muerte de los grandes teatros. [9:173]

Azorín leaves it to the readers, actors, and producers to decide whether or not this applies to Spain, and tacitly shows that he believes it does.

In a satirical essay entitled "Un estreno sensacional," [5] dedicated to "Los amigos de las novedades teatrales a ultranza," Azorín invents a situation which exaggerates Pirandellian tendencies in order to show where the new techniques are leading. It is also possible that he was thinking of the imitations which, according to Bishop,[6] were abundant in France in the 1920s. In this essay he describes a play entitled "Cambio a la vista" in which the change of the stage settings becomes the complete play. The audience, informed that the play would begin at 11:00 sharp, sits before closed curtains, although perceiving from the sounds that the play is actually going on behind the curtain. After one half hour of this, the lights go out, three knocks announce the beginning of a play, and the curtain goes up to reveal the stage setting, which the stagehands proceed to change for the next act "despaciosamente, con arte, sin atrope-llamientos" (8:512). Azorín, who is a member of the audience, comments: "Comencé yo entonces a comprender: Vi que Nemesio Pajares [the playwright] con intuición genial, había comprendido, a su vez, que lo que actualmente interesa en las obras dramáticas no son los actos, sino los entreactos. Y valientemente, convirtió los entreactos en actos" (8:512). The play is greeted with enthusiasm by the public: "el público había ya 'entrado' en la obra, como se dice en la fraseología de los escenarios; llevaba camino 'Cambio a la vista' de ser uno de los más grandes éxitos del teatro, no sólo en España sino en Europa" (8:513).

In his essay "Comedia del arte" (1923) Azorín exaggerates another aspect of Pirandellism by showing situations in which the boundaries between reality and the stage have been erased. An old professor of Cartesian philosophy comes to visit Azorín to discuss the play he has "written" in the *commedia dell'arte* tradition, "Los burladores burlados." It is to be a play-within-a-play; the primary setting is a drama school during the final examination period. The artificial examinations of the conservatory are replaced by "el arte de la vida y de la verdad" (8:74). The previous year the examination consisted of a scene in a café where adulterous lovers were surprised by the woman's husband. The customers in the café thought fiction was reality, there was a scandal, and the director of the drama school even had to pay a fine for disturbing the peace.

This year's students will pretend they are demented and will descend upon a clinic in which there is a great specialist in mental illness. However, without the knowledge of the students the doctor has been informed of the plan and will be acting also.

> ¡Cuántos procedimientos de examen extravagantes, enorme-mente disparatados, les aplica a estos enfermos ante la estupe-facción y el asombro de los actores! Ellos venían a divertirse con el doctor y se encuentran con que este doctor se ha vuelto loco de repente. Los actores todos (el doctor y los enfermos) tienen aquí un amplio margen para su estro festivo. [8:875]

In this essay Azorín states that the *comedia atelana* of ancient Rome is the precursor of the *commedia dell'arte*. His own theoretical examples take the *commedia dell'arte* a step further than Pirandello by actually mixing fantasy with life completely removed from the theater to make the differentiation between the play and life psychologically impossible.

Azorín is aware that Pirandello's systematic disintegration of form could eventually lead to a destruction of theater or to an anti-theater.[7] Pirandello, of course, was also conscious of this as he explains in the preface to his trilogy.[8]

This leads to the problem of aesthetic distance, which many of Pirandello's techniques decrease or destroy. When the spectators actually participate in the play or seem to do so because of spectator-actor interventions, direct address by actors to the audience, or actual scenes which take place in the auditorium among the spectators, they lose the ability to contemplate the work of art objectively as an artistic entity separate from them.[9] Among all of the new devices which cause the spectator to lose his detachment Azorín reveals a particular fascination for that of authentic audience participation in the play. In an article written in 1947, he makes an observation not directly parallel to any of Pirandello's ideas; rather it is more an outgrowth—Azorín's sensitive understanding of genuine audience-actor *rapport* which contributes to the perfect total expression on the part of the actors.[10]

The article is a meditation about Felipe Sassone's desire to dispense with footlights. Azorín thinks that the footlights, by blinding the actor, prevent him from modulating his role delicately according to the reactions of the particular audience. Azorín suggests that Sassone should also leave on the auditorium lights to remove completely the barrier between actors and audience. However, he realizes that in the light the audience would have a different attitude toward the play and would feel more responsible.

> Pero, con la sala iluminada, ¿cuánto cambiaría la actitud del público? No se conduce lo mismo un espectador en la oscuridad que a plena luz; no se aplaude o se desaprueba lo mismo en las tinieblas, cuando nadie nos ve que cuando todo el mundo puede vernos: la responsabilidad—responsabilidad moral, por el aplauso o por la desaprobación—surge en cuanto la luz resplandece en la sala. En la oscuridad esa responsabilidad no existe. [9:122]

Azorín constantly reminds his readers that nothing in the world is new, and he is particularly insistent upon underlining the kinship between Pirandello and Calderón. In his essay "Al margen de un Pirandello" (1946) he quotes one of Calderón's titles, "En esta vida todo es verdad y todo mentira," and goes on to say that in Pirandello's world also everything is true and everything is false; one cannot distinguish between reality and fiction. "Todo es contingente, todo puede ser y todo puede no ser. Puede ser como nos lo presenta el autor y puede ser al revés de como nos lo presenta el autor" (9:151). In "El teatro de Pirandello," (1925) Azorín quotes from *La vita che ti diedi*: "E allora basta che sia viva la memoria, io dico, e il sogno è vita, ecco!" (9:148). Yes, says Azorín, life is a dream, and this thought inevitably leads to Calderón and to the statement: "En esas palabras calderonianas puede resumirse exactamente todo el teatro de este gran dramaturgo, que tanto parecido tiene—en la poderosa facultad de abstraer—con el gran Calderón" (9:148).

"Los seis personajes y el autor" (1924) is not about Pirandello's play at all, but is a description with Pirandellian overtones of Calderón's *auto sacramental, El gran teatro del mundo*. Azorín explains the title of his article in the conclusion, in which he qualifies the two plays as "obras análogas" (9:44) because they present the chaos of human destiny.[11]

In the same article Azorín gives a very interesting resumé of pre-Pirandellism in Spain:

> El teatro, fuera del teatro,[12] tiene antecedentes en España; no reputemos por novedad lo que es sólo reminiscencia. Teatro fuera del teatro es la presente obra de Calderón; y *Los payos en el ensayo,* de don Ramón de la Cruz, y *La crítica del Sí de las niñas,* de Ventura de la Vega, (con precedentes en *La crítica de la escuela de las mujeres* de Molière), y *Un drama nuevo,* de Tamayo (con sus antecedentes del San Ginés, de Rotrou, y el Hamlet), y hasta *Los intereses creados,* de nuestro gran dramaturgo Benavente. [9:44]

Azorín's awareness of historical and ideological precedents is constantly evident. He acknowledges the influence of Maeterlinck and Rilke in his own plays[13] and translated Maeterlinck's *La intrusa* in 1896.[14] Azorín translated Simon Gantillon's *Maya* which Bishop calls one of the "two prominent examples of experimental plays of the twenties reflecting Pirandello's multiple personality concept."[15] He also translated *El Doctor Frégoli* by Nicolai Evreinov, who, as Büdel points out, "saw the world as permeated by pantheatricalism, and the artist's duty for him consisted in an active theatricalization of life. Pirandello's ideas go in the same direction, and his theoretical thinking as well is influenced by this concept."[16]

Azorín is also aware of the relationship between Pirandello's work and psychological experimentation. In his essay "De Claparède a Pirandello" (1927) he describes a psychological experiment in which a grotesquely dressed individual who enters the classroom for a few seconds cannot be identified by the students a week later. Azorín then discusses the difficulty of understanding historical figures,when even living personalities cannot be understood. "No existe una personalidad en cada uno de nosotros; pero los demás—¡ay!, para nosotros mismos también—, para los demás, es como si nosotros nos reflejáramos en diez o doce espejos a la vez" (9:177). He finishes this essay by stating: "El doctor Claparède, director del Laboratorio de Psicología en la Universidad de Ginebra, ha precedido a Luis Pirandello. El sabio suizo justifica—con muchos años de anticipación—al dramaturgo italiano." Azorín adds that among his papers he has found a pamphlet entitled "Expériences sur le témoignage," published in Geneva in 1906. "Deben leerle cuantos admiran y estudian las comedias de Pirandello" (9:177).

Considerable space is also devoted to a discussion of the differences between Jean-Victor Pellerin's ideas expressed in *Têtes de rechange* and those of Luigi Pirandello (9:169). The entire article "Libros sobre el teatro" concerns French playwrights, most of whom have been influenced by Pirandello.

Azorín's comparative studies also lead him to the classics, especially to Plautus. He thinks nothing more Pirandellian exists than Plautus's *Anfitrión* or *Los menecmos:*

> En el *Anfitrión* el pobre Soria no sabe quién es él mismo; existen dos Sorias; no es posible discernir cuál es el verdadero y cuál es el falso . . . Añada usted a esas comedias de Plauto un poco de imaginación moderna, de teorías científicas modernas (los sueños, el amor, la relatividad, etc., etc.) y tendrá usted, en Plauto, un pirandelista formidable. [9:158]

The autonomous characters present in Pirandello's work have often been compared to their Spanish counterparts such as Unamuno's Augusto Pérez or Cervantes's Don Quijote.[17] Azorín also introduces the topic of the autonomous character in "Sobre el teatro," in which "un amigo mío, dramaturgo" describes the playwriting process:

> Lentamente, el dramaturgo va siendo arrastrado por su obra. Los personajes protestan, se rebelan cuando el autor intenta

proceder contra lo vivo y lo humano. Los personajes han comenzado ya a vivir por sí mismos. El autor no es ya dueño de sus personajes. [9:81]

The author has traced the general outlines of his work and within these outlines the conflicts and situations. But when the characters face each other the situation which the author had imagined does not occur—something else does. While the play is being developed the author does not carry it within himself—it develops itself in relationship to the environment. A reading, a conversation overheard, a thousand details from daily life transform the characters.

Los accidentes del medio exterior los van fortaleciendo, agrandando. Y a medida que los personajes son más fuertes, el autor tiene menos imperio sobre ellos. Llega un momento, en fin, en que la obra camina rápida, vertiginosamente, hacia un desenlace. [9:82]

Azorín's concept of the autonomous character in this essay, then, is that he is an entity with freedom to act separately from the author; however, there is no actual conflict with the author—rather his concept seems to imply that exterior events inspire the playwright, whose characters then evolve automatically. Unexpected things happen, but they are still in harmony with their creator.

In "Breve sainete" Azorín describes the work of a playwright as something like automatic writing: "No pienso nada; piensan los personajes, y yo voy escribiendo lo que ellos piensan. Si pensara yo por ellos . . . no serían ellos los que pensaran" (8:876).

The implications of the autonomous character as applied to playwrighting in general have interested Azorín. In "Al margen de un 'Pirandello,'" which is inspired by Walter Starkie's book on Pirandello, he soon forgets that his original intention was to comment on this study and goes on to speculate about the consequences of *Sei personaggi* applied to dramatic characters. He fails to understand why characters would look for an author when an author usually causes trouble for them, and he wonders why they cannot be satisfied with "el mundo indeterminado, incircunscrito, indefinido, en donde reposaban" (9:149). He then creates scenes in which the characters of *Don Alvaro* complain to the Duque de Rivas about what he is going to do to them, "¿No tienes escrúpulos en hacer de mí lo que piensas hacer?" (9:150), and state their intention to flee from him. In this particular essay Azorín again alters the meaning of Pirandello's half-formed characters, who already have been created to a certain point before being abandoned by their author and who have an inner compulsion to act out their story.

Azorín admires "el ilustre dramaturgo italiano" and has been considerably influenced by him, but he seems to be more fascinated by Pirandellism in theory than he is in actually incorporating true Pirandellism in his own plays. Ramón Gómez de la Serna reports his conversation with Azorín about *Angelita,* which the latter was preparing at the time to be performed by amateurs in a village *corral.* Ramón inquired how many acts the play would have and Azorín answered: "Varios . . . Tres, o cuatro, o quizá cinco—a mitad de la comedia, el primer actor avanzará hacia el público y le preguntará si desea más actos, verificándose uno o dos actos más si el público lo pide." [18] In the final version of *Angelita* this invitation to the audience to participate in planning the play does not appear and Azorín probably was not serious when he suggested this possibility.

Old Spain (1926) is one of the most significant of Azorín's plays influenced by Pirandello, a debt he acknowledges in the "Prólogo Sintomático." In this prologue there are diverse opinions about the dénouement. The actress, the actor, and the producer all desire different endings and present their points of view to the author. The *maquinista* explains that each of them is imagining his own dénouement and reveals that the dénouement is exactly the discussion that the people of the stage have every day when the author is not present. The audience loves the play, thinks the mixture of levels of reality is marvelous, admires the new tendencies, and calls the play "pirandélico." The author congratulates himself for the three dénouements in one and affirms that this was the *maquinista*'s idea. Everything will be fine, he adds, as long as the next day they don't tell him it was borrowed from an Italian or Irish or Russian author.

Old Spain is preceded by a prologue which was certainly written under Pirandello's inspiration. An actor tells the audience that he has just come from a friendly argument backstage with the stage director and the author. Mr. Brown, a *commedia dell'arte* tradition clown, constantly interrupts the actor, who cautions him that there can be no play if he overhears his remarks to the audience. At the end of the prologue Mr. Brown attempts to join the audience by jumping over the footlights, but they are too high. He tries to exit via the prompter's shell, but it is occupied. Azorín thus shows that he will go only so far with this type of action—just to the end of the prologue. The twentieth-century Spanish stage is still self-contained and cannot overflow into the audience.

Basically, the technique of this play is conventional. The innovations for which the prologue prepares us are not forthcoming. Although Mr. Brown is a very important character in the play, he is the only person who appears both in the prologue and in the play. It is not until the second *cuadro* of the last act that the play-within-the-play appears. The Spanish countess is staging a skit with the help of hired actors to convince Don Joaquín (an American whom she hopes to marry) that she can be as "extravagante" as he. However, this will be "una broma inocente y muy española, de buen gusto," [19] which seems to sum up Azorín's attitude toward technical innovations in his plays. In the skit, which Don Joaquín is to come upon without knowing it is pretense, Don Quijote appears, and the "Condesita" herself is the "nueva Dulcinea del Toboso."

In this play Pirandellism may be a symbol of the foreign innovations which many members of the Generation of '98 thought would partially solve the problem of Spain. We know that Azorín admired writers who incorporated foreign influence while still remaining thoroughly Spanish. He remarks for example: "Ha sido netamente española Emilia Pardo Bazán, y ha tratado siempre de injerir lo extranjero, como elemento fecundador, en lo nacional." [20] The image employed in this quotation is strongly reminiscent of the advice given to the Spanish countess when she is contemplating marriage to the American, whose mother was Spanish: "¿No ganará usted al fundar en el viejo tronco un árbol nuevo? La Humanidad es eso: renovación, continuación del pasado; pero añadiendo al pasado una fuerza nueva" (4:914).

The thematic content of *Old Spain* makes it a prototype of the work of the Generation of '98 which criticizes isolation, decadence, the deterring effect of religion, and resistance to outside influence and progress, but which at the same time shows great appreciation and love of the traditional values of Spain. Therefore, it seems reasonable to assume that the Generation's formula for the solution to the problem of Spain, innovation plus tradition, is symbolically represented in *Old Spain* not only by the marriage of the Spanish countess to an American whose mother was Spanish, but also by the use of Pirandellian innovations in combination with elements from the Spanish tradition. Azorín is constantly aware of the Spanish precedents for Pirandello's innovations and the Italian's techniques appear in the play accompanied by Spanish pre-Pirandellism, represented in *Old Spain* by Don Quijote and Dulcinea.

Cervantes, o La casa encantada (1931) also emphasizes the relationship between the Quijote theme and Pirandellism.[21] The play-within-the-play represents the delirium of a poet, except for the first scene and the epilogue which treats the manner of preparing the audience for a play based on the subconscious adventures of a poet. The poet, Victor, is the protagonist of the play-within-the-play and he drinks a potion to increase his imaginative power, which in act 3 enables him to visit Cervantes. Don Quijote also arrives, and the surprised Victor exclaims: "¿Es Don Quijote? ¿Existe Don Quijote?" Cervantes inquires: "¿Lo pregunta un poeta? ¿No sabe el señor poeta que los entes de nuestra imaginación son más reales que la misma realidad?" (4:1128). "Don Quijote," however, is only a neighbor, Jacinto, who has served as a model for Cervantes's creation and who has also taken on some of Don Quijote's characteristics through force of suggestion: "a fuerza de oirme llamar Don Quijote, y llevado por mi amor a ese gran personaje, he ido poco a poco, sin darme cuenta, acomodando mi figura a la del caballero inmortal" (4:1130).

Thus, several of Pirandello's techniques and ideas appear, but they are transformed into something quite different—the poet's illness caused him to withdraw into himself, enabling him to discover in his subconscious the true essence of his being. He has found a synthesis of the past and the present and the end of the play calls for a forward surge toward a new world: "alegría, animación. Nuevo el mundo, el cielo, nuevas las nubes . . ." (4:1139).

Angelita (1930), a manifestation of Azorín's preoccupation with time, is his most completely Pirandellian play—it is almost a sampler of Pirandello's techniques and ideas. Azorín calls attention to the theater as such through the use of theater-within-the-theater methods. After Angelita has turned her magic ring twice to make two years pass, she suddenly finds that she is the wife of a playwright, Carlos, who raves about the difficulties he is having in producing his play. In *Angelita,* as in Pirandello's plays, the simultaneous presence of several planes of reality is an indispensable element. Carlos complains that the leading lady is not interpreting properly a scene in which she is to pretend she does not know her husband. The situation in Carlos' own life (although he does not know it) is similar to the scene in the play. He thinks his wife is acting very convincingly when she refuses to recognize him as her husband, but she is not acting—she really does not know him. The confusion of reality and illusion preoccupies Azorín's protagonists: "Y ¿quién te dice a ti que el ensueño no sea la realidad, y la realidad no sea el ensueño? Cuando dormimos, ¿nos acordamos de las imágenes que han pasado?"[22]

Immediately after these questions Angelita and Carlos discuss the relationship of an author to his characters. Carlos claims that he is a prisoner of his images and his characters. Angelita shouts: "¡Acudan, acudan a ver a un hombre que fabrica damas y caballeros, y luego todos mandan en él!" (5:471), which is also quite reminiscent of Galdós' La sombra.[23] There is also a play-within-the-play in Angelita when Angelita and Carlos invent a skit while they are wondering what will be going on in their home five years from then: "Comienza el drama o la comedia; ¡arriba el telón!" (5:472).

The personality problem is also important in this play. Angelita says she depends upon her husband to help her know herself: "para reaccionar contra mí misma y entrar más hondo en mi propia personalidad" (5:474). In the third act, three Angelas appear to show the options for Angelita's future. The first is a New York reporter, the second a married woman usefully employed in organizing the life of her scientist husband, and the third is a social worker. Angelita selects the third possibility. This illustrates the many potential personalities which are contained within the same woman, but is, of course, not quite the same as Pirandello's multiplicity of personality. Another important difference between Azorín's treatment of personality and Pirandello's is that Angelita *succeeds* in discovering her true self.

> Soy yo, que al fin sé lo que debo saber. Sé que para el perfeccionamiento humano se necesita el recogimiento sobre sí mismo. Debemos conocer nuestra personalidad; debemos poner todas nuestras fuerzas, todo nuestro espíritu, todo nuestro fervor, en la realización del bien. [5:504].

The change from first person singular to first person plural converts this personal salvation into a symbol of the salvation of Spain. The members of the Generation were looking for a solution to the problem of Spain and therefore the lack of resolution which characterized many of Pirandello's works would not have been appropriate for them. Angelita has found herself in the same way in which Azorín and other members of the Generation of '98 hoped that Spain would discover its essence. What seems to appeal to Azorín about Pirandello and is pertinent to the problem of Spain is the struggle to define personality.

Azorín's *Comedia del arte* (1927) is a play about actors. The first act ends in an improvisation based on *Oedipus at Colonus* by a young actress Pacita Durán and the leading man, Valdés. After many years art has become life—the actor who played the part of Oedipus is blind. Pacita has become a great actress and when she returns from America she wishes to watch Valdés coach a young actor in a practice session (a "comedia del arte," one of the actors calls it) when Valdés does not know that she is there. The acting lesson involves a scene from *El trovador,* which Valdés interrupts frequently; and the scene ends when he senses that Pacita is present.

In the third act the blind actor, Valdés, who is playing the title role of *Oedipus at Colonus* has been carried away by his part to the point of improvising, and the emotion causes him to faint. The conversation backstage concerns the influence of the audience, a theme which also appears in Azorín's essays. "No veía el público, pero sentía su presencia. Y era algo así como si me fueran apretando el corazón. Me sentía yo en ese momento visto, observado con ansiedad por la muchedumbre" (4:1019).

As happens so often when Azorín destroys the boundaries between art and life, he mentions the life-dream theme or *El gran teatro del mundo* theme of Calderón: "El mundo, hijo mío, es un teatro. Un teatro en que se representa la misma función desde hace siglos, desde que comenzó a vivir la Humanidad. Cambian los personajes, los trajes, las decoraciones; pero la obra es la misma" (4:1021). Valdés dies while the actors recite verses from Calderón.

Azorín employs none of Pirandello's exaggerated theater-within-the-theater techniques, that is, all the action takes place on the stage, for the most part the direct address to the audience appears in the prologues, and the personality problem is resolved at the end—there is no chaos in Azorín's work. However, in his plays Azorín does erase the boundaries between art and life in a very Pirandellian fashion. He is also very much the self-conscious artist. He consistently uses the gamut of theater-within-the-theater techniques involving the mention of theater as such, the problems of actors and the stage, the autonomous character, and Pirandellian themes such as reality versus illusion, conflicting points of view, multiplicity of personality, and madness. The four plays which have been discussed owe the most to Pirandello, however *La guerrilla, Farsa docente,*

Brandy mucho Brandy, and *Lo invisible* also contain certain Pirandellian characteristics.

Several of Azorín's novels are also undoubtedly part of the Pirandellian literary current. Américo Castro believes that he has identified the essence of the Italian's art when he points out that Pirandello forces one to view the painting together with the palette and the paint brushes with which it is painted.[24] Similarly, Azorín often mentions his "cuartillas" and even titles the first chapter of *El libro de Levante* (1929) "El lapicerito de oro," a reference to the pencil he will use to write the novel. Several of Azorín's novels have the creative process as subject, and the novelist, who is Azorín only perfunctorily disguised, is the hero. In *El caballero inactual* (1928), Azorín has given one of the best examples of self-conscious creation, for by observing Félix Vargas, the poet who is the main character in the novel, the reader gains what seems to be a very authentic insight into the unexplainable process of literary creation.

Among the self-portraits of women which Azorín has included in *Capricho* (1943) there is a little masterpiece which concisely relates much that needs to be known about Azorín's purpose in focusing on the process of writing rather than on the story. Adriana Campos must write a short autobiography. She slowly carries blank paper to her room, checking on the cleanliness of her home as she walks and obviously feeling pride and pleasure in what she sees. She enters her room "llevando en la mano como una banderita blanca, las blancas cuartillas" (6:942). She enjoys in anticipation what she confidently feels will be her success in writing: "Si a mí me gusta tanto la limpieza, ¿cómo mi prosa no iba a ser limpia?" (6:942). She continues to procrastinate, however, and confesses that writing is more difficult than she thought it would be. When she finally begins, the dull facts she relates are in obvious contrast to the very human understanding of Adriana that the reader gained from her wanderings and hesitations before she actually started to write. Azorín ends this short chapter very soon after Adriana actually begins to tell about her herself in order to emphasize the fact that as in the entire novel of which this is a small part, it is the process which reveals personality and emotion and not the conventional story which is important.

The interior duplication which accompanies the emphasis on the creative process in literature of this type is quite complex in some of Azorín's novels, as Livingstone describes it:

The novelist-within-the-novelist-within-the-novelist of *El escritor* who is also a novelist-against-the-novelist is but one revealing example of the virtuosity of Azorín in the application of the principle of interior duplication. Among the many writers who have adopted this general technique perhaps none has involved himself more consciously and intentionally and more irretrievably than he.[25]

Azorín seems to have been intrigued by the possibilities inherent in the idea of character creation, and autonomy is one of his favorite devices. In *El libro de Levante,* the readers witness the birth of the character, who later converses with Azorín, affirming his autonomy although he still doesn't have a name: "Usted cree que yo soy su creación, y yo lo que soy es un ente distinto de usted, y libre" (5:377). The character insists that the writer has created him and then tries to become like him instead of the other way around. The author, he believes, becomes the prisoner of the character. In *Capricho* Azorín is quite magnanimous toward his autonomous characters, as he tells them: "Haced lo que queráis, personajes de esta novela. Soy el autor; no os he tratado mal. Si queréis, vais a la casa misteriosa; si no queréis, dejadlo" (6:946).

One element associated with autonomous characters which Américo Castro has commented about in his essay is also quite important in Azorín's novels:

> Pirandello . . . tiene la gentil audacia de arrojar a las tablas del teatro a unos sujetos sólo medio cocidos en la fantasía del autor, que esgrimen agresivamente sus inconclusas personalidades. Asistimos a la elaboración de las sustancias artísticas, penetramos en el subsuelo donde las raíces forman planes de arboleda.[26]

In *Capricho* Azorín tells his characters that they are in a decisive moment, they are in a formative stage, and they will soon become tangible. In *El libro de Levante* the character is very vaguely drawn and never seems to become a completely formed entity of fiction. Azorín's autonomous characters, however, have the possibility of future growth, unlike Pirandello's who seem forever doomed to remain at the stage of creation in which their author left them.

In *Capricho* Azorín does something very strange with his characters. Although they are supposedly people from the publishing world who are to help him write his novel, actually they turn out to be the characters in the novel. Again we have a reversal in which describing the attempt to form a literary work *is* the work of art itself. In this novel the people in the publishing business can be compared to the theatrical people in Pirandello's trilogy. The literary critic, the financial editor, the director, and the chief editor, among others, collaborate with the writer in the same way that Pirandello's director and actors attempt to cooperate in making the characters appropriate for the stage.

Another Pirandellian trait found in Azorín's novels is the impression often given that the book has not really been written yet. The reader must ask himself whether he is reading a novel, or, to use the equivalent theatrical terminology, whether he is merely witnessing the backstage preparations for the real performance. *El libro de Levante* is a "prenovela gaseiforme" [27] and in *Capricho* Azorín gives the choice of several endings.

The question of where reality ends and illusion begins and the intermingling of these apparent opposites, a concern so often characterizing Pirandellian writings, also interests Azorín. One of his purposes in *El escritor* seems to be to reveal how a character is formed of elements which come from the spheres of fantasy and reality, and how it is impossible to identify the origin of different aspects of the character:

> No acierto a esclarecer, empero, el personaje central del libro. No sé si ha de ser auténtico o imaginario. La vida cotidiana me ofrecería sus ejemplares; no tendría yo sino bordar, cual en un dechado, con sedas o estambres de distintos colores. Sobre la realidad pondría yo los accidentes de la fantasía. Poco a poco me iría acercando al personaje, y éste quedaría cada vez más definido. Llegaría un momento—así lo espero—en que el personaje hablaría y accionaría con independencia de mi voluntad. ¿Con más vida, siendo imaginado que real? Y ¿quién puede discernir en la vida lo auténtico de lo ficticio? [6:324]

Quiroga, the novelist-within-the-novel, who really is Azorín, then says that even in the most subtle analysis it is impossible to distinguish between reality and fantasy and that the more deeply one goes into the examination of a character, the more risky the exploration becomes. But now he sees on the blank pages before him the distant image of a character who has just left the chaos of the uncreated and begins to be visible in life. He now lives and has a name: Luis Dávila. But who is he? He feels attracted toward books, but, "Does he write?" inquires Quiroga. Quiroga decides that Luis Dávila will be a writer, so at this point in the novel it seems that Dávila is really Quiroga's (Azorín's) creation. Throughout, the novel creates the strong impression that Dávila represents a younger Azorín, and he is certainly partially Azorín. When Dávila adds his own comments to the novel he remarks that his style resembles Quiroga's.

The relationship between *** and Délago in Pirandello's *Quando si è qualcuno* is an appropriate comparison here. In both cases writers in their mid-sixties invent young counterparts, and the experience turns out to be extremely traumatic, even more so in Pirandello's play than in Azorín's novel, however, because Pirandello shows coexistence to be impossible.

On the other hand, in keeping with Azorín's purpose of making the coalescence of reality and illusion so complete in his central character that he is both real and illusory and yet neither, it is impossible to assert that Dávila is not drawn from reality. Azorín finds a book written by Dávila, and then his friends and acquaintances discuss Dávila with him. The initial conflict between the old and young writers seems insurmountable, but finally they become close friends. Martínez Cachero has even attempted to identify this young writer, suggesting that it is Dionisio Ridruejo, to whom the book is dedicated. Azorín also stated in an interview, Martínez Cachero tells us, that the book is about the contrast between a prewar and a postwar writer.[28]

The way in which Azorín combines reality and illusion disorients some of his characters. In *Capricho* the theatrical critic "Unía en su desorientación dos realidades igualmente ficticias. ¿Era o no la estación del Norte estación de verdad?" (6:901). Also, in the same novel Azorín confesses: "Todos los personajes de este libro andan un tanto perplejos; habrá que reconocerlo" (6:914). But the stance which has been noticed in Cervantes and Pirandello is not lacking in Azorín either, for the little philosopher also comes to the conclusion that reality is what is represented in the imagination: "Lo real es lo que nuestra imaginación nos representa. Nada más vital que la creencia" (6:987).

While the new art is important in many of these novels, and in fact the original title of *El libro de Levante* was *Superrealismo,* an exact comparison cannot be made between the technique of this novel and artistic surrealism. Nevertheless, Azorín's terminology often suggests that he has pictorial representation in mind and it is quite legitimate to show certain traits of modern artistic movements in many of his novels.

Of course the very title of the novel *Capricho* suggests that Azorín knows that playfulness is part of the new artistic approach, and he inquires: "¿Por qué no deportarse en las cuartillas, como nos deportamos, tras el trabajo, en deleitable campo?" (6:887). But then he explains that he is capricious in the same way as is a goat, whose capers account for the origin of the word. He is playful, but at the same time is sure-footed when he is treading the brink of a chasm.

Finally, in his novels as in his plays, Azorín suggests the Cervantine origin of many of the twentieth-century themes and techniques. This is especially true of *Capricho*. In this novel Azorín compares the four autobiographies to Cervantes's interpolated novels, he even inserts a paragraph from Cervantes without using quotation marks (giving warning in the introduction that he will do so), and Don Quijote is among the autonomous characters from Spanish classics who appear in the novel to collaborate in writing it.

Azorín's admiration of and affinity for Pirandello are undeniable and Pirandellism is an essential component of his work. However, the aesthetic fascination which Azorín felt for his ideas and techniques only partly accounts for the importance of Pirandello in Azorín's writings—perhaps even more significant is the fact that Pirandello's introduction into Spanish literature is particularly appropriate for the Generation of '98. Azorín often reminds the reader of pre-Pirandellism in Spain, especially in Calderón and Cervantes. Pirandellism combines with Golden Age Spanish techniques and ideas and Azorín's own original art to symbolize the tradition plus innovation formula which the Generation of '98 so often suggests as the solution to Spain's problems.

The fluidity-of-the-human-personality theme, which in Pirandello's writings often results in chaos, is modified by Azorín to conform to his generation's needs. When Azorín discusses how Pirandello treats multiplicity of personality, he clearly shows that he understands and appreciates that Pirandello dramatizes the complete impossibility of capturing the human personality. However, in Azorín's plays, although the struggle for self-knowledge can be an important theme, as in *Angelita,* the final solution must contain a reintegration of personality, for the Generation of '98 tried to solve the problem of Spain in their work. Spain had to find itself and the answer had to be based on practical reality. The "costruirsi" element in Pirandello's writings would have been fatal here; especially since one problem at this time was the false image many Spaniards had formed of their country, an image which allowed them to live in the dream world of the past. When the mask is torn away there must be something remaining to replace the broken image.

In addition to his practical reasons for modifying Pirandello's techniques and ideas must be added Azorín's own artistic temperament. It is doubtful that the little philosopher ever truly feels the depth of Pirandello's torment; certainly his writing is not Pirandellian in tone. Even in the essay where he describes in minute detail his reaction to Pirandello's search for personality, the aesthetics of this search seem to be more intriguing to Azorín than is the examination of the agonizing human problem. Although a Pirandellian concept is often a point of departure, Azorín's basic optimism and originality always lead him to something quite his own.

Azorín relates Pirandello to his total background, showing himself to be a true comparatist. He is familiar with the psychological, historical, and literary influences which contributed to Pirandello's art and he knows about Pirandello's followers, especially in France. Perhaps most significant of all, Azorín is conscious of the wide implications of Pirandello's innovations. Although he hesitates to incorporate the exaggerated techniques in his own plays, he is certainly aware of the possibilities. He understands that the theater is dying within four walls, that it must recapture the *rapport* with the audience which he imagines it had in the religious theater of the Middle Ages,[29] that a destruction of form is implicit in the new techniques, and that the barrier between life and theater has been broken down. In many ways he seems to anticipate contemporary studies about the implications of Pirandello's innovations.

MANUEL AND ANTONIO MACHADO

Although generally unnoticed, Pirandello had a profound influence on Manuel and Antonio Machado, who actually mention "Pirandelismo" twice in their *Las adelfas* (1928). In so doing they refer to two of Pirandello's chief contributions: the theme of ambiguous personality and the contrast between the fantasy of theater as opposed to the reality of life. In act 1 of *Las adelfas,* Salvador, the hero, introduces himself by saying he is "el otro," [1] to which the heroine, Araceli, scornfully replies, "Pirandelismo." Instantly we have the problems of identity, multiplicity of personality, impossibility of mutual understanding, and changing character of opinions which so preoccupy Pirandello. In act 2, when Salvador is reading a short play that he has written for Araceli in order to help her view her situation objectively, Araceli interrupts his recitation by exclaiming, "Me apesta el pirandelismo" (p. 67), in this case referring to another facet of Pirandello's art: the fantasy of theater opposed to the reality of life, often expressed by Pirandello through similar theater-within-the-theater techniques.

The scornful tone in both of these examples does not necessarily mean that the Machados disapproved of Pirandello himself. Thomas Bishop discusses the imitations which were common in France in the 1920s: "Pirandellism became a derogatory term, referring to dramatic wizardry that covered up a lack of basic substance." [2] Proof of the Machados' admiration for Pirandello himself is that, especially in the two plays written in 1928, *Las adelfas* and *El hombre que murió en la guerra,* there is clear influence which goes much beyond the brief mention cited above. In *Las adelfas* there is constant awareness of the Italian's technique and themes. *El hombre que murió en la guerra,* while having only a line or two of theater-within-the-theater technique at the end of the play, contains much confusion of a character's identity such as we find in *Come tu mi vuoi* and *Ciascuno a suo modo*.

The Machados, however, are basically conservative and never use exaggerated Pirandellian techniques such as scenes in the lobby and entrance from the audience. All action in their plays takes place on the stage. Also, the personality theme is not as excruciating, as destructive, as deeply felt as in Pirandello's works. The Machados prefer to have everything understood or to give a promise of future satisfaction before the final curtain. Pirandello's influence in the Machados' plays may be characterized as an echo, a reflection adapted to traditional theatrical techniques and their own mild personalities.

The theater-within-the-theater scene in *Las adelfas* which causes Araceli to object to Pirandellism, for example, is certainly not an exaggerated form of interior drama. Salvador reads a manuscript to Araceli which he says is a play he is writing. This is a rather whimsical theatrical sketch entitled "Matarse por no morir o resucitar difunto," with four and one half characters (the half being the confidant), and which includes a speech by the author addressed to the public.

Most of the Machados' efforts to break into the illusion of the theater are much more subtle, usually consisting of a word or two which indirectly reminds the audience that this is only a play. The characters protest that they do not want to hear "frases de teatro" (p. 39), that they do not wish to be tragic heroes (p. 16), or that they have been assigned a grotesque role (p. 70). A typical direct reference by the authors to the theater appears in the second act of *Las adelfas* after a servant has made a comical gesture, when Araceli tells Carlos, "Apunta un dato curioso: siempre que mengua una casa como en el teatro, pasa el racionista a gracioso" (p. 61).

Such examples of Pirandellian technique would not be overly significant without the accompanying Pirandellian themes which are found in *Las adelfas* and *El hombre que murió en la guerra*. The theater-within-the-theater technique is not exclusively Pirandello's and the Machados' delicate use of the technique could almost find closer kinship with the interior-drama tradition of Spain that Cervantes, Calderón, Tamayo y Baus, and Unamuno employed. The thematic similarities and at times even the exact vocabulary are more truly Pirandellian. In *Las adelfas,* Araceli speaks about "verdad oculta" and "falsa apariencia" (p. 15). The following, also spoken by Araceli, could almost be a summing-up of the father's complaint in *Sei personaggi in cerca d'autore:* "los caracteres sostenidos son un hecho en el teatro; en la vida el asunto es más complejo" (p. 88).

In *El hombre que murió en la guerra,* which is more intensely Pirandellian in theme than *Las adelfas,* the Machados frequently use the word "fantasma." Even more characteristic of Pirandello, however, is the use of the word "mask," which appears, for example, in the scene where Guadalupe begins to suspect Juan's true identity. She tells him that if she correctly understands the situation, she is speaking to Juan de Zúñiga, disguised as Miguel de la Cruz. Miguel answers: "Es decir, enfrente de dos máscaras, una sobre otra. No, eso que usted imagina, o que usted sospecha es el mayor absurdo de todos" (p. 148).

More important, however, in *Las adelfas* Araceli is endeavoring to understand her deceased husband's personality; she feels that she never truly knew him and this has become important to her because she wishes to forget her past unhappiness and begin a new life. Here, then, are the Pirandellian themes of being and seeming, truth and illusion, the unreliability of human opinions, and the difficulty of discovering the truth. First of all, Araceli saw her dead husband Alberto in one way; his friends and acquaintances saw him in another. She is beginning to think that for her Alberto never really lived, that she failed to understand him. Her discovery that she had not really known her husband makes her doubt that she knows anyone. When Salvador comes to see her for the first time, her father asks: "Pero ¿te vas a quedar a solas con un extraño?," and Araceli answers:"¡Bah! Nunca lo será más que los conocidos" (p. 39). Araceli wants Alberto's friends to talk to her about him—after his death she hopes to be able to understand the man she did not know when he was living, as she believes this will help her decide whether or not to remarry. She must know why he committed suicide before she can free herself from his memory. Carlos, one of Alberto's friends, objects that it will be difficult for her to find Alberto mirrored in him.

As in *Come tu mi vuoi,* where there is a painting of the dead girl, *Las adelfas* uses a photograph to evoke the presence of Alberto. Salvador tells Araceli that Alberto was much better looking than the photograph indicates, and Araceli acknowledges: "Lo vivo vale más que lo pintado" (p. 65). Salvador goes on to tell her:

> Si usted quiere la figura
> de su marido evocar

guarde esa mala pintura
que es buena para olvidar.
¿No piensa que acaso diese
el pobre Alberto en suicida
por no encontrar en su vida
mejor retrato que ése?
Que fue en cartón
toda su iconografía,
y él, acaso, la quería
pintada en un corazón. [p. 65]

Immediately after Araceli has said she despises Pirandellism, she expresses her intense longing to understand Alberto:

El Alberto que yo quiero
conocer no es un fingido
personaje, es mi marido
que fue un hombre verdadero. [p. 67]

Salvador reminds her that she was ignorant of her husband's true personality.

Araceli's obsessive desire to understand Alberto leads her to speak to his mistress, Rosalía. When Araceli asks her "¿Quién era Alberto?" (p. 71), Rosalía is naturally surprised and hesitates to answer, then responds evasively; she does not understand what Araceli is trying to discover and therefore Araceli must explain more clearly:

Es lo cierto
que yo no conocí a Alberto,
y ustedes van a ayudarme
a recordarlo, de suerte
que yo sepa cómo fue
en la vida el hombre que
se me reveló en la muerte. [p. 72]

Rosalía also tells Araceli that the photograph which she keeps looking at is not Alberto, that he didn't know how to pose and that he only looked for a mirror in which he could lose himself. She goes on to say that her Alberto was humble in his own way, but Araceli states that her Alberto was disdainful, cold, and proud. The act ends with another point of view, that of the servant Pablo, who tells Araceli that people liked her husband and explains how grief-stricken his acquaintances were when he died.

Las adelfas contains the Machados' version of how the many-sided nature of truth prevents complete knowledge of another's personality, a theme found constantly in Pirandello's plays. However, in theme as in technique, the Machados do not carry Pirandello's ideas to the extreme, for in the last act everything is explained satisfactorily.

El hombre que murió en la guerra, the most cerebral play the brothers wrote, even more truly suggests the Italian's thematic preoccupations. There are very few decorative motifs. Most of the Machados' plays are set in Andalusia, and the elements of Andalusian life are notably present: gypsies, flowers, music, fiestas, dances, and patios. *El hombre que murió en la guerra,* however, could very well be performed on a bare stage—here only the dialogue and thought are important.

The situation is that Andrés's illegitimate son Juan was reported dead in the first World War, but his body had never been found. In the first act the tenth anniversary of his supposed death is being commemorated. Andrés has not had another son, therefore the son he believes dead is extremely important to him now, and he has formed an image of Juan in his imagination:

> Yo no he conocido realmente a mi hijo; eso es cierto. La criatura de dos meses que entregué al ama Juliana en mi cortijo de Guadix; el niño de siete años que llevé al colegio de Inglaterra . . . Sí, sí. Pero luego he pensado constantemente en él, y con tal intensidad, que he logrado reconstituir completamente su figura y penetrar su espíritu y su caracter. [p. 119]

Although Juan is now about thirty years old, Andrés thinks of him as an adolescent. One of the minor characters, Juan's nurse Juliana, also shows the Pirandellian tendency to believe what is not true in order to make life easier, although the belief seems to be more superficial than in Pirandello's work:

> Como yo le di el pecho en puesto de mi Ramoncillo, que se murió, recién nacido, pues . . . que . . . sé yo, me haría de cuenta que aquel niño era el mío . . . Aunque, por otro lado, bien se echaba de ver que no lo era. [p. 121]

After supposedly having been dead ten years, Juan returns to his father's home. However, he says he is Miguel de la Cruz, Juan's war companion, and that he has visited the family because Juan had asked him to do so. He tortures and confuses his father with his ideas about illegitimacy, which he believes makes one the child both of everyone and of no one. He praises the generosity of a father who gives life and demands nothing in return. He says that Juan had offered to change identity with him, but that he had refused.

Perhaps it is Guadalupe who most completely shows the tendency of many of Pirandello's characters to live according to images which they have formed of reality. Guadalupe's uncle, Don Andrés, had encouraged her interest in Juan before his death, and although they did not know each other, they had corresponded, and she was his "madrina de guerra." Juan cannot help thinking of her as Penelope, the woman who waits while her man is away many years with little hope for his return. She suspects the truth of Juan's identity, but hasn't faced it yet when she says to Andrés: "¿Usted ve a Juan a través de ese hombre? A mí me sucede todo lo contrario . . . Sus palabras me lo ocultan, me lo borran, deshacen la imagen de Juan que yo había concebido. Y que estaba aquí, que está aquí, firme, firme" (p. 140).

She speaks to the photograph which Juan has given the family, and which, of course, is really a photograph of Miguel: "Óyeme, Juan, por lo que soñé contigo, por lo que te he esperado, verdad que tú no eres como ese hombre dice, ese Miguel, ese intruso en nuestra vida . . . , ese pobre, no, ese malvado que quiere matarte otra vez en mi alma" (p. 140).

Juan explains to Guadalupe the switch of identity which he and Miguel had discussed: "un trueque en beneficio mío, una suplantación completa de la personalidad de su ilustre apadrinado, con todos los medios para realizarla" (p. 142). Juan tells her to imagine what would have happened then:

> Pude venir a esta casa como Juan de Zúñiga, y entonces—procure usted imaginarlo—qué grave conflicto sentimental para Ud. Porque hubiera tenido usted que alegrarse al ver a su prometido, vuelto inesperadamente a la vida, llorar de alegría, Guadalupe, y hasta desmayarse . . . Y sin embargo, qué horrible desilusión. Porque yo no hubiera sido nunca el Juan de Zúñiga que Ud. ha soñado. Claro que el Juan de Zúñiga que usted ha soñado tampoco era el Juan de Zúñiga verdadero, mi noble amigo, a quien usted no ha conocido. [p. 142]

Juan, who is beginning to fall in love with Guadalupe, is exasperated by the fact that his rival is a "fantasma" which Guadalupe has formed from a combination of novels and films, plus his letters written many years ago and what she has been told about Juan by people who did not know him very well. However, at the end of act 3 of the four-act play, Guadalupe is very close to realizing that the man who says he is Miguel is really Juan, although in his last line of the act Juan denies it.

In act 4, Juliana, Juan's old nurse, is the first to recognize Juan. He cannot continue to deceive her as she knows instinctively who he is; besides she had always loved him for himself, and he has no wish to deny her. After Juliana leaves the room, Guadalupe enters —one look at Juliana's face has given her the final proof of what she already suspected. She tells Juan she knows that he has returned in order to kill the Juan of their memories and also to make sure that the identity of Juan is dead in his own soul. She also tells him that she will continue to wait for him: "Mi papel es aguardarte en el mío [mi mundo]. Muchos años te he esperado, sin esperanza; los mejores de mi vida. Ahora, ¿por qué no he de seguir esperándote?" (pp. 166–67). At the end of the play, then, there is no complete resolution—the problem of identity still exists: Juan does not wish to reveal himself to his father yet and his search for his true identity is not over. However, unlike Pirandello, the Machados more optimistically hint that a complete resolution of this identity problem is possible—it is only a question of time. The Machados also are much kinder to their protagonist than Pirandello is when, for example, he does not permit the heroine of *Vestire gli ignudi* to die in dignity under the veil of the story she has invented for herself, or when, as in *Così è (se vi pare)*, there is outside interference which makes the protagonist fight for a continuation of pretense. In *El hombre que murió en la guerra,* the two people who know Juan's secret will keep silent until he is ready to reclaim his position in life. Also, the audience is not confused in the Machados' plays, as it often is in Pirandello's; it is in the traditional position of knowing more than do most of the characters.

In addition to the brief intrusion of reality at the end of the play when Guadalupe says that since they are not characters in a play the wedding is not necessary, the two themes which appear constantly are those of identity and parenthood. The identity theme of Miguel-Juan is not the same as that in any one Pirandellian play or novel. Rather, it contains elements of many. As in *Come tu mi vuoi,* the war caused the family to lose an heir, and the protagonist returns after ten years to investigate his or her former environment. Unlike *Come tu mi vuoi,* however, in which L'Ignota is not the Cia who disappeared in the war, but tries to make believe she is, Juan really is Andrés's son, but says he is Miguel. However, both L'Ignota and Juan seem to be searching for something similar: a true, human identity rather than the one imposed upon them by society.

In many ways this theme is similar to that of *Il fu Mattia Pascal.* Juan has taken advantage of the war to escape from his true name and situation, which he no longer wanted. Mattia Pascal profits from a corpse identified as his to abandon an unsatisfactory way of life. Mattia Pascal, however, struggles under the handicap of having no substitute identity—the lack of "stato civile" plagues him. Juan solves this problem: "(Sacando sus papeles.) Aquí lo dice. Esto es muy serio. Mira: 'Miguel de la Cruz, soldat, légion étrangère, Espagne.' Con estos papeles ando yo por el mundo. Ya no sería fácil probar que soy Juan de Zúñiga. Si lo intentara, tú misma dudarías. Además, aquí constan mis servicios militares" (p. 163). However, Juan is still an outsider in life as is Mattia Pascal and many other Pirandellian characters.

Guadalupe represents another aspect of Pirandello's art; she has lived for ten years with the image she has formed of a man she should have believed was dead. Here she is like Martino Lori of *Tutto per bene,* who cultivated the memory of his dead wife, characters in *Ciascuno a suo modo,* who invent their own reality, and the mother in *La vita che ti diedi,* who will not believe that her son is dead. In *Come tu mi vuoi,* Cia's relatives show Guadalupe's attitude: after ten years they still think they know Cia—they have formed their image of her and expect to recognize her when they see her. Guadalupe and Elvira, of Unamuno's *Sombras de sueño,* also seem to be cut from the same cloth.

El hombre que murió en la guerra treats the parenthood problem in several different aspects which are also important in Pirandello's theater. The illegitimacy and childless-women themes are too much a part of world literature to attribute this influence completely to Pirandello. However, the idea, so characteristic of Pirandello, that parenthood is much more than merely giving birth, as in *L'innesto,* for example, in which affection gives a man more right to call himself father than the real father has, is also a very important theme in *El hombre que murió en la guerra.* Juliana, the nurse who took Juan into her home when he was very young, is the first to recognize him. She knows; no one can deceive her about "her" son. At the same time Juan's father does not even suspect who "Miguel" really is.

Unlike the profound personality similarities which have been noted in the works of Unamuno and Pirandello, and which caused Unamuno, upon reading one of Pirandello's works to remark "lo mismo habría dicho yo," [3] the Machados have profited from Pirandello's psychological studies without involving themselves deeply. The psychiatric problem of being and seeming has been translated into their own terms. In *El hombre que murió en la guerra,* the Machado play most characteristic of the Generation of '98, the problem of identity evolves to meet the need of that generation to know themselves and Spain deeply and to search for a new life and new values. The prologue of this play explains that Miguel-Juan needed to break with the past, to renew and recreate his life. Participating in the search of the Generation of '98 for a new identity, a new combination of tradition and progress, and in this particular case a new direction in which Miguel-Juan symbolizes Spain as a whole, the Machados could not allow themselves the artistic luxury of leaving the protagonists in "il caos" which Luigi Pirandello so dearly loved.

FEDERICO GARCÍA LORCA

The dramaturgic revolution incited by Pirandello extended to even so autarkical a personality as García Lorca who transformed and poetized this influence to such an extent that its presence in his work still passes almost unobserved. Unlike certain dramatists who obviously set out to write plays in the mode of Pirandello or who wished to experiment with his techniques and ideas, García Lorca certainly did not wish to be inspired by Pirandello or by anyone else. However, he unconsciously absorbed knowledge of everything which was present in the literary world. Angel del Río's comment is especially pertinent: "He had an extraordinary facility for assimilating for his own purposes whatever literary or artistic current was at the moment in the air: a few allusions, some conversations, or some cursory reading sufficed. It was almost like a sixth sense, a physical attribute." [1]

In spite of the fact that almost all Lorca commentators mention the characteristic defined by del Río, the names of García Lorca and Pirandello have been associated only peripherally. Eric Bentley, for example, remarks that after the deaths of García Lorca and Pirandello, Spain and Italy had to be content with the histrionics of Franco and Mussolini. [2] Francis Fergusson states: "After Pirandello—to take him symbolically rather than chronologically— the way was open for Yeats and Lorca, Cocteau and Eliot," [3] and he later affirms that Eliot, Lorca and Yeats all belong to the movement which is a quest for a contemporary poetry of the theater. Edwin Honig has perhaps come closest to actually pointing out the relationship between these two dramatists:

> If one remembers how eagerly Lorca sought freedom for his imagination in the theatre, how he attempted to break down the

barrier between stage and audience, it is possible to see why
surrealist devices should have interested him. Certainly there
has never been anything in the theatre which one might call a
surrealist *form*. Lorca's experiment in this direction, however,
was not particularly original. Maeterlinck, Pirandello, O'Neill,
Strindberg, and Čapek had used, with both marked and indifferent success, certain new imaginative formulas on the stage,
by which critics learned to argue new terms—Expressionism
Symbolism, Constructivism, etc. Quite as daring were the attempts of Azorín, Gómez de la Serna, Alberti, Cocteau, Breton,
and a host of lesser surrealists who combined earlier technical
innovations with their own fanciful projections, striving for a
more startling "reality" or "super-reality" on a transformed
stage.[4]

Even García Lorca's own mention of Pirandello in a lecture does
not reveal much:

> Al público se le puede enseñar—conste que digo público no
> pueblo—; se le puede enseñar, porque yo he visto patear a De-
> bussy y a Ravel hace años, y he asistido después a las clamorosas
> ovaciones que un público popular hacía a las obras antes recha-
> zadas. Estos autores fueron impuestos por un alto criterio de
> autoridad superior al del público corriente, como Wedekind en
> Alemania y Pirandello en Italia, y tantos otros.[5]

The fact that Pirandello's actual influence on García Lorca has not
been seriously considered is easily explained: his most beautiful and
popular plays show almost no Pirandellism. It is necessary to go to
his experimental theater to find it, and only two parts of *El Público,*
by far the most important play in this respect, are available.[6] In
addition, these two parts, "Reina Romana" and "Cuadro Quinto,"
have been neglected because they do not give the enjoyment expected from García Lorca's writings; they are a confusing conglom-
eration of images, the surrealist elements seem to excuse one from
really understanding, and the homosexual overtones somewhat obscure the important artistic messages which are the main theme.

On the whole *El Público* has proved somewhat embarrassing to
scholars. Its very existence demands at least mention in any survey
of García Lorca's theater and critics have solved this problem in
various ways. Some have said that the fragmentary nature of the
play makes an attempt at analysis "absurd," or that it is not im-

portant, although García Lorca himself clearly stated that his experimental plays meant much to him.[7] Some recent studies of García Lorca's plays limit themselves to repeating and quoting passages from earlier commentaries, or summarizing the action of the play. Others simply discuss *Así que pasen cinco años* and *El Público* as a pair. Amid this, Jean-Louis Schonberg's blunt statement that the *key* to the play is the passage which suggests love of two boys for each other and his further declarations that the "Desnudo" being crucified is the church and that in this play García Lorca shows his decision to make the stage a court to discuss social problems is at least a refreshing approach.[8]

Some have conjectured that Lorca intended *El Público* as a violent blast against the commercialized theater,[9] and even suggest that Lorca expressed his anger and disdain toward the public in this play, although this seems to contradict the attitude that Sánchez shows he had toward the audience.[10] The playwright's own statement about the impossibility of presenting the play and the wrath it would cause if it were performed is frequently repeated.[11]

However, several critics have made important contributions to the understanding of this play. Alfredo de la Guardia, in his chapter entitled "Revolución en el teatro," suggests its relationship to Pirandello: "Por su pensamiento, si ha de buscarse en el título, la obra podía tener una relativa filiación pirandelliana, pues afirmaba Lorca que se proponía la intervención de los espectadores en el espectáculo."[12] He goes on to say that García Lorca understood in time that this was not the road his theater should take, although he admits that the idea of participation by spectators fascinated the playwright. Del Río points out that *El Público* seems to have been inspired by the problem of reality and poetic "superreality" on the stage and in real life.[13]

Edwin Honig states that the fragments "excite and confound expectancy by the enormous promise they reveal," but he sees a confusion in dramatic focus.[14] He also feels that something in *El Público* and the later poems is elusive: "we can say that what escapes us are the signs, the first birth pangs, of a new dramatic language, even a new dramatic orientation, based on a necessity of the imagination to break through the impasse of sterility, already so insistently documented in his last three plays."[15] María Teresa Babín states that *Así que pasen cinco años* and the available scenes of *El Público* "penetran la zona de la estética en su dimensión más abstracta y encarnan ideas que trascienden de la vida externa a la vida del espíritu y del pensamiento."[16] Indeed, *El Público* is an extremely important document and it shows Garcia Lorca's very special reaction to Pirandello.

Luigi Pirandello, in the Premise to his trilogy explains how the three plays are similar:

> Formano come una trilogia del teatro nel teatro, non solo perché hanno espressamente azione sul palcoscenico e nella sala, in un palco o nei corridoj o nel ridotto d'un teatro, ma anche perché di tutto il complesso degli elementi d'un teatro, personaggi e attori, autore e direttore-capocomico o registra, critici drammatici e spettatori alieni o interessati, rappresentano ogni possibile conflitto.[17]

Almost the same words could be used to describe the action of *El Público*.[18] Although Garciá Lorca shows most of the possible conflicts Pirandello suggested, the emphasis on the spectators' intervention in the play corresponds especially to *Ciascuno a suo modo*. In *El Público* the spectators argue, and they show even more violence against theatrical people than in Pirandello's plays: they ask that the director be killed, they want the poet to be dragged by the horses, they kill the actors after forcing them to repeat a scene, and they kill the "verdadera" Juliet after stuffing her under a theater seat, still alive, gagged, and whining.

As for the many levels of reality represented in *El Público*, García Lorca could almost be said to outdo Pirandello, except that so far as can be discerned from this fragment, all of the action takes place on the stage. The spectators' violent actions are narrated by representative members of the audience who appear on the stage and by allegorical figures. Thus, to begin with, there are two planes of reality: the action on the stage and the action which is narrated. The persons who appear on the stage represent three levels of reality: the allegorical figures, the prompter, and the members of the audience. The narrated action also contains figures which correspond to these three levels: the allegorical figures (Elena, who is the personification of the moon, and the horses), the stage director, and the audience which, swarming through every possible area of the theater, is the main protagonist of this narration. In the narration there are three additional levels: the poet (playwright), the actors, and Juliet (the character).

Both dramatic authors allow the audience to see the interior mechanics of the stage. In Pirandello's plays this is a basic theme; in *El Público* it is the cause of the revolution.

Intrusion of reality into the illusion of the stage comes about, as in Pirandello's plays, because mistakes made by the stagehands interrupt the action. The prompter has sent the thieves onto the stage too soon, and then there is a delay because José de Arimatea's beard has been lost. Later, nature disrupts the illusion when a nightingale sings (symbolizing death) before the script called for it—an uncontrollable natural element of life can govern the stage action.

Both playwrights are conscious that these theater-within-the-theater techniques lead to chaos, destruction, and confusion. This is one of the main themes of *El Público,* and Pirandello explains in his Premise:

> Ove la commedia è da fare, come nel primo, da recitare a soggetto, come nel terzo, il conflitto, non uguale, né simile, anzi precisamente opposto, impedisce che la commedia si faccia e che l'improvvisazione sia governata e regolata e giunga seguitamente a una conclusione; ove la commedia è fatta, come nel secondo, il conflitto ne manda a monte la rappresentazione.[19]

The decrease or disappearance of aesthetic distance is one particularly significant result of the theater-within-the-theater techniques Pirandello and others use, which include in their extreme form devices such as participation by actors who appear to be members of the audience, interruptions by actors or prompters which destroy the illusion, and direct address to the audience.

Stated in the simplest terms, the problem of aesthetic distance is concerned with the observer's need to be somewhat remote from the art form he is contemplating: that is, he must be psychologically and physically detached in order to view objectively the work of art as such, without being so distant that he is detached from it completely. Any dramatic technique which does not allow the play to exist as a detached entity for aesthetic contemplation, because it actually attempts to involve the spectator, destroys aesthetic distance. Edward Bullough, the British psychologist, published an important study on aesthetic distance as a factor in art appreciation in 1912,[20] and recently Oscar Büdel has discussed its implications in the contemporary theater.[21] Bullough and Ortega y Gasset have been paired in Rader's *A Modern Book of Esthetics* under the caption "Theories of Psychological Detachment,"[22] and, following his lead, P. A. Michelis has commented on the relationship of these two men.[23]

Aesthetic distance is both a physical and an intellectual phenomenon. Treatments of the problem include everything from the arrangement of the theater seats to the individual spectator's most intimate mental attitudes which enable him to view a play subjectively or objectively according to his own experience or state of mind.

The *form* of Pirandello's theater-within-the-theater plays decreases or destroys the aesthetic distance between players and spectators because they feel varying degrees of almost physical contact with the stage. The *content* of these plays increases aesthetic distance to the utmost because the human story with which the spectators can emotionally identify has been removed to the plane of the idea—the characters are no longer replicas of human beings acting out human conflicts—they represent abstract ideas or are *fantasmi d'arte*. Thus Pirandello's plays illustrate minimum physical aesthetic distance in combination with maximum ideological distance. Büdel, who makes it clear that his article concerns form only, uses Pirandello as a major illustration of the breakdown of distance in the contemporary theater. Ortega y Gasset, who treats ideas, thinks *Sei personaggi in cerca d'autore* is the perfect example of the increase of distance in new art. He is, of course, referring to the increase of intellectual distance, the placing of an idea beyond the immediate grasp of *las masas,* in short, "deshumanización."

In *El Público* García Lorca centers on the destruction of poetic illusion wrought by the breakdown of aesthetic distance that theater-within-the-theater techniques in their extreme form cause. The audience begins by intervening in the play, and, its appetite thus whetted to discover in full the mystery of poetic creation, forges ahead until it kills almost everyone involved with the theater, including the "true" Juliet. This beautiful, poetic character is destroyed by the public who, like children, tear her apart as if she were a rag doll to see what is inside her. Not even Juliet, a character probably used here because *Romeo and Juliet* was one of García Lorca's favorite plays, can continue to exist under these circumstances and suffers the great indignity of being gagged and stuffed under a theater seat before she is dead. Thus García Lorca dramatically illustrates the end results of the destruction of illusion found in the contemporary theater. The following paragraph from Büdel's article could almost be used to summarize the thesis of *El Público:*

Whereas the Expressionist revolution may have been a salutary reaction against an era of "illusionism" (and as such stressed again the theatricality of theater), its implications seem to have created tendencies which perhaps have gone beyond original intentions. These tendencies may destroy more than mere theatrical "illusionism"; they indeed seem to reach to the very roots of theater. One of these trends appears to point toward a destruction of aesthetic distance with reference to the spectators, thereby reducing or eliminating the tension between actor and spectator, between stage and audience, which seems to be a *conditio sine qua non* for the theater.[24]

In *El Público* Lorca stresses this idea of initial confidence that the new techniques would be salutary for the theater, followed by disillusionment when it became obvious that they could lead to disaster. A lady, representing the audience, expresses her own illusion and subsequent disillusion by saying that when they were climbing over the hill of ruin (in the context of the play this obviously means when the theater-within-the-theater techniques permitted them to wander over the stage) they thought they saw the light of dawn, but they stumbled against the curtains, and her shoes are now stained with petroleum.

The stage director has had a similar experience. He is the initial cause of the revolution because he opens the stage traps to allow the audience to see the inner workings of the stage. He soon discovers that under these circumstances all of his skill is insufficient to maintain theatrical illusion: "El director de escena evitó de manera genial que la masa de espectadores se enterase de esto, pero los caballos y la revolución han destruído sus planes" (p. 1075).

In addition, the revolution has escalated beyond imagination. No one could have anticipated it would touch such time-established masterpieces as *Romeo and Juliet:* "Era un drama delicioso y la revolución no tiene derecho para profanar las tumbas" (p. 1069). However, García Lorca does not limit himself to these more subtle forms of lamenting the destruction of aesthetic distance. After the students' argument about exactly why the revolution started, Lorca clearly states why the theater is dying:

Aquí está la gran equivocación de todos y por eso el teatro agoniza. El público no debe atravesar las sedas y los cartones que el poeta levanta en su dormitorio. Romeo puede ser un ave y Julieta puede ser una piedra. Romeo puede ser un grano de sal y Julieta puede ser un mapa. ¿Qué le importa esto al público? [p. 1070]

Later, he reinforces his message that a spectator should never take part in a play and that aesthetic distance must be maintained. When a student complains that the attitude of the public has been detestable, his friend answers: "Detestable. Un espectador no debe formar nunca parte del drama. Cuando la gente va al acuarium no asesina a las serpientes de mar, ni a las ratas de agua, ni a los peces cubiertos de lepra, sino que resbala sobre los cristales sus ojos y aprende" (p. 1075).

A comparison of Ortega y Gasset's *La deshumanización del arte* (1925) and García Lorca's *El Público* (1930) [25] is surprisingly fruitful. It may seen incongruous to compare the work of the philosopher of the *minorías selectas* whose essay has a clearly defined thesis with that of the poet of and for the people whose surrealist play under analysis is not available in its entirety. However, the images García Lorca employs show an amazing similarity to those his predecessor used, which makes it conceivable that part of *El Público* may be García Lorca's unconscious surrealist distortion of some of Ortega y Gasset's ideas. Of course Ortega y Gasset is concerned with all "arte nuevo" manifestations and García Lorca refers only to the new theater.

Ortega y Gasset is certainly the most likely ideological inspiration for ideas regarding aesthetic distance in *El Público,* not only because of the common language, but because García Lorca had opportunities to be exposed to these ideas: the two men frequented the Residencia de Estudiantes in Madrid during the same period, and when García Lorca was in New York one of his friends was Ortega y Gasset's translator, Mildred Adams. Even if we reject the possibility of direct inspiration, this reaction to the same phenomenon of two writers who are otherwise diametrically opposed in almost every way is extremely interesting.

In spite of the similarity of images denoting interest in the same theatrical situation, most of the time these two writers react to distinct facets of the phenomenon. Although occasionally Ortega y Gasset's statements could refer to the breakdown of aesthetic distance caused by theater-within-the-theater techniques, his chief concern is to study the phenomenon of ideological content in the new art which has become too distant for most of the people to understand. García Lorca, despite definite examples of dehumanization in his play, illustrates the results of the breakdown of physical distance between the poetic illusion and the audience caused by the theater-within-the-theater techniques.

Another important difference is that García Lorca definitely shows his disapproval and rejection of these techniques which have caused the destruction of theater. Although Ortega y Gasset clearly states that he is merely moved by the desire to try to understand the phenomenon, motivated neither by ire nor enthusiasm, and admits that new art has produced nothing worthwhile, in his essay there is felt a tacit approval of the dehumanized art which makes a clear intellectual distinction between the select minority and the masses which are forced to recognize their inferiority because of their inability to understand the new art. In fact, the social implications of the intellectually aristocratic ideas conveyed by Ortega y Gasset almost overshadow his discussion of aesthetic distance. However, a comparison of Bullough's article and Ortega y Gasset's essay reveals that they are treating the same fundamental psychological problem.[26]

Ortega y Gasset's statement which most clearly describes the situation treated in *El Público* appears at the end of his chapter "La vuelta del revés" in which he calls *Sei personaggi in cerca d'autore* the first "drama de ideas":

Se advierte ejemplarmente la dificultad del gran público para acomodar la visión a esta perspectiva invertida. Va buscando el drama humano que la obra constantemente desvirtúa, retira e ironiza, poniendo en su lugar—esto es, en primer plano—la ficción teatral misma, como tal ficción. Al gran público le irrita que le engañen y no sabe complacerse en el delicioso fraude del arte, tanto más exquisito cuanto mejor manifieste su textura fradulenta.[27]

This irritation of the audience Ortega y Gasset describes is one of the main themes of *El Público,* of course, but there is a passage which specifically echoes the above-quoted concepts. The audience is angry and asks that the poet be dragged by the horses; even though it was a "drama delicioso" and the tomb scene was well developed, they discovered the lie when they saw Juliet's feet, which were extremely small. One lady's opinion is that this was "delicioso" and impossible to criticize, but a boy answers that they were too small to be a woman's feet. They were too perfect and too feminine. Obviously they were male feet, feet *invented* by a man, and this is horrifying.

The confusion the new art or new theater causes the audience is treated by both writers, Ortega y Gasset because the work of art is

intellectually too distant from them: "Tan pronto como estos
elementos puramente estéticos dominen y no puede agarrar bien la
historia de Juan y María, el público queda despistado y no sabe qué
hacer" (p. 357); and García Lorca because aesthetic distance has disappeared and they have approached closely enough to see the interior mechanics of the theater: "¿Y qué han sacado en claro? Un
racimo de heridas y una desorientación absoluta" (p. 1076).

Naturally in *La deshumanización del arte* the conversion of
human forms into nonhuman ones is a prominent theme. "Convenía
libertar la poesía, que, cargada de materia humana se había convertido en un grave, e iba arrastrando sobre la tierra, hiriéndose
contra los árboles y las esquinas de los tejados como un globo sin
gas" (p. 371). Ortega y Gasset believes that in the new epoch the
symbol of art has again become the magic flute of Pan, which makes
the goats dance on the edge of the forest. He inquires what the
young people want the poet to be, in contrast to the romantic poet
"quien quería siempre ser un hombre" (p. 371). He rejects the possibility that they want him to be "un pájaro, un ictiosauro, un
dodecaedro," believing that they only want him to be a poet.

This "deshumanización" aspect is quite prominent in *El Público*.
There are many figures which are not quite human, and a constant
theme is the possibility that all forms can represent poetic reality.
For example: "Es una cuestión de forma, de máscara. Un gato
puede ser una rana, y la luna de invierno puede ser muy bien un
haz de leña cubierto de gusanos ateridos" (p. 1071). Of course the
Panlike figures who dance and play the flute in "Reina Romana"
are directly reminiscent of Ortega y Gasset's opinion about the new
epoch.

Both authors realize that aesthetic distance is necessary. This is
one of the main ideas of García Lorca's play, and he underlines it
by saying that the audience should not go beyond the silk and
cardboard that the poet sets up in his room, and that people who
go to the aquarium move their eyes over the glass and learn, so why
should they not do the same in the theater? Ortega y Gasset states:

> Ver es una acción a distancia. Y cada una de las artes maneja un
> aparato proyector que aleja las cosas y las transfigura. En su
> pantalla mágica las contemplamos desterradas, inquilinas de un
> astro inabordable y absolutamente lejanas. Cuando falta esta
> desrealización se produce en nosotros un titubeo fatal; no sabe-
> mos si vivir las cosas o contemplarlas. [p. 370]

The stage directions of *El Público* also allude to the cinema: "La luz toma un tinte plateado de pantalla cinematográfica" (p. 1075). This stage direction appears immediately after the "Desnudo" disappears and the man appears in his place and just before the statement that the spectator should not form part of the drama. It obviously suggests that this new genre has a lesson for the theater because spectator participation in the film is impossible.

Both writers show the ironical or farcical essence of new art. Ortega y Gasset believes that the new inspiration is comical, ranging from buffoonery to a slight ironical wink, even though the content of the work is not comical. Art mocks itself. García Lorca uses the joy and laughter of the students in an episode toward the end of the play to create an emotional about-face: the vitally important situation which had been treated with complete seriousness until then is suddenly made the object of jest when one of the students throws Juliet's shoe at his friend. This shoe was apparently taken from the dead performer originally with the intention of conserving it as a relic.[28]

Youth is an important element of the phenomenon which both artists observe. Ortega y Gasset believes that "Todo el arte nuevo resulta comprensible y adquiere cierta dosis de grandeza cuando se le interpreta como un ensayo de crear puerilidad en un mundo viejo" (p. 384). In García Lorca's play youth is hopeful of finding the solution, is helpful in leading the older people, and is willing to destroy the old doctrines of the past.

Finally, both writers see that young people want to start from scratch, as Ortega y Gasset states: "Los jóvenes quieren crear de la nada" (p. 356), and García Lorca's young people intend to burn the book from which the priests read the mass. Also, they both realize the need to find another road, which is neither the present one nor the traditional one, as Ortega y Gasset says: "A las objeciones habría que añadir otra cosa: la insinuación de otro camino para el arte que no sea este deshumanizador ni reitere las vías usadas y abusadas" (p. 386), and García Lorca expresses this idea by showing the young people looking for this path at the end of the play: "Alguna puerta será la verdadera" (p. 1079).

Pirandellism and the problem of aesthetic distance seem to clarify García Lorca's message in *El Público:* the central figure of "Cuadro Quinto" is a "Desnudo viejo" who is dying ("agoniza"). Although most commentators consider this figure to symbolize the poet, his more specific function may be to represent the theater or the spirit of the theater. This would appear to be true because the text states "el teatro agoniza," and because he is an old man and is lying on a bed "como pintado por un primitivo" which would suggest the ancient art-form of the theater. Also, he is naked, which in addition to stressing the analogy of his death with the crucifixion of Christ would show why the theater is dying—it has been stripped of its clothing which would symbolize the distance placed between the illusion of the theater and the audience.

In "Cuadro Quinto" the male nurse is extracting blood from the nude figure with his complete consent and cooperation. García Lorca once stated: "Now I am writing a poetry which demands the opening of veins—a poetry freed from reality," [29] suggesting that this figure of the theater must also be freed from the close contact with reality which the theater-within-the-theater techniques have forced him to accept.

The figure is being crucified. Although no cross actually appears, many other symbols of Christ's crucifixion are present, including the thieves. As Saez points out,[30] in *Poet in New York* the figure of Christ crucified carries with it the implied hope of resurrection. Obviously the crucifixion has the same significance here, because a nurse, a figure associated with healing, is arranging for his death. There are other very strong symbols of hope at the end of the play; that is, the students have lanterns in their hands and are leading the adults in their search for the right door. The reason for the great importance given to the students in this play is clear if it is remembered that after his return to Spain from New York García Lorca organized a university theater.

The audience asks that the stage director be killed. The director, exemplified by Dr. Hinkfuss of *Questa sera si recita a soggetto,* is one of Pirandello's most prominent agents for breaking into the illusion of the stage. The members of the audience are indifferent to the dying theater, probably because they are unaware of its ancient grandeur, so cluttered has the stage become with all the artifices which make true theater impossible.

The spectators are completely confused because they have approached the dramatic work too closely and can touch the props and clothing of the actors. All illusion is destroyed and nothing can be found to replace it. At the same time, perhaps to emphasize man's commitment to and need of theater, the spectators cannot find an exit from the burning theater.

Horses are an important symbol in "Cuadro Quinto," where they seem to represent uncontrollable force and freedom. They help break down the barriers between stage and audience. At the beginning of the "Cuadro" they accompany the director who has instigated the revolution by opening the stage traps. But when the revolution gets out of hand, and the director finds that he can no longer maintain poetic illusion, the horses are still aligned with the revolution which is now destroying the director's efforts. When everyone else is desperately looking for an exit from the burning theater, the horses escape by breaking a hole through the stage roof.

The first bomb of the revolution kills the professor of rhetoric—at least the new techniques are spontaneous—which enables his wife, whose name is Elena or Selene, symbolizing the moon, to work so much "que tendrá que ponerse dos grifos en las tetas" (p. 1067). They say that she used to go up to the terrace with a horse, so she is associated with both freedom of poetic expression and the destruction of artificial barriers. In fact, she is the one who sees what was happening in the theater and gives the call of alarm. The poets try to kill her, but she keeps shouting and the crowd arrives to help. Thus the role of the moon in *El Público* validates Gustavo Correa's explanation of the very complex moon symbolism in García Lorca's writings: the moon is an affirmative but ambivalent symbol, corresponding to the changeable nature which the moon's phases give to it. The moon symbolizes vital renovation and "plenitud de realización" and at the same time it destroys life implacably and inevitably. "Se halla así el hombre bajo la influencia inescapable de un signo que es a la vez su salvación y su propia destrucción. Apartarse de él es penetrar en el caos desmoralizador y agónico de una vida sin sentido." [31]

Juliet, the character who is stuffed under the seat, is not completely comparable in nature to Pirandello's "Sei personaggi" because she is not in search of dramatic form for her story. Allowing for a certain surrealistic distortion of time, she is somewhat like Delia Morello of *Ciascuno a suo modo,* who suffers in the audience when the story of her life is represented on the stage. Like Pirandello's "Sei Personaggi," however, she seems to represent superior artistic creation, destroyed in *El Público* to show the most horrible effects of the revolution.

At the same time García Lorca illustrates that the dramatic illusion, which has been destroyed, is superior to whatever reality the "verdadera" Juliet represents. When a friend tells him that Juliet was played by a disguised boy, "un truco del director de escena," and that the true Juliet has been gagged and placed beneath the chairs, the student comments: "¡Pues me gusta! Parecía muy hermosa, y si era un joven disfrazado no me importa nada; en cambio, no hubiese recogido el zapato de aquella muchacha llena de polvo que gemía debajo de las sillas" (p. 1077).

As part of the disorientation theme in this play, the spectators disagree about why the revolution began. However, one student states: "Se amaban los esqueletos y estaban amarillos de llama, pero no se amaban los trajes y el público vió varias veces la cola de Julieta cubierta de pequeños sapitos de asco" (p. 1070), a remark which echoes one García Lorca made in an interview: "El teatro necesita que los personajes que aparezcan en la escena lleven un traje de poesía y al mismo tiempo que se les vea los huesos, la sangre" (p. 1634). This is a plea that a profound humanity which communicates itself directly to all men combine with the compensating distance factor of poetic illusion.

The ritualistic element of "Cuadro Quinto" cannot be overlooked. Büdel points out the audience-participation factor which religious ceremony and contemporary theater have in common:

> On our modern stage, in comparison, the audience is to be made part and parcel of the whole performance; it is to be dragged, as it were, into the play. With this we move toward the concept of theater as rite, as the liturgical celebration of a community; indeed a situation not unlike the one from which theater originally sprang.[32]

In *El Público* the sacrifice of the "Desnudo" is carried out according to strict ritual—the prompter is in charge of preparing the necessary instruments: "Sólo faltan los candeleros, el cáliz, y las ampollas de aceite alcanforado" (p. 1073). The timing, although thrown somewhat out of kilter by the prompter's mistake, is obviously intended to follow a preestablished ceremony.

The ceremonial death of this figure is also shown to be intimately connected with the fate of man, because when the "Desnudo" dies, the revolving bed turns to reveal a man in evening clothes, representing the spectator, who is also dying. He is complaining about the loneliness of man who has been deserted by the spirit of theater: "Agonía. Soledad del hombre en el sueño lleno de ascensores, trenes donde tú vas a velocidades increíbles. Soledad de los edificios, de las esquinas, de las playas, donde tú no aparecerás nunca" (p. 1079).

Spain possesses a unique art which is a perfect synthesis of theater and ritual, the bullfight. Of this García Lorca said in his essay *Teoría y juego del duende:* "la liturgia de los toros, auténtico drama religioso donde, de la misma manera que en la misa, se adora y se sacrifica a un Dios" (p. 45). And the bull symbol appears in *El Público* twice. Near the end of the play one student states: "Yo tengo cuatrocientos toros. Con las maromas que torció mi padre los engancharemos a las rocas para partirlas y que salga un volcán" (p. 1078). Perhaps the elements associated with the bullfight, then, offer a partial answer to the problem of the theater.[33]

Soon after the bulls are mentioned the prompter announces: "Señores: clase de Geometría descriptiva." In *Teoría y juego del duende* García Lorca stated: "En los toros [el duende] adquiere sus acentos más impresionantes, porque tiene que luchar por un lado, con la muerte que puede destruirlo, y por otro lado con la geometría, con la medida base fundamental de la fiesta" (p. 46), which restates a fundamental problem of the theater—that somehow a way must be found to fit the life force, which is essentially noncontrollable, into the art forms which separate aesthetic experience from life.

In *El Público* García Lorca demonstrates that although the revolution in the theater, that is, Pirandellism, was greeted with enthusiasm by the members of the audience, they soon become confused and unhappy because these same techniques, by removing aesthetic distance, made poetic illusion impossible. After extreme forms of Pirandellianism cause the death of the theater a new path must be found to enable its resurrection. At the end of the play, the young people, carrying lanterns and leading the adults, are looking hopefully for this path. As García Lorca said in an interview in 1934: "Caminos nuevos hay para salvar al teatro. Todo está en atreverse a caminar por ellos" (p. 1624).

Before *El Público* García Lorca had employed theater-within-the-theater techniques to a limited extent. In the "farsa guiñolesca," *Los títeres de Cachiporra,* there is a prologue ("advertencia") in which Mosquito speaks to the audience to ask for silence and to explain that he and his company have escaped from the bourgeois theater in which the spectators slept during the performance, in order to perform for simple people.[34] The little farce proceeds normally until the fifth *cuadro* when, while Cristobita is sleeping, Fígaro points out that his head is made of painted wood, shows the knots on his head, and suggests that he perspires resin. The exposure of Cristobita as a puppet is made complete in the last *cuadro,* for when he dies it is discovered that he has no blood and Cocoliche emphatically announces: "¡Cristobita no era una persona!" (p. 689). Thus one puppet calls attention to the fictional nature of another, and although the effect should not be too startling in a farcical puppet show, it exemplifies another case in which art self-consciously points to itself and destroys the illusion in the process.

La zapatera prodigiosa (1930) also begins with an address to the audience by the playwright in which he differentiates between his own attitude toward the spectators and the attitude traditionally exhibited by playwrights who address the "respectable público." This phrase, he believes, shows a certain fear of the audience, a fear which in the past prevented many playwrights from using poetry on the stage. He does not ask for benevolence but only for the spectators' full attention.

He explains that he has decided to embody the dramatic example in a "zapaterita popular" who is a poetic creature: "Ella lucha siempre, lucha con la realidad que la crea y lucha con la fantasía cuando ésta se hace realidad visible" (p. 822). While the author is speaking, the *zapatera* shouts from backstage that she wants to come out. The author reminds her that she is dressed in the torn outfit of a shoemaker's wife and not in "un traje de larga cola y plumas inverosímiles" (p. 822). But now it is time to begin and she may come out just as people do every morning when they awaken from the world of dreams to go to the markets. Before the playwright withdraws he performs a magician's trick, for when he takes off his hat a green light shines out of it, and then when he tips it a shower of water falls, after which he leaves the stage "lleno de ironía" (p. 822). Sánchez comments: "Nada podía ser más teatral, nada más falso, pero la intención de Lorca es perfectamente clara. Después de invitar al espectador a acompañarle en su mundo de fantasía, quería poner en claro la magia que es esencia del teatro."[35]

As in many of García Lorca's plays, fiction is shown to be more important than truth. Throughout the play the *zapatera* values illusion more than reality, and the prosaic quality of her life contrasts with her fantasies. At the same time she is incapable of recognizing the elements of beauty which do exist in her life. For example, while she is telling her husband about her imagined prenuptial suitors, she speaks about Emiliano who rode a black horse and was very elegantly dressed. The shoemaker remarks that once he had a cape similar to the one she describes, but she scornfully tells him that a shoemaker could never have such clothing. The shoemaker, who is dressed quite decently in a velvet suit with silver buttons and a red tie, asks her if she cannot see him, but she is already back in her dream world thinking about another suitor. The *zapatera* does have admirers who are in sharp contrast to her imagined ones and probably the best example is Mr. Blackbird, a ridiculous man dressed all in black.

But as soon as the shoemaker leaves home, distance permits illusion because the *zapatera* converts him into a poetic figure, mounted on a white horse, dressed in a black suit, red silk tie and four golden rings which shine like four suns. The shoemaker returns in disguise as a puppet master.[36] The story he tells about a saddle-maker and his young wife is really his own story, and the *zapatera* recognizes her own situation in this interior drama. When the *zapatera* ardently defends the husband she thinks is absent, the shoemaker believes that it will be possible to return home, but as soon as he reveals himself and thus steps down from the pedestal upon which he had been idealized, the *zapatera* returns to her former nagging ways.

Within the limits of this minor genre, the puppet farce *Retablillo de don Cristóbal* (1931) is quite Pirandellian. In the prologue the poet addresses the audience. He tells something about the play, asks for complete silence, and states that he is going to eat a little bread and then iron the company's costumes. He looks around to see if he is being observed before he confides "Yo sé cómo nacen las rosas y cómo se crían las estrellas del mar" (p. 930), but he is abruptly interrupted by the director who tells him to be quiet, that the prologue ends where he says that he must iron the company's costumes, and that the poet does not have the right to reveal the secret with which they all live. The poet is subservient because he obviously depends upon the director for his living, but he ventures to say that he knows that basically Don Cristóbal is good. The director insists that the poet tell the audience that Don Cristóbal is evil. This initial doubt about how to interpret the central character shows the multiple possibilities of personality and the error which is often committed in the theater of showing only one aspect of a character. This could be compared to the complaint of the father in *Sei personaggi* whose whole life will be represented on the stage by one scandalous event.

The director calls Cristóbal and Rosita and tells them to come out because the spectators are waiting. Don Cristóbal disputes the director's decision that he is to be a doctor in the drama, but the director reminds Cristóbal that he needs money in order to get married, thus persuading him to comply.

At one point the poet intervenes to complain about the director's interpretation of the characters because he has not permitted them to be poetic creatures. But the director again goads him into silence. At the end of the play the director has the last word and destroys the poetic illusion because he seizes the puppets and displays them to the audience. He then explains the long tradition of this type of farce, relating it to Monsieur Guiñol of Paris, Harlequin, and the Galician Bululú.

The plot of García Lorca's short play called *Amor de don Perlimplín con Belisa en su jardín* (1931) may have been partly suggested to him by Pirandello's treatment of the problem of identity and the idea of life as a play—themes Pirandello vitalized in the twentieth century. In this play Don Perlimplín, an old man who is married to a young woman, knowing that his age prevents her from loving him, disguises himself as a young man. Belisa receives messages from him and sees him in the distance wrapped in his cape. Perlimplín tells her that he knows this young man, says that he understands, and further excites her love for the mysterious figure by talking about him: "Yo me doy cuenta de las cosas. Y aunque me hieren profundamente, comprendo que vives en un drama" (p. 914). Perlimplín thinks that this figure which he has invented is the triumph of his imagination.

At the end of the play, dressed as the young man and asserting that he is the youth, Perlimplín staggers into Belisa's presence, saying that Perlimplín gave him his death stab with an emerald dagger and then escaped. The personality problem becomes rather intricate here because Perlimplín has been represented as soul and the young man as body, but when Perlimplín stabs himself and insists as he is dying that he is the nonexistent suitor, he somehow obtains a fusion of body and soul. Influenced by Perlimplín, Belisa, who before had been only body, now has a soul, because the dying man relates that Perlimplín said while he was stabbing him, "Belisa ya tiene un alma" (p. 926). The symbolic meaning of the emerald green dagger is important because here it suggests sensuality,[37] so when Perlimplín plunges this symbol of physical love into his heart, he somehow gains in death the double dimension of body and soul. As he is dying and still pretending to be the young man, he calls Perlimplín a "viejo verde" who will not be able to enjoy

Belisa's body because it was meant for young men and affirms that he himself only loved her in a sensual way. When Belisa asks what he has done, he seems to regain his identity as Perlimplín as he explains to her, "Yo soy mi alma y tú eres tu cuerpo" (p. 927), and that in his last moment he wishes to embrace her. Thus it seems that in death Perlimplín has achieved the possibility of uniting opposites, and he will be buried in the red cape which he has used to give the impression of youth.

As Perlimplín dies in Belisa's arms, she exclaims that she did not realize that he was so complicated. Although she knows the truth when she sees his face, she cannot really absorb it. She asks her servant: "¿Pero quién era este hombre? ¿Quién era?" and the servant replies: "El hermoso adolescente al que nunca verás el rostro" (p. 928). She now feels love for Perlimplín: "Le quiero con toda la fuerza de mi carne y de mi alma," but asks confusedly: "¿Pero dónde está el joven de la capa roja? Dios mío; ¿dónde está?" (p. 928). The marvelous young man whom Perlimplín invented will continue to live in Belisa's imagination, and Perlimplín willingly pays with his life in order to gain a perfect fictional existence in the mind of his loved one.

In *Así que pasen cinco años* (1931), García Lorca again shows the powerful hold which illusion exerts over human beings and how in its extreme form illusion can even destroy the possibility of living a fairly happy life in the real world. The entire play can be interpreted as a daydream which occurs in the young man's mind,[38] but, within the dream, present pleasure is rejected in favor of anticipated future happiness, symbolized by the hero's statement that when he was a child he always kept his candy to eat later.

In the third act of *Así que pasen cinco años* a small stage appears in the middle of the large one, the curtains are closed for most of the act but finally open to reveal a reproduction in miniature and in paler colors of the setting for the first act. This does not seem to provide the opportunity for a play-within-the-play in the usual sense of the word, but rather serves to recall the lost opportunities of the past and the complete changes of attitude which occur as time passes.

The power of illusion to dominate over reality, which in Cervantes and Pirandello can also be interpreted as the sagacity of madness, is a prominent theme in *La casa de Bernarda Alba* (1936), for María Josefa, Bernarda's insane mother, cuts through the hypocritical environment in which she is forced to live with the voice of poetical truth. Unlike the inhibited daughters, madness gives her the liberty to shout her desire to marry and have children and the ability to believe that this is possible. In a moment of lucidity she explains that she knows that the lamb which she has been treating like a child is a lamb, "Pero ¿por qué una oveja no va a ser un niño? Mejor es tener una oveja que no tener nada" (p. 1434).

Thus, although in *El Público* García Lorca rejects techniques which destroy aesthetic distance, in certain of his own plays written before *El Público,* he himself experimented with devices which could possibly derive from the Pirandellian "revolution" combined with Spanish tradition. After *El Público* he seems to have abandoned the technique completely, which would support the theory that this play is actually a rejection of Pirandellian aspects that destroy aesthetic distance. At the same time there is a fundamental thematic affinity between Pirandello and García Lorca, for they both create characters who invent personal truths which have the power to impose themselves on life and which in the end are shown to be preferable to unadorned reality.

ALEJANDRO CASONA

Several of Alejandro Casona's plays are enveloped by the Pirandellian mist which Azorín discusses in his article "El arte del actor:
Neblina en 1925." The influence in Casona's plays is subtle, and
much of it may also be attributed to other sources. Charles H.
Leighton considers Pirandello's influence to be minimal and points
out the differences between the two writers' reactions to the prevail-
ing literary atmosphere.[1] However, if we consider the totality of
Pirandellian themes in Spanish literature Casona's work becomes
quite relevant, and a survey of certain of his plays adds yet another
dimension to the study of Pirandellism in Spain.

A significant connection between the Italian and Spanish playwrights can be seen in *La sirena varada* (1929) where Casona creates
an environment in which an individual is able to reject the reality
of a world which does not permit him to live according to his individual ideals. The beginning of the play is strongly reminiscent
of Pirandello's *Enrico IV* because Ricardo, a central figure in
Casona's play, has withdrawn from the world to create his own
environment in the company of servants who humor him. He states
his intention to form a republic in which common sense does not
exist; his desire is to build a new life, to dream impossible dreams
in the company of other similarly motivated individuals.

This strange world is inhabited by people whose personalities
manifest the combination of reality and illusion in varying degrees
of intensity. Pedrote, Ricardo's loyal servant, distinguishes clearly
between reality and fantasy, but in a panzaic way is willing to
cater to his employer's whims. Ironically, the most fantastic character, "el fantasma," is the one who soon tires of participating in the
game, but he is forced by Ricardo to continue playing the ghost's
part.

Daniel is especially comfortable in Ricardo's special environment. He is a painter who has led everyone to believe that he keeps his eyes blindfolded in order to invent new colors in his self-imposed darkness. At the end of the play his actual blindness is revealed when the blindfold is torn away. However, he insists upon replacing the blindfold because he prefers to continue in the belief that he can really see, and thus turns out to be the only truly Pirandellian character in the play.

Florín, a temporary visitor, represents the voice of reason. In a manner akin to characters in many of Pirandello's plays such as *Così è (se vi pare)*, who do not accept the need for fantasy, he desires to know the truth.

The title character is a girl who in her madness thinks she is a mermaid. Ricardo falls in love with her and does not wish to be swayed by Florín's desire to discover the truth about her: "Sirena es una deliciosa mentira que no estoy dispuesto a cambiar por ninguna verdad." [2] Ricardo, however, does not really have the power of his convictions, for he soon tries to discover the girl's true identity.

The general situation, the attitude toward reality, and the apparent superiority of fiction over reality in the first part of the play result in a scene which suggests the thematic content of Pirandello's work. However, in the last act Casona leads the reader firmly back to a stable world, rejecting fantasy in favor of reality which is reconquered by Sirena because she is about to become a mother. Had Sirena been allowed to continue in the belief that she was a mermaid, the insane illusion would probably have caused her death. Attracted by the magnetic thought of being the daughter of the sea, Sirena had once before thrown herself into the water and would undoubtedly have done so again if the fact of prospective motherhood had not effected the triumph of reality over illusion.

The first character to be released from his role is the ghost who is granted his desire to be a gardener and thus is free to enjoy the simple pleasures for which he has yearned. Daniel is the only character who cannot return to reality because his irremediable physical defect is more bearable when he believes and causes others to believe that he is not blind. Ricardo wavers between illusion and reality because he is in love with Sirena and wants to know the truth. However, when he sees the effect the removal of the blindfold has on Daniel, he fears that something similar might happen to Sirena, who might be unable to live with the memories of her sordid past (she was the mistress of the circus strongman) if she were forced to face the truth. Ricardo attempts to persuade Sirena to return to the sphere of fantasy, but she of her own volition clings to reality for the sake of the child she is soon to bear.

In Pirandello's *La nuova colonia,* motherhood redeems a woman as it does in the case of Sirena. Another Pirandellian parallel is the subtheme about the identity of the father of Sirena's child. Casona resolves this problem in a manner similar to Pirandello's solution in *L'innesto:* Ricardo will accept the child as his own, and the identity of the real father is immaterial. However, although Casona uses the multiple relationships of truth and fantasy as a foundation for his work, the manner of his solution does not correspond to Pirandello's general treatment of the theme.

Las tres perfectas casadas (1941) is another of Casona's plays which may be considered as part of the Pirandellian current. The great difference which exists between appearance and reality is made clear when three men who considered their wives to be perfect are suddenly given information to the contrary. Ironically, the source of information is a letter written by their best friend (which was not to be read until after his death) stating that he has had sexual relations with all three wives. The reactions of the men are varied —Jorge wants to know the whole truth; Javier suggests that they should deceive themselves: "Echemos esa carta al fuego, como si nunca se hubiera escrito y jurémonos guardar silencio. Ferrán ha muerto con su secreto. Ellas guardarán el suyo. Guardemos nosotros el nuestro . . . Y respetémonos mutuamente . . ."[3] This reaction brings to mind the desire of everyone except the wronged wife in *Il berretto a sonagli* to keep peace by pretending that infidelity does not exist. Máximo, in the most extreme type of Pirandellian reaction, really deceives himself. He believes that his wife is worthy of his faith in her because he must believe this in order to go on living. He will never question her and will respect her more than ever.

The situation becomes more involved when Ada, the wife who has faltered only once, but who is perfectly loyal to her husband and who suffers great remorse because of her one indiscretion, goes to Ferrán and asks him to commit suicide after writing another letter saying that he had lied in the first. He agrees, on the condition that she allow him to deliver the letter to her personally in his home. His intention, of course, is to repeat his previous conquest. When he attempts to kiss her, she seizes the gun and in the struggle Ferrán is shot. It is uncertain who actually pulled the trigger, although Ferrán, as he is dying, assures Ada that it was he.

Thus, there are certain Pirandellian overtones in the doubt about Ferrán's true motives, the different reactions of the men to their wives' infidelity, and the doubt at the end of the play about who actually pulled the trigger. Needless to say, however, the play does not pose any very tantalizing problems. The audience knows all of the important facts, and the question of who actually pulled the trigger is in actuality rather insignificant.

The most Pirandellian of Casona's plays is *Los árboles mueren de pie* (1949). The story briefly is as follows: the "director" has created an organization whose purpose it is to help people find happiness. Balboa comes to him with a problem. His grandson is a ne'er-do-well who left twenty years ago to go to Canada. In order to make life bearable for the grandmother, Balboa wrote false letters from the grandson, in which the grandson he invents is a reformed man who became an architect, held an important position, and married. But one day "La vida se metía en la farsa" (p. 607) and the grandson wires that he is returning. The immediate problem of the return is conveniently "solved," however, by the sinking of his ship. Balboa wishes to avoid a tragic experience for the grandmother by having the "director" play the part of Mauricio during a short visit. Isabel, a newcomer to the organization, plays the part of Mauricio's wife. The visit is a great success, but again life and theater cannot be separated, and Isabel really falls in love with her make-believe husband. But the real Mauricio, "el otro," returns as he had not been on the ill-fated ship after all; his purpose in returning is to obtain money from the family. Isabel and Mauricio unsuccessfully attempt to prevent him from seeing the grandmother. However, when the old lady is alone with "el otro," she tells him that she has known about him since the previous evening, so he can no longer gain anything from the family. She decides that she is going to continue in the pretended belief that the man who is masquerading as her grandson is really the authentic Mauricio, because she wishes to bring joy to the people who have given so much of themselves in order to rescue her from a life of despair.

There is much about *Los árboles mueren de pie* that is Pirandellian. The "director's" organization exists for the sole purpose of bringing poetry into the often harsh reality of life: illusion enables people to live happily. The headquarters of the organization at first almost seems like an insane asylum. The difficulty of comprehending the surroundings is dominant: "A primera vista, todo lo que estamos presenciando aquí solo puede ocurrir en un teatro o en una filmadora de películas o en un circo" (p. 594). Art is better than life, just as the imitation of a lark sounds more beautiful than the singing of a real lark and the "invented" grandson is, of course, much better than the real one: "¿Qué importa ya el nieto de mi sangre? Al que hay que salvar es al otro; al de las cartas hermosas, al de la alegría y la fe . . . , ¡el único verdadero para ella!" (p. 608).

Another similarity to Pirandellian thought is found in the idea that an artist's creation will exist forever, whereas the real object will die and be forgotten:

> Entonces, ¿de verdad crees que el arte vale más que la vida? Mauricio: Siempre. Mira ese jacarandá del jardín: hoy vale porque da flor y sombra; pero mañana, cuando se muere como mueren los árboles, en silencio y de pie, nadie volverá a acordarse de él. En cambio, si lo hubiese pintado un gran artista, viviría eternamente. [p. 632]

This concept can be compared to the father's often-quoted statement in *Sei personaggi* in which he maintains that the man will die, but the character will live forever.

In *La dama del alba* (1944) a situation occurs which is based on the interplay of illusion and reality and a human life is even sacrificed in order to perpetuate the belief in a beautiful lie. In this play Angélica has supposedly been dead for four years, but her body was never found in the river where she was thought to have drowned. Her reputation for beauty and goodness are legendary in the region in which she lived. One day a young girl, Adela, is rescued from the river by Martín, Angélica's husband. Adela's solitary position in the world moves her to accept the invitation to live with the family, and little by little she comes to occupy Angélica's place. Even Martín falls in love with her, but he is the only one who knows the truth about Angélica: she is not dead but has run away with her lover. Martín plans to leave because he knows that he cannot marry Adela. But Angélica returns, broken by her difficult life in the city after her lover has abandoned her. The only person present in the house to greet her when she arrives is a fantastic figure: death personified in the form of a pilgrim. The pilgrim persuades Angélica to drown herself. It is preferable to die and perpetuate her legend as a saint than to live the sad existence of a fallen woman. Accordingly, Angélica does throw herself into the river and when the people discover the body they think a miracle has occurred because it is still fresh. The legend of Angélica's saintliness will become part of the undying folklore in the region. As in many of Pirandello's plays, the lie triumphs over reality, and this is shown to be beautiful and just.

In conclusion, an assessment of the prevalence in Spanish literature of the themes which have come to be associated with Pirandello necessitates the inclusion of certain plays by Casona. While it is more than possible that he did actually learn something from the Italian playwright, either directly or indirectly, it is undeniable that his original treatment of the interpenetration of reality and illusion certainly has earned for him a prominent place among Spaniards of all centuries who have been fascinated by the topic.

JACINTO GRAU

The study of Jacinto Grau's relationship to Pirandello has been confined to discussions of *El señor de Pigmalión*[1] primarily because this work, like Unamuno's *Niebla*, is marked by the use of the autonomous character, the device employed so masterfully in *Sei personaggi in cerca d'autore*. Pigmalión has made dolls who resemble human beings and trains them to act in his plays. The dolls escape from him and kill him when he pursues them. These large animated dolls are like human beings physically, but mentally they are shallow creatures whose escape from Pigmalión is no more significant than schoolchildren playing hookey. The comparison between them and the autonomous characters which have been discussed must be a limited one because they do not radiate a deep sense of humanity as do Pirandello's *fantasmi d'arte* or Unamuno's Augusto Pérez. Nevertheless, it appears that Pirandello himself must have been attracted to this play, for he directed a performance of it in the Teatro d'Arte in Rome,[2] and it tantalizingly approaches the Pirandellian attitude toward art and life, the problems of the stage, various levels of reality, and the autonomous character.

While the literary affinity between Grau and Pirandello has been clearly established by *El señor de Pigmalión,* if the entire Grau / Pirandello relationship were based on this play alone, the subject would not lend itself to much comment. If, however, we focus attention on three other plays which have not been studied in this connection[3]—*Tabarín, Las gafas de don Telesforo o un loco de buen capricho,* and *Bibí Carabé* written consecutively between 1946 and 1954—Grau emerges as a full-fledged member of the group of playwrights inspired by Pirandello and Pirandellism.

Las gafas de don Telesforo (1949) is one of the most interesting Spanish plays written under Pirandello's aegis. It follows a pattern found in certain of Azorín's plays which were also inspired by Pirandello: direct influence of the Italian playwright plus clear acknowledgment that Spanish writers also shared many of his attitudes toward life and art.

In the plot Violante, Telesforo's wife, wishes to send him to an asylum because she can no longer stand his strange actions, such as putting on rose-colored glasses to view the world. Besides, she is passionately in love with another man. She is unsuccessful in her attempt to have her husband declared insane, however, because the doctor realizes Telesforo is not mad at all.

The second act reveals that for months Telesforo in disguise and under the name of Félix Miranda has been courting Violante, a deception he is forced to reveal because Violante wants to divorce him as Telesforo in order to go away with Félix. The third act takes place in Telesforo's toy store, in which there is a toy theater, and in one scene the head and shoulders of a handsome boy appear. He says he is the devil, and that he has come to induce Telesforo to reveal a secret formula, and, giving the episode Faustian overtones, offers to return Violante to Telesforo's arms in exchange for the formula. Telesforo refuses, but Violante returns anyway, because, although she knows that Félix Miranda is her husband's creation, she cannot live without the illusion he provides.

Several aspects of Pirandello's work are obvious in this play: the madness-sanity theme, illusion versus reality, the problem of identity, and various levels of reality. But, most interesting of all, Grau seems to have adopted a character whom Pirandello rejected. It has been pointed out frequently that Pirandello's short story, *La tragedia d'un personaggio* (1911) contains the nucleus of *Sei personaggi in cerca d'autore*, because in it appears an autonomous character who is searching for an author. In this story Pirandello relates that it is his habit to hold interviews every Sunday morning from eight to one with prospective characters for his future stories. One Sunday he arrives late because the previous evening a novel kept him awake until three in the morning, since Fileno, one of the characters, "l'unico vivo tra molte ombre vane" had suggested so many possibilities to him, although the author "Non aveva saputo assumere intera coscienza di questo personaggio."[4] When Pirandello arrives in his office he finds Dr. Fileno himself waiting to see him. Fileno begs that Pirandello undo the damage which has been done to him and complains bitterly about the way his own "imbecilic" author has suffocated him in an artificial world. Although Pirandello sympathizes, he regretfully but firmly refuses, triggering the famous autonomous character's tirade, part of which appears later in *Sei personaggi in cerca d'autore*.[5]

Fileno is only a character in outline. He believes he has invented an infallible method to enable people to bear the misfortunes of life: one must read history books from morning to evening, endeavoring all the while to imagine that present events really have long since occurred and now form part of the archives of the past. One must contemplate sad events as if he were looking through the reverse end of a telescope, making things seem far away. Fileno applies this philosophy, which he calls "La filosofia del lontano" and about which he has written a book, when his daughter dies, making his friends' consolation superfluous.

After Pirandello refuses him, evidently Fileno proceeds to follow the writer's suggestion that he should "picchiare alla porta di qualche altro scrittore."[6] Fortunately, he found behind this door a Spanish author who was willing to attend to his plea, for he is the hero of *Las gafas de don Telesforo*. A change of name was quite in order, because this was one of his complaints against his original author: "Ma guardi . . . Fileno . . . mi ha messo nome Fileno . . . Le pare sul serio che io mi possa chiamar Fileno? Imbecille, imbecille! Neppure il nome ha saputo darmi! Io, Fileno!"[7]

Under the circumstances, the facts Pirandello gives about this character can only contribute a small portion of the total personality with which he emerges in Grau's play, however, the source of the original inspiration is unmistakable. Pirandello says the following about Fileno: "Rappresentava un pover uomo, un certo dottor Fileno, che credeva d'aver trovato il più efficace rimedio a ogni sorta di mali, una ricetta infallibile per consolar sé stesso e tutti gli uomini d'ogni pubblica o privata calamità."[8] And Grau's Telesforo relates: "El dolor físico es insufrible, pero los dolores morales, las angustias del alma o del espíritu, pueden sortearse y vencerse fácilmente. Tengo la receta infalible para ello."[9]

Like Fileno, Telesforo has a telescope: "uno con lentes que disminuyen y alejan de nosotros esos hechos negros y conflictos terribles. Vistos a distancia pierden todo lo aplastante de una desesperación inmediata" (p. 104). He illustrates his philosophy by explaining that when his mother died he suffered tremendously; now, twenty years later, his sorrow is quite different. "De ahí la benéfica utilidad de ese anteojo que aleja y disminuye los objetos. Proyéctelo en los hechos y al considerarlos en una lejanía mudan de aspecto" (p. 104). Later, because of this philosophy, he is not upset when his daughter elopes.[10]

There are other signs of Pirandello's influence in this play. The uncertain boundary which exists between madness and sanity is a subtheme. Although he is eccentric, the "loco de buen capricho" is not really crazy at all, but seems so to others. Certain aspects of this situation remind the reader of *Enrico IV* and *Il berretto a sonagli*. Grau also handles the illusion-reality theme in an extremely Pirandellian manner; even the language seems to suggest direct inspiration. Telesforo, in a sentence reminiscent of *Così è (se vi pare)*, tells the doctor: "Pues lo mismo que los niños, deben hacer las personas mayores y elegir la ilusión que más les plazca vivir con arreglo a ella, en la seguridad de que la ilusión escogida, no es menos real que lo que llamamos realidad" (p. 102). And nothing could be more Pirandellian than: "¡Esa es precisamente mi verdad! ¡Que no hay nada verdad!" (p. 104). Grau, aware of the humoristic aspect of Pirandello's work, suggests that this play is also humoristic: "Tan cierto como es humorístico mi caso y tan absolutamente real, como pueden ser reales las cosas que sentimos y vemos en este mundo" (p. 108).

Telesforo echoes Fileno's claim to being more alive than the author: "Dentro de equis años, lo que usted llama realidad, su caudal atesorado, que dilapidarán sus hijos, y su persona, no serán nada, ni un recuerdo, mientras que mis apuntes científicos y mi filosofía de la ilusión seguirán existiendo y comentándose. ¡La realidad soy yo!" (p. 119).[11]

The way in which the first act ends seems to indicate Grau's intention to combine Pirandello's themes with Spanish pre-Pirandellian tradition: when the nurse enters, Don Telesforo has on his large rose-colored glasses, and the doctor is holding up a lantern to observe him more clearly. Telesforo remarks that anyone who saw them would think that they are insane, just as the nurse probably does, and the doctor answers that from their point of view they would be right, suggesting the theme of *Così è (se vi pare)*. Telesforo goes on to say that in spite of everything they are probably the two most sane people in the world, the doctor says it is possible that he is right, and the last sentence of the act affirms that notwithstanding the very marked foreign inspiration, Spanish tradition is strongly present: "Sí, señor. Tengo la razón de la sinrazón, como Don Quijote" (p. 109).

Don Quijote remains a presence throughout *Las gafas de don*

Telesforo because Telesforo has Cervantes's book at hand. Also, the setting of act 2 includes large dolls in the form of Don Quijote and Sancho. During this act, when Telesforo puts on his rose-colored glasses, he sits between Don Quijote and another doll in the form of Joan of Arc. Later when the devil says that illusion is the instrument which he uses to give the initial impulse to all brilliant human actions, Telesforo responds that illusion motivated Joan of Arc and Don Quijote. The devil answers: "Que yo les infundí, alucinando al uno con el espejismo de ideales nobles y fingiéndome una voz de Dios, a la otra" (p. 151). Reason, they agree, is a gust of cold polar air and life without illusion causes despair, like the despair shown by Don Quijote's dying words in which he rejected his "locura sublime" without which he would not truly have lived, "quedándose en un pobre e insignificante hidalguillo de gotera, de los del montón, desaparecido, apenas muerto, en el más absoluto anónimo" (p. 151). This emphasizes the idea that in the long run the character is more alive than a person, the exact thought which Pirandello expressed, giving Don Quijote's companion as an example: "E per vivere eterna, non ha mica bisogno di straordinarie doti o di compiere prodigi. Mi dica lei chi era Sancho Panza!" [12]

Nor does Grau neglect other Spaniards who show pre-Pirandellian characteristics in their work. In *Las gafas* he alludes to Calderón: "Viendo que toda la vida y el mundo vienen a ser, cual dijo el clásico, un puro o impuro sueño, una ilusión, me propuse, hace tiempo, ver al mundo y a la vida a través de otra ilusión más agradable y divertida que la idea que tenemos de la realidad, idea que es tan mentira como la ilusoria que yo me construyo y además mucho menos hermosa" (p. 100). Echegaray's *O locura o santidad* contains a statement similar to this of the doctor's: "Claro. Un santo, un genio, un héroe, sin estar locos, pertenecen a un orden superior y son por tanto anormales" (p. 93). Telesforo, in his insistence upon making duty his highest value also follows in Lorenzo's (the hero of *O locura o santidad*) footsteps, although he seems to be more aware of the subjective nature of such values: "Cada cual elige la ilusión más de su agrado y medida y yo prefiero la del deber, aunque me haga infeliz y me mate, a todo el resto de las ilusiones" (pp. 152–53).

Azorín has seen that the plays of Benavente and Pirandello have something in common when he lists the Spaniards who have used theater-within-the-theater techniques,[13] and Grau expresses an attitude similar to that found in *Los intereses creados:* although the lovers have been led to each other through deceit, love itself is the highest truth, and makes all other elements of secondary importance. Telesforo tries to explain to his wife the basic truth of the lie: "¿Fingido? Más verdad que la misma verdad, porque el amor y su atracción, que alucina y prolonga el mundo, es la verdad más fuerte y patente de la vida" (p. 158). Benavente ends his play with a passage in which he compares human beings to dolls, moved by strings, most of which represent the baser human motives, but occasionally the thread of love descends to move the heart and makes men seem divine, "y nos dice que no todo es farsa en la farsa, que hay algo divino en nuestra vida que es verdad y es eterno, y no puede acabar cuando la farsa acaba." [14] The two Spanish playwrights show the idealization of love in combination with the theme of the vagueness of the boundary between art and life.

In *Las gafas de don Telesforo* the idea of religion has the same Pirandellian overtones as in Unamuno's *San Manuel Bueno, mártir*. Telesforo stresses that his illusion is a dynamic one like an old wine whose odor alone is enough to intoxicate. The happy state does not end as quickly as that caused by wine and is much stronger. This is reminiscent of Don Manuel's wish that the lake be converted into a special kind of wine that would make people happy without the ill effects of alcohol. Also, Telesforo approves of illusions "que nos ayudan a vivir contentos y optimistas y nos sirven de tónico, más eficaz que los medicinales" (p. 103)—vital, optimistic illusions, which lead men to give their best to improve the world until God is reached. When asked what happens if God is not found, Telesforo answers that it does not matter if the journey is pleasant and we enjoy happiness along the way, which is certainly similar to the ideas of Unamuno's Don Manuel, whose whole life was a "piadoso fraude," dedicated to his parishioners so that they would live "lo más contentos que puedan en la ilusión de que todo esto tiene una finalidad." [15]

The plot of Garcia Lorca's short play *Amor de don Perlimplín con Belisa en su jardín,* may have been partly suggested to him by Pirandello's treatment of the themes of identity and life as a play. Don Perlimplín, an old man who is married to a young woman who does not love him, disguises himself as a young man and causes Belisa to fall in love with him (see p. 142). Although Grau's play, unlike Lorca's, has a happy ending, the result is the same: even after the lie is exposed, the woman who has fallen under the spell of beautiful illusion refuses to surrender it—fiction is stronger and more real than truth, echoing the need for self-deception and consciously accepted illusion so often found in Pirandello's plays.

The play-within-the-play, so closely associated with Pirandello, is only of minor importance in the work just discussed, but the technique fascinated Grau enough so that he developed it to a considerable extent in *Tabarín* (1946–47). Theater-within-the-theater in this play is brought up-to-date by means of an element unknown in Pirandello's plays. At the beginning of the first act an actor addresses the spectators saying that what they are going to see on the stage is really happening in another theater. This is made possible by the use of an amazing television set which shows distant events exactly as if they were occurring in front of the spectators' eyes. The actor tells the prompter to turn on the television. The impresario, who is the first person to speak, introduces Tabarín, a clown who customarily performs in public squares with Mondor, who sells patent medicines after the performance. As he finishes speaking, an usher rushes down the aisle to inform him that children are rioting outside because they want to enter. The impresario hurries away to see what can be done, and returns to ask the audience to wait while the police clear the street. This is a very confusing mixture of levels of reality, especially since the audience had been asked to believe that everything is taking place elsewhere. Then, spectators intervene in a way very similar to the interventions in Pirandello's *Questa sera si recita a soggetto*. Four women rise from their seats in the audience and approach the stage. They complain to the impresario that their husbands have stopped working in order to attend all of Tabarín's performances. The impresario asks them to be seated, they answer him rudely, and he calls for a policeman. But then the women see their husbands, who are just arriving, and fearfully scurry away. The manager announces that the last performance of Tabarín and Mondor will now begin. He leaves the stage, an usher shows the three husbands to their seats, the curtain goes up, and Tabarín and Mondor appear. The spectators speak to Tabarín, asking him not to leave town and shouting terms of endearment and approbation. After the comedians' recitation of jokes, they offer their medicines to the spectators who rush to the stage, surround them, and eagerly make purchases. Some stagehands join them, and at the height of the commotion the lights suddenly go out. A voice tells the audience not to be alarmed, the television has been turned off, but soon they will be able to continue seeing scenes from Tabarín's life through this marvelous apparatus which enables them to view action exactly as it happens, undistorted by historians.

Considerable detail has been given here in order to show that Grau has imitated the scandalous effect caused by spectator-actor intervention in *Questa sera si recita a soggetto*. This is especially significant because although many Spanish playwrights have employed Pirandello's ideas and techniques, they have rarely dared to break down the barriers between the stage and the auditorium so completely, except in the *sainetes*. The date of the play suggests that there is quite possibly some connection between Grau's work and the experiments of the "Arte Nuevo" group (see chapter 14). Another factor is that the spectator-participation techniques employed by Pirandello result in the destruction of aesthetic distance; that is, the spectators can no longer contemplate the work of art as such but are drawn into it.[16] Grau, by introducing television, adds a new dimension to this technique, which probably increases the confusion, but which, if understood intellectually by the audience, could result in spectator participation without loss of distance, since everything is supposed to be happening elsewhere.

Apparently Grau completely satisfied his desire to experiment with this method in the first act, because in the remaining three acts of the play he does not again remind the spectators that they are supposed to be watching television, and there is no further audience participation. The second act contains the exposition of the play which traditionally appears in the first act.

The third act reveals that Tabarín's exact resemblance to the King of Birlandia has been noticed by the king's mistress, Countess Charambambá, who conceives the idea of replacing the king with Tabarín so that she and her lover can leave the country together. Tabarín secretly worships the Queen of Birlandia, and even carries with him a life-sized doll in her likeness, so he accepts the plan, and disguised as a secretary, lives with the king for a while in order to learn how to fit unobserved into his new life. Unfortunately, when the great moment arrives in which Tabarín is finally alone with the queen (who is ready to forgive her husband although she has been neglected by him for many years), she is naturally unable to believe that Tabarín's emotion is real. When Tabarín sees that he has failed to win her love as the king, he tries to confess who he really is: "Yo no soy Roberto IV, yo soy Tabarín, el hazmerreír de las plazas, el famoso bufo de las ferias y prefiero que me prendan, que me azoten, que me ahorquen, a que me creáis un farsante cuando digo . . . que toda mi vida sois vos." [17] But this convinces her more than ever that he is acting; she accuses him of performing a grotesque comedy and stalks from the room, telling him to erase her from his memory forever. Tabarín laments as the curtain falls: "¡Ah, torpe payaso! ¡Te creíste una cosa y eres otra! ¡Eres un pobrecillo títere de barraca! . . . ¡Toda tu experiencia del mundo no supo que la verdad y la nobleza pueden ofender más en los palacios, que la astuta mentira!" (p. 194).

In *Tabarín* Grau shows several variations on the life and art theme: theater into which life intervenes, the life of an actor which is dominated by the theater, and pretense which becomes an irrevocable part of life, involving the very identity of the person.

In *Il fu Mattia Pascal* which Pirandello wrote early in his career, he treats the personality problem which occurs when a person tries to change his identity. Later he portrays the attempt to fit into another's life in *Come tu mi vuoi*. In both cases the protagonist fails to adapt himself to the change. Spanish writers have developed this general theme in *El otro* by Unamuno, *El hombre que murió en la guerra* by Manuel and Antonio Machado, and *¿Quién soy yo?* by Luca de Tena.

In *Bibí Carabé* Grau also treats the theme of life and the theater. Much to his dismay and annoyance, Bibí's simplest action or most straightforword statements cause his fellow workers and family to smile. A circus manager, having heard about this characteristic, hires him as a comedian. Bibí's debut is a disaster. He has stage fright and is shouted off the stage. Marione, a dramatic actor, explains that life and the theater are usually reversed: people who are comical in life become great tragic actors and people who seem sad become comedians on the stage. Bibí, under Marione's direction, is very successful as a tragedian. Conversely, Leonor, Bibí's wife, becomes an excellent comedienne and is completely changed by her success. During an argument Bibí kills Leonor because the conflict between them is too great to resolve.

The last act of the play takes place in a side show of a fair, where there are cardboard caricatures of famous people such as Napoleon, Garbo, Chaplin, and Bibí Carabé, who is portrayed strangling his wife. A painter has set up this show in order to study and sketch the reactions of the simple people who visit it. The police have been informed that Bibí is hiding there and arrive to arrest him for the murder of his wife. The inspector remarks: "Por lo visto quiso usted también ser, en la vida real, un personaje de tragedia, como las que tan genialmente representaba" (p. 272). Thus in *Bibí Carabé* Grau has examined the effect of acting on personality, a problem which was also treated by Pirandello in *Trovarsi*.

In each of the three plays Grau approaches Pirandellism in a different way. In *Tabarín* he shows many levels of reality, the theater-within-the-theater, spectator participation, and the identity problem. *Las gafas de don Telesforo* forms a collage combining many of Pirandello's ideas and techniques with Spanish pre-and post-Pirandellian influences. In *Bibí Carabé* he treats the problem of actors whose dramatic roles change their personalities and whose lives are thus destroyed by the theater.[18] This Pirandellian trilogy clearly provides new perspectives on the relationship between Grau and his Italian colleague and it is at the same time yet another example of how the Spaniards have assimilated twentieth-century Pirandellism into their own tradition.

JUAN IGNACIO LUCA DE TENA

Excellent examples of the problems involved in Pirandello-Spanish comparisons are found in the plays of Juan Ignacio Luca de Tena, who is included in the *Enciclopedia dello Spettacolo* among playwrights influenced by Pirandello.[1] Luca de Tena even mentions Pirandello in the prologue to one play when he evaluates an act as being "Pirandellian in reverse." [2]

Luca de Tena's *De lo pintado a lo vivo* was performed on 28 March 1944, the centenary of José Zorrilla's presentation of *Don Juan Tenorio.* As the author explains in his dedication, this play is a "comedia sobre comedia," following the tradition of Shakespeare's *Hamlet.*

The first act of *De lo pintado a lo vivo* begins with the dress rehearsal in 1844 of *Don Juan Tenorio,* played for six minutes exactly as Zorrilla wrote it. Then the actor who portrays José Zorrilla stands up in the first seat of row three to criticize the actors, and from this time on there are frequent intrusions into the illusion of the stage by actors who inject comments about their personal lives or criticize each other. A transparent curtain falls between the acts of this rehearsal to separate the two levels of fiction: the play and the lives of the actors. Behind this curtain Alverá, the stage father of Don Juan, invites to dinner the girl who is a nun in the play. The Duque de Rivas visits Zorrilla and he and Latorre listen to Zorrilla's self-criticism, taken by Luca de Tena from Zorrilla's memoir.

At the end of the first act there is a hint that under the influence of his role Latorre may find himself attracted to the girl, even though in real life he is a happily married family man. Latorre's progressive transformation continues in the second act, "La capa de Don Juan," which takes place backstage during the première of *Don Juan Tenorio,* at the end of which Latorre is unable to abandon his stage personality, and, aided by Brígida, who plays the procuress in the play, he arranges a date with the girl.

The third act, "Un personaje se escapa de su autor," in which Zorrilla compares his role as author to the position of God, takes place the following day in Zorrilla's study and concerns the repercussions of the previous evening's activities. When Latorre speaks to Zorrilla he explains how he has been excited by the role and completely controlled by it, and thus is not able to return to reality after the performance. Zorrilla tells Latorre that he does not have the right to escape from his author. Latorre agrees and asks his pardon and his help in repairing the damage he has done in the one night when he let the role of Don Juan carry over into his real life.

This play is a treatment of the problems and mechanics of the stage and it begins with a rehearsal, as does *Sei personaggi in cerca d'autore*. It contains several interwoven levels of reality—Zorrilla's play, the lives of the actors, the lives of the actors influenced by the play, and the author Zorrilla as man and as creator. Intervention from the audience abruptly shatters illusion.

We find a personality problem similar to that of the actress Donata Genzi in Pirandello's *Trovarsi* who has sacrificed a normal life by immersing herself completely in her roles in the plight of Latorre: "He pasado mi vida dedicado a los demás, sin pensar en que yo también existo. Para salir de mí mismo y comunicarme con el mundo exterior necesito el gran público. Ése me entiende y a ése le entiendo yo" (p. 1265).

However, Luca de Tena is misleading when he affirms that the third act of *De lo pintado a lo vivo*, "Un personaje se escapa de un autor," reverses the action of *Sei personaggi in cerca d'autore*. In Pirandello's play the "personaggi" represent an author's characters before they have been given dramatic form. They are not people, nor are they actors, although Pirandello seems to think that they are more alive than either. They are autonomous "fantasmi" or "creature d'arte." Luca de Tena, on the other hand, uses the word "personaje" here to signify the actor who continues to live his part after the play is over. The artistic creation does not escape; the actor merely suffers a personality change for one evening under the influence of his role, which is a completely different concept.

An integral element of the plays in which Pirandello opposes art to life is the torment of the playwright himself (although he does not appear on the stage) as he struggles to give his inspiration dramatic form. Luca de Tena, using the circumstances of a well-

known play of a century ago instead of his own experiences as a
playwright, gives greater literary dimension to the torment of creation through this interesting version of Zorrilla's experience.

Precedents for many of the aspects of Pirandellism in Luca de
Tena's play can also be found in the Spanish theater. For example,
Tamayo y Baus' *Un drama nuevo* is very similar to *De lo pintado
a lo vivo*. Both plays are behind-the-scenes accounts of plays in the
making which reveal the mechanics of the stage and include
prompters as important figures. The manner in which Zorrilla takes
part in *De lo pintado a lo vivo* is very similar to the treatment of the
character Shakespeare (although he is not the author of the new
play) in *Un drama nuevo*. In both plays the author attempts to help
the actors who are having trouble in their personal lives due to
problems caused or complicated by their stage roles. In both plays the
lives of the actors are more important than the play, and an actor
allows his role to carry over into his private life. The dire results of
such an overlapping in the Tamayo y Baus play remind one of the
tragic consequences in Pirandello's plays; in *De lo pintado a lo vivo*
the consequences are less serious because they affect only a brief
interlude in the life of Luca de Tena's character.

In Luca de Tena's play when Zorrilla compares his role as author
to that of a god, one is reminded of Calderón's *El gran teatro del
mundo* in which man appears in the world, is assigned a role, but
possesses free will, and thus sins or lives a praiseworthy life under
his own responsibility. Zorrilla feels he has created and determined
the characteristics of his protagonists, but they sin without his permission: "Como un dios en miniatura he creado seres y he presidido
sus destinos, sus culpas y sus inconsciencias. Pero han pecado, como
los humanos creados por el Dios verdadero, sin quererlo yo" (p.
1285). In his "nivola" *Niebla*, when Unamuno has a confrontation with the character Augusto Pérez, he also participates in this
tradition of comparing the author-character relationship to that of
God and man. In addition, Unamuno's *El hermano Juan o el
mundo es teatro* may have influenced Luca de Tena in this play.
Although Unamuno's play is completely different in concept and
purpose from *De lo pintado a lo vivo*, it also combines the world-as-
theater concept of Calderón and a presentation of Don Juan in contemporary society, "el hermano Juan" being Unamuno's original
psychological interpretation of Don Juan's character.

Although *¿Quién soy yo?* (1935) contains none of the theater-
within-the-theater techniques of *De lo pintado a lo vivo*, the identity

problem is certainly extremely Pirandellian. Colomer, an exceptional man, perfect to a fault, but not very likeable and completely lacking a sense of humor, is characterized in act 1 ("La Comedia") as a very busy and successful minister of finance in the imaginary country of Saldaria. However, his success is marred because he wants to marry Claudina, who admires but cannot love him.

Brandel, who has obtained an interview with Colomer's friend and adviser, Astófano, arrives disguised as an old man. When he removes his beard and wig, Astófano is astonished to find that Brandel is the exact double of Colomer. Brandel, knowing that the social duties connected with his office bore Colomer, has come with the proposition of substituting for him in public functions for a salary and maintenance.

Colomer accepts, and in act 2, "La Farsa," Brandel happily and successfully carries out his agreement, playing his part so well that "algunas veces yo mismo me creo que soy él" (p. 986). He calls Colomer "el otro" and speaks as if he himself were the complete figure represented by a combination of the two men. Even Astófano becomes somewhat confused about the identity of Brandel, who tells him: "En fin de cuentas, cada uno es lo que parece. Yo parezco, luego soy. ¿Qué soy yo ahora mismo? ¿Quién soy yo?" (p. 989).

In act 3, "La tragedia," Colomer, unhappy because Claudina has fallen in love with Brandel, decides to rid himself of his double and rival. A struggle between the two men occurs behind opaque glass so that the identity of the survivor will be uncertain.

The second "cuadro" of the last act begins with the voice of the actor which says "¿Quién soy yo?" There has been a *coup d'état* which will make Mario Colomer chief of state. When he comes out, the stage directions state: "¿Colomer? ¿Brandel? El autor no lo sabe aún ni le importa" (p. 1016).

In Luca de Tena's play the personality theme is neither so profound nor ambiguous as it is in Pirandello's *Così è (se vi pare)*. Only after the murder at the end of *¿Quién soy yo?* is there actual doubt about the identity of the protagonist, and the Pirandello-like statement appears that his true identity does not matter. Pirandello's play, however, is based on a confusion of identity which is never solved. Signora Ponza of *Così è (se vi pare)* willingly consents to be for each person what he wants her to be and for herself no one. She remains a mystery to the other characters and to the audience. Brandel, on the other hand, knows who he is, in spite of the artificial confusion created by the shout "¿Quién soy yo?" He insists that he is Colomer because he thinks that only in this way will he have a public identity, for as Brandel he had no position in life at all.

Another personality problem of *¿Quién soy yo?* reminds us of *Quando si è Qualcuno:* when a person's reputation is made and his solid public image is formed he can do little to change it. In *¿Quién soy yo?* the characters discuss a woman admirer who thinks Colomer is going to speak on the radio but who hears a communist speech in error; believing it is Colomer, she makes the following comment: "¡Qué cosas más raras ha dicho hoy Colomer! ¡Pero cuando él las dice!" (p. 987). Brandel applies this to his own situation when Astófano fears he will be found out: "No tengas miedo, hombre: Yo ya tengo hecha mi reputación." Astófano exclaims: "¿Usted?," and Brandel answers: "Bueno, el otro, que en determinados momentos, ahora, por ejemplo, soy yo. Los que con fe ciega creen en mí, bueno, en el otro, seguirán creyendo por muchas tonterías que me vean hacer" (p. 987).[3]

¿Quién soy yo?, although definitely Pirandellian, is even more similar to a Spanish ancestor: Unamuno's *El otro* in which one brother kills the other and then refuses to reveal which of the twins he is (see p. 89). In many ways the essence of Unamuno's drama is just as alien to Luca de Tena as is that of Pirandello. However, the basic plot and the terms "¿Quién soy yo?" and "el otro" seem to imply that Luca de Tena partly used Unamuno's play as a model. *¿Quién soy yo?* is certainly more similar to *El otro* than it is to anything Pirandello ever wrote. In both plays there are look-alikes who are incapable of living without their own individual personalities. In both the one survivor, having killed his double in a battle motivated by envy and the love of a woman, then refuses to identify himself and tries to take on the identity of the other.

In the playbill distributed in the fall of 1968 at a performance of *¿Quién soy yo?* Luca de Tena himself comments about his predecessors:

El tema no es nuevo; no hay nada nuevo bajo el sol. Había inspirado ya numerosas obras de la literatura dramática universal. Desde Plauto hasta nuestros días, pasando por Molière, Tirso de Molina y, hace menos años, Unamuno y Pirandello, fueron muchos los autores que han desarrollado igual tema en serio o en broma, colocando casi todos al margen del protagonista la figura de una mujer.[4]

Two years after *¿Quién soy yo?* Luca de Tena wrote its sequel, *Yo soy Brandel.* After the prologue, which is a resumé of the previous play, the first act begins with a scene between Astófano and Brandel, in which after a half-hearted attempt to convince Astófano that he is Colomer, Brandel admits his identity and asks Astófano to help him govern the country. He has not inherited the political skill of Colomer and also seems to have lost his own attractive personality.

Al morir se llevó una parte de mi alma, y no me dejó la suya. Esa es mi tragedia. Mi vida es desde entonces, una continua reacción de mi personalidad a la suya. Pero en muchas ocasiones, cuando ya he conseguido dominarme y 'ser' él, mi yo verdadero se rebela y vuelvo a ser Brandel. En mis sueños se me aparece el muerto y me da consejos. Y como cuando vivía, estoy harto de él. [p. 1082]

Although Colomer is dead, he intervenes in this play in the form of a "sombra," projected by a film, which Brandel is able to call forth at will. After Brandel reveals the truth to Claudina, Colomer's shade explains to him that he has only existed in Brandel's imagination, in the unconsciousness of the masses, in Claudina's romantic head, in the egotism of Astófano. Colomer's shade tells Brandel that Brandel can kill him completely just by truly wanting to do so. Finally freed from Colomer, Brandel and Claudina leave: "Adiós. Mario Colomer ha muerto hoy por segunda vez, pero ahora definitivamente . . . Juan Brandel ha vuelto a nacer" (p. 1118).

The fact that Luca de Tena thought that his play *¿Quién soy yo?* needed further development to resolve the identity problem shows that a true ideological relationship between him and Pirandello does not exist. Also, at the end of the play all of the apparatus which has been used to show that there actually were two people is rather artifically turned into a split-personality situation. Indeed, the way the playwright directed the staging of the last scene in the excellent 1968 production makes a sequel superfluous. In the original version the last line the protagonist speaks is an emotional "¿Quién soy yo?," whereas in the latest production, by gesture and facial expression, he indicates to the audience that he is Brandel.

In spite of these objections, some traits of *Yo soy Brandel* do resemble certain aspects of Pirandello's *Come tu mi vuoi.* Both treat the problem of an unknown person who is consciously assuming an identity not his own. In *Come tu mi vuoi* L'Ignota knows she is not

Cia, but in order to escape from her own sordid existence she accepts the opportunity to go to the home of a girl who had disappeared ten years previously during the war and whom she resembles so closely that the relatives believe she is Cia. L'Ignota is desperate for a new, beautiful life which she feels can be embodied in the life of Cia.

In Luca de Tena's plays Brandel is not escaping from an existence. He is an unemployed, professionless man who decides that a part-time impersonation of an important person whom he exactly resembles would be a pleasant way to make a living. The similarity to *Come tu mi vuoi* begins after Brandel kills Colomer in self-defense and is left to complete the assumption of the latter's personality. The result of this action is similar in both of these plays. L'Ignota cannot keep up the false existence as Cia and goes back to her previous life. Brandel is unable to continue existing as Colomer and at the end of the play he leaves Saldaria with Claudina.

The motives behind these two actions are quite different in the two plays, however. In *Come tu mi vuoi* the problem is much more profound: L'Ignota cannot bear the fact that Cia's relatives continue to try to recognize Cia in her physical appearance, when she feels that she could truly embody Cia's beautiful soul, and therefore her actual identity does not matter. Brandel abandons his assumed identity for the practical reason that he does not have Colomer's political acumen and is unable to reconcile two completely different personalities.

In 1944 Luca de Tena wrote *La escala rota* in collaboration with Miguel de la Cuesta. In this play Marta, the leading lady, Federico, the leading man, and the author form a triangle around which are woven the themes of life opposed to art, the effect of acting on personality, and the author's control of the actors through his characters.

When the play opens, the author is reading aloud a love scene from the play-within-the-play, "La escala de Jacob," which involves the love of Luisa and Rafael, a sculptor. The author intends the play to show the fulfillment of his own love for Marta, but the actor Federico thinks that the protagonists of "La escala de Jacob" represent Marta and himself.

In act 2, when the play is about to be performed for the hundredth time, Marta is ready to rebel: she is tired of being controlled by her role. But Federico tells her that she never plays her role twice in exactly the same way. He explains that when she improvised a scene because a minor character forgot to appear, she showed her own creative spirit and her happiness at being liberated from the author.

Act 3 begins with the love scene of the play-within-the-play. The author is playing the leading role, ostensibly to celebrate the hundredth performance, but actually to try to make real his fictional conquest of Marta. Seeing them act together, Federico thinks that Marta returns the author's love. Saying that he has had enough of the play and of the theater and that he intends to leave the company, Federico then reveals the artificiality of the props which are present on the stage, such as the cardboard which represents books. But Marta assures Federico that she really loves only him. She tells the author that they are not puppets, that the new play in which she will perform is life itself, and that life, and not the author, will distribute the roles.

At the end of the play the author is left alone on the stage. He observes with his back to the audience while the stagehands remove the furniture. When the prompter asks why he is watching so attentively, he explains: "No son decoraciones, amigo. Es mi hogar . . . que se deshace" (p. 84).

Luca de Tena indirectly suggests that he may have had Pirandello in mind when he wrote *La escala rota* by naming the actress Marta, a name which even Pirandello did not give the heroine of *Trovarsi* although Marta Abba was his model and the play is dedicated to her. The theme of *Trovarsi,* which is the difficulty the heroine finds in combining art and life, is very similar to the problem illustrated in *La escala rota.* However, in the former, the actress returns to her career, and in the latter it is assumed that she will abandon her career for marriage. Although this conventional ending in the Spanish play weakens Luca de Tena's attempt to portray a woman whose life is dedicated to the theater, both playwrights do show the personality problem of an actress who finds it difficult to combine life and art.

Luca de Tena may also have had Pirandello's *Diana e la Tuda* in mind when he made the hero of his play-within-the-play a sculptor. In this play Pirandello portrays the rebellion of life, represented by a model, against art, represented by sculpture. Luca de Tena also suggests the desire of a work of art, symbolized by the actress, to rebel against the fixity of art, symbolized by the play.

Although several levels of reality are also represented in *De lo pintado a lo vivo,* Luca de Tena more nearly approximates Pirandello's approach in *La escala rota* because the action is brought up-to-date and the play-within-the-play is Luca de Tena's own. Also, this is the play in which Luca de Tena most aggressively breaks into the illusion of the stage, competing thus with the effect obtained in Pirandello's *Ciascuno a suo modo*.

La escala rota contains the element of improvisation, which is so characteristic of Pirandello and constitutes one of his main themes: the opposition of art and life. When Marta of *La escala rota* is forced to improvise because a minor character forgets to appear, she is more of an actress and more of a woman than when she follows the lines written for her. Pirandello's improvisation scenes usually show the impossibility of communicating on the stage the dramatic impact of life, but Luca de Tena suggests that when Marta improvises a short scene within the framework of the play she liberates herself from all restraint.

Although Pirandello is one source of Luca de Tena's inspiration in this play, we cannot overlook his Spanish precedents. *De lo pintado a lo vivo* recalls Calderón with the idea that the author is a superior, Godlike being whose relationship to his character is equivalent to that of God to man. The play-within-the-play technique is like Tamayo y Baus's *Un drama nuevo* and Echegaray's *El gran galeoto*. The author as character receives similar treatment in *El gran galeoto* and in Moratín's *La comedia nueva,* although in the latter a satire against inferior playwrights is Moratín's only concern. Manuel and Antonio Machado also wrote about a dedicated woman artist in *La Lola se va a los puertos.* Their *cantaora* disdains marriage with any of her admiring coworkers in order to dedicate herself to her career which is her complete existence, but like Pirandello's Donata Genzi, Lola is more consistently attached to her career than is Marta of *La escala rota.*

Luca de Tena wrote an *entremés* for the opening of the Alvarez Quintero Theater in Sevilla which, in a fashion similar to the brothers' play written for Valera (see pp. 45–46), presents the Quinteros' characters Malvaloca and Consolación on the stage. The first part of the play consists of Consolación's visit to Malvaloca's home to invite her to attend the opening of the Alvarez Quintero Theater. Malvaloca demurs, but suddenly Consolación tells her that they are already there and asks her to look at the audience. Malvaloca can't see anything until the house lights are turned on. Consolación and Malvaloca then turn their attention to the spectators, remarking how many beautiful women and well-dressed men there are. They recite a few lines in the style that the Alvarez Quintero brothers used to end their *entremeses* and finally request applause for themselves as actresses, using their own names.

In contrast to the many Pirandellian characteristics of Luca de Tena's plays, the basic differences between the two playwrights are very striking. Perhaps the most important distinction is that Pirandello glorifies fiction, which in his plays is usually more vibrant than life itself and which can even become reality (such as when Enrico IV's playacting becomes his life or when Signora Ponza of *Così è* [*se vi pare*] continues her complicated pretense in spite of her neighbors' efforts to destroy this fiction). When Pirandello does demolish the beautiful illusion of pretense, as in *Vestire gli ignudi* and *Come tu mi vuoi,* the deep vacancy of the nothingness left in life reaffirms the deeper value of art. Luca de Tena, on the other hand, systematically rules in favor of life: Brandel gives up the role of Colomer to go away with Claudina and live his own life. It is understood that Latorre, after one night as a fictional character, will no longer be tempted to stray, and Marta gives up her brilliant acting career for marriage.

Luca de Tena's plays translate the deeply human problems which torture Pirandello's characters into a lighter type of conflict, which is usually resolved satisfactorily in order to provide the happy ending the theater-going public enjoys. Luca de Tena, then, shows the direct influence of Pirandello amply supported by Spanish theatrical tradition and modified by his approach as a popular playwright.

PEDRO SALINAS

Although the poetry of Pedro Salinas has been the subject of numerous studies, his activity as playwright is usually omitted or at most barely mentioned in discussions of twentieth-century Spanish theater. Although some reviews and articles which serve to introduce the subject appeared after three of his plays were published in 1952,[1] the first important study was published only recently.[2]

A playwright in exile in a country where his native language is not spoken suffers from a handicap unknown to exiled novelists or poets. Even though university groups performed some of his plays,[3] it is understandable that they are not considered part of the mainstream of twentieth-century Spanish theater. However, these lyrical stories in the form of plays share at least one characteristic found in the Spanish theater of the twentieth century and thus form an integral part of its history. This characteristic is the imprint of Pirandello.

Salinas has, for example, written a play, *El precio,* in which the center of interest is the autonomous character. Briefly, the story is as follows: Alicia and her father, who is a psychiatrist, are spending the summer in the country. One day Alicia meets a girl who does not know where she is going nor who she is. Alicia takes the girl home and names her Melisa. She is an exquisite, poetic creature who makes Alicia very happy with her imaginative pastimes. She exists in time without knowing the meaning of yesterday and today, and she sings a song which tells her story, although she does not understand it, nor can she explain how she learned it.

Jáuregui, a writer, arrives in search of Melisa. He explains that he knows her completely, although he has never seen her. At ten o'clock one morning a week earlier he began to write a description of a morning: "Una mañana para ella . . . que se ajustara a su modo de ser humano, que fuese como el traje en que el mundo la envolvía, y que con ser tan inmenso, le cayese a ella justo, perfectamente, a la medida" (p. 215), and through this morning she escaped from him. He explains that he has created her; she is a fictional being, a poetic lie. He had her half formed, he loved her more than anyone, and now she will remain incomplete, "y yo, igual, ella sin su pasado, que yo tengo, y yo sin su mañana, sin su otra mitad, que iba a darle, sin su vida entera" (p. 217). When Alicia brings Melisa to him she simply embraces him, saying: "A ti vuelvo . . . Ya sé quién soy . . . Quiero vivir . . . ¡Tuya, tuya . . . !" (p. 218), and dies in his arms. Death is the price she must pay in order to continue living as a fictional character.

Like Pirandello's six characters, Melisa is a half-formed character who has left her author. Also, Salinas indirectly expresses an idea similar to Pirandello's that corporal life is worth less than the eternal life enjoyed by a fictional character. Finally, Melisa's initial appearance is especially reminiscent of the appearance in *Sei personaggi* of Madame Pace who comes to the stage lured by the setting which has been prepared for her.

However, there are many differences between Salinas's and Pirandello's versions of the autonomous character, the main one being that Salinas's play lacks the conflict between character and author. Melisa is docile and places herself completely in her author's hands. She had escaped only because the author created a situation in which she could not do otherwise. Pirandello's autonomous characters, both in his short story *La tragedia d'un personaggio* and in his famous play, are characters who are said to be poorly formed or half-formed by another author and who appeal to Pirandello in the first case and to the stage manager in the second to be given their proper vehicle of expression. They are disgruntled, frustrated entities who complain bitterly about the treatment which they have received.

The most famous Spanish autonomous character, Unamuno's Augusto Pérez, is also at odds with his author, as is Azorín's autonomous character in *El libro de Levante*.[4] André Lebois suggests this basic characteristic of autonomous characters by entitling his article on the subject "La révolte des personnages."[5] In fact, one main purpose of autonomy seems to be the creation of a clash between art, represented by the character, and life, represented by the author, which results in a deep questioning of the nature of both.

Thus, in contrast to the other autonomous characters who con-

front their author, Salinas has given Melisa what seems to be a
rather purposeless autonomy. However, the very contrast between
the typical character who acts independently from his author and
Melisa seems to underline the aspect of instinctive perfect communication which is so important in Salinas's poetry and is here transposed into theatrical terms. The Pirandellian point of departure in
El precio could possibly have led Salinas to show conflict between
character and writer; instead, the result is an expression of perfect
harmony.

Several of Pirandello's themes are found in Salinas's play *La
estratoesfera*. Alvaro, a poet who occupies a table in the café called
"La estratoesfera," contemplates life through the eyes of fiction.
When Felipa enters the café with her blind grandfather, who sells
lottery tickets, the poet associates him with Oedipus and her with
Antigone. A group of actors enters: César, who is playing Don
Quijote in a film; Ramón, who is Sancho Panza; Luis, the Duke;
and Rita, the Duchess. Noticing Felipa's agitation, Alvaro asks her
to confide in him, and when she hesitates he assures her: "Pero soy
tu amigo . . . Te conozco de tiempo . . . Y vas a ser mucho,
chiquilla . . . ¿No ves que te estoy haciendo personaje? Te estoy
inventando . . . Déjame que te invente . . ." (p. 83). Felipa tells
Alvaro that four years ago when César (whom she knew as Juan)
was in her town, Toboso, he had made love to her, recited to her
from *Don Juan Tenorio,* promised to marry her, and then had dishonored her. Alvaro approaches César, and finds it convenient to
confuse fiction with reality:

> Dialogo con Don Quijote de la Mancha, creación inmarcesible
> del Manco de Lepanto . . . Con el defensor de la honra ultra-
> jada y la virtud escarnecida, con el amparo de los inocentes . . .
> Y compenetrado, como debe usted estar, con su personaje,
> calcúlese lo que en esta peripecia, tomada de la vida real, habría
> hecho el Caballero de la Triste Figura. . . . [p. 87]

César does not share Alvaro's tendency to confuse reality with
fiction, nevertheless he is willing to speak to Felipa as Alvaro suggests, telling her that he is Juan's twin brother, that Juan had gone to
America in order to earn enough to marry her, and that he had
died there. Thus Alvaro, with César's cooperation, has given Felipa
a beautiful lie which she believes, and which will give her dignity:
"Es que soy otra, es que ahora me atrevería yo a ir a mi pueblo y a

mirar a tós así cara a cara, sin bajarle los ojos ni al más pintao. ¡Es que me quería, no lo ha oído usté!" (p. 90).

The mixture of fantasy and reality in this play is very true to the spirit of Pirandello. The hero is a poet within the play and sees everything through the veil of poetic imagination. He "invents" Felipa, superimposing on her real self, which is that of an ignorant village girl, a classical heroine. When he makes her believe that her honor is unsullied, his fiction becomes a very powerful force in the life of the girl, who will no longer be bowed down by the shame of her past.

Although Salinas is much kinder to his heroine than is Pirandello, and although Pirandello's heroines are both conscious of the deception, whereas Felipa is not, this theme recalls *Vestire gli ignudi* and *Come tu mi vuoi* in which attempts are made to give dignity to a rather sordid past by covering it with the veil of fiction.

As has been pointed out, Cervantes and Pirandello have much in common,[6] and in the plays of Azorín and Grau which show the influence of Pirandello, there are also allusions to Cervantes. Salinas, by using actors who are performing in a representation of *Don Quijote*, underlines the fact that Spanish tradition provides a firm precedent for the interplay of fiction and reality. Indeed, the characters chosen by Salinas to represent Cervantes directly suggest the levels of reality in the *Quijote*, for in the second part of Cervantes's novel the Duke and Duchess create a situation where Don Quijote can actually believe that the fantasy which he has created is truth. The fact that Felipa is from Toboso also recalls Cervantes and the way in which Alvaro "invents" Felipa parallels Don Quijote's invention of Dulcinea.

The invention of a character is also a theme in Salinas's *El chantajista*, which concerns Lucila, who writes unique and beautiful love letters and "loses" them in a cinema. Lisardo, "el chantajista," finds them. He writes to Lucila, asking her to send Eduardo, the young man to whom the letters were supposedly written, to meet him if she is interested in recovering her letters.

The play opens when Lisardo arrives to find Lucila, disguised as a man, waiting for him in the park. He turns down the money she offers him, stating that the price for the return of the letters is the key to Lucila's garden gate, which she gives to him.

In the second *cuadro* Lisardo appears in Lucila's garden masked and dressed as Romeo. Lucila tries to explain to him that nothing is a lie, not even his costume or mask. "También ellos tienen su verdad . . . , se les ve la verdad" (p. 135). She leaves him and reappears as Eduardo, saying that she will give Lisardo ten minutes more with Lucila, but only if he promises to tell her the truth. When he is alone he tells how much the game has confused him; he can no longer separate truth from falsehood. He does not know whether he has deceived Lucila or not, and he feels that his emotions are completely authentic although they are covered by superficial falsehood. When Lucila reappears she tells Lisardo that when he read the letters he gradually took on the features and shape of her lover, exactly as she wished him to be. He admits that while reading the letters he was longing to be Eduardo, and adds, "Tú me has hecho" (p. 142).

Although this play is very much Salinas's own, it clearly belongs to the age of Pirandello, and the way Salinas explains the process at the end of the play seems especially Pirandellian. Although Lisardo cannot really have any serious doubts about his identity, he appears to be dubious as he questions: "¿Quién soy yo?" (p. 138). And the remark Lucila makes that she has created him places her in a position similar to that of the author who creates a character.

The phenomenon of a fictitious situation which becomes reality appears in such Pirandello plays as *Ma non è una cosa seria,* where a woman is so much changed by the experience of being a wife that the man who married her for convenience falls in love with her. Of course there are many differences between this situation and that of *El chantajista,* but in both dramas fiction triumphs over reality and then becomes reality.

As is true of many Spanish plays reminiscent of Pirandello, *El chantajista* also contains Spanish precedents. Benina, in *Misericordia* by Galdós, invented Don Romualdo; Don Quijote invented Dulcinea; and Augusto Pérez tried to invent Eugenia. However, Salinas's character is far more successful in superimposing fantasy on reality than any of these.

In *La fuente del Arcángel* Salinas again combines illusion and reality in a great variety of ways. Claribel and her sister Estefanía are spending the summer vacation with their Aunt Gumersinda in Alcorada, an Andalusian town. The young ladies have led a sheltered existence, and Gumersinda does not want them to see a nightly spectacle which occurs outside their window where there is a fountain with a statue of the archangel on it. It is the custom for lovers to meet there—they hold hands and even kiss. Since it is a local superstition that the archangel protects lovers, Gumersinda wants to move the statue to the church so that the lovers will no longer be attracted to the fountain. But when she speaks to Padre Fabián about her project, he reveals a carefully guarded secret: the statue is not really the archangel but the pagan Eros in the angel's garb.

Claribel and Estefanía had been given permission that night to go to a magician's show, and while Gumersinda is speaking to Padre Fabián, a painting which is hanging on the wall becomes transparent to reveal the stage of the casino where the magician Florindo is performing. By means of a counterpoint technique two conversations are heard at once—first the conversation of Gumersinda and Fabián in which the secret is being revealed: "Las cosas no son todas lo que parecen . . . Ni siquiera las personas . . ." (p. 35); and then the speech in which Florindo is speaking about illusion: "Este número es ilusionismo puro . . . Porque, señores y caballeros, todos sabemos, desde que lo afirmó en sus inmortales décimas don Pedro Calderón de la Barca, que las cosas no son lo que parecen. Y mucho menos las personas . . . Todo apariencias, señoras y caballeros . . ." (p. 34). Fabián is referring to the true pagan nature of the statue which seems Christian, and Florindo is alluding to the much more beautiful and spiritual aspect of illusion.

Florindo's most impressive act is to turn members of the audience into characters of other epochs. Claribel volunteers and is changed into Teodora, the Byzantine empress. After this experience, she is no longer quite the same: "Yo no sé, pero siento como si me bailaran dentro del cuerpo tres o cuatro Claribeles juntas . . . , vamos, como si yo fuese otras cuantas más que yo . . ." (p. 39). This lyrical description of her sensations is a unique variation on the multiplicity of personality theme.

As in *Così è (se vi pare)*, the idea that there can be different interpretations of a situation depending upon point of view is also important in *La fuente del Arcángel*. Several persons contemplate the same scene of the lovers at the fountain but interpret it in different ways. Gumersinda thinks the lovers are extremely wicked and is scandalized. Estefanía thinks it is all rather strange, does not really like to see it, and says "no es para nosotras . . ." (p. 41). Claribel invents a beautiful poetic conversation which she tells her sister she can hear. However, unlike Pirandello, Salinas permits the audience to know the truth, which is none of the truths seen by the observers: Honoria and Angelillo, whose names reveal what Salinas thinks of them, are discussing the furniture they will have in their home. This conversation brings fantasy down to a more prosaic level because Angelillo believes that Honoria's desire to have a wardrobe with two mirrors and a flower-painted basin and pitcher with which to wash their hands with perfumed soap is far above their way of life: "Y dale con la fantasía . . . ¿Pero qué te crees tú, que vamos a está lavándono la mano a ca rato . . . Mía la señorita . . ." (p. 40). Probably Salinas would like fantasy to triumph even in their lives, because he sets their wedding for the day of San Juan, traditionally the time when magic events are believed to occur in Spain.

At the end of the play the archangel comes down from the fountain, dressed as a trapeze artist, and takes Claribel away with him. The exact identity of this figure is not really clear; he seems to be a combination of many people. As Cowes explains: "La persona con que Claribel se va de Alcorada es el Arcángel y no es el Arcángel, es Eros y no es Eros, es el caballero Florindo y no es el caballero Florindo, es el mundo de la madre y no lo es." [7]

In spite of the fact that the exact identity of the man is not quite certain, the end of the play suggests that Claribel knows and is sure of her destiny. Perhaps his identity does not matter, for the play shows the triumph of illusion over the prosaic life of Alcorada which Claribel has exchanged for what seems to be a beautiful future.

La bella durmiente also treats the identity problem. This play takes place in an exclusive resort for celebrities who wish to spend a vacation in absolute anonymity. Soledad, which is not her real name, is spending her vacation there to escape from the unwanted fame which has accompanied her ever since she has modeled for a mattress company's publicity campaign. She explains the joy she feels at being liberated from her public identity: "¡Qué gusto ser desconocida, salirse de la imagen de una que tienen los demás, dejar de ser la que se figuran los otros que es! Yo lo comparo con volver a casa después de un baile aburrido y quitarse el traje y el color y todo, y meterse en el agua y sentirse verdadera" (p. 167).

Alvaro is there to escape the public attention accorded to a millionaire and is, by coincidence, the owner of the mattress company for which Soledad has modeled. Alvaro and Soledad fall in love, but she feels it is necessary to explain to him who she is, as she feels tainted by what has happened to her. She especially resents the owner of the company, although she does not know him. Alvaro never reveals his identity to her, telling her only that for reasons she does not understand, their marriage would be impossible.

Of course Soledad's personality and real self are never involved, thus the reader is not convinced that the situation is desperate enough to warrant the torment she suffers; nevertheless this play may be considered Salinas's translation into his own terms of the type of conflict Pirandello presented in *Quando si è qualcuno,* where a famous writer feels trapped by the public image from which he would like to escape.

And if the identity of a living person is a problem, in *Ella y sus fuentes* Salinas shows that the search for historical truth is likely to result in an unconscious creation of fiction by the historian. Don Desiderio has devoted his life to writing the biography of Julia Riscal, a national heroine. He is proud of the accuracy of his account, having based it on documentary evidence. However, Julia shatters his whole image of her when she visits the earth to tell Don Desiderio the truth. The truth is so elusive that it takes a miracle to uncover it.

Another theme of Pirandello's theater, illusion which attempts to conquer death, is found in Salinas's *Sobre seguro.* In this work insurance agents decide that their business would develop in the imaginary city, Serenia, if the inhabitants were to see the benefits of insurance. Therefore, they arrange for one of the insurees, Angel, a retarded boy, to die in a boating "accident." His body is not recovered. The father, sister, and brother believe that Angel is dead, need the money, and urge the mother to sign the receipt so that they may collect the indemnity. But she believes that as long as she does not sign he is not really dead: "Si yo firmara, entonces sí que se habría muerto . . . ¿Lo entienden ustedes? Cada vez que digo 'no firmo' le siento vivir, sin verle, como le sentía en los primeros meses de su vida, dentro de mí, como un latido. No, yo le guardo su vida" (p. 293). Up to this point the play is realistic, but after Petra is left alone, the money, which the insurance agents have left overnight in order to tempt her to sign, comes to life to tell her, in a speech reminiscent of *Poderoso caballero es don dinero,* that no one can resist it. But then Angel returns in a confused state, remembering only that he felt a blow when he was in the boat. He has spent the five days since the occurrence with a couple in the country. The mother decides that she and her son will go away together to a place where no one can buy him. In spite of the fantastic scene in which money talks, it seems that the return of the son was not illusory.

Of course Salinas's play is quite different from Pirandello's *La vita che ti diedi,* because the mother's faith is rewarded in the Spanish play. But at the point when she has been told that her son is dead and has no reason to doubt it, she shows the exact attitude of the mother in Pirandello's play, who creates for herself the illusion that her son still lives.

Salinas wrote fourteen plays,[8] and practically all of the plays which have not been discussed also contain certain Pirandellian details because the interplay of illusion and reality is the main substance of his theater. To give two more examples, in *La isla del tesoro*[9] Marú rejects her attractive suitor in order to await the appearance of the man who has written a diary which she has found in a hotel room, and *Judit y el tirano* is a play in which the tyrant does not permit his subjects to see his face, as his entire personality has been invented. "Todo eso de la apariencia y la voz es histrionismo, puro teatro malo. El es un cualquiera que ha dado con esa artimaña para imponerse a la gente" (p. 308).

Salinas was a professor of literature and a literary critic, thus he probably had more than a superficial knowledge of Pirandello's plays. Also, by the time he wrote his dramatic pieces Pirandellian tendencies were found in many writers and could be said to float in the atmosphere, to use Unamuno's phrase.[10] It is interesting to find these traits in Salinas's plays because his basic view of life is diametrically opposed to Pirandello's. Love, joy, optimism, perfect communication, and faith in the ability of the writer to clarify reality[11] all characterize the poetry and plays of Pedro Salinas. Pirandello, on the other hand, usually sees only the sensual side of love; MacClintock has called him "The Perfect Pessimist,"[12] his protagonists usually cannot communicate, and he seems to love chaos.[13]

Salinas's plays are in many ways isolated from other Spanish plays of his epoch, but they nonetheless contribute a chapter to the history of Spanish theater because they show how even a playwright who had little in common with the Italian entered the Pirandellian door leading to thematic innovation. In this way, Salinas joined his fellow-countrymen—Unamuno, Azorín, the Machados, García Lorca, Casona, Grau, and Luca de Tena—who all show either direct influence of the Italian playwright or characteristics which reveal their affinity for him.

OTHER CONTEMPORARY
PLAYWRIGHTS

In 1945 a number of playwrights and critics, among them Alfonso Sastre, José Gordon, Alfonso Paso, Medardo Fraile, Carlos José Costas, José Franco, and José María Palacio formed the Arte Nuevo group in an attempt to reinvigorate the Spanish theater. Many of the plays they wrote show the frankly acknowledged influence of other writers. For instance, Oscar Wilde appears as a character in *Tres variaciones sobre una frase de amor* by José María Palacio, a play which also mentions the author of *Navidades en la casa Bayard,* and Alfonso Paso subtitled a little play entitled *3 Mujeres 3* "Farsa para hombres, en prosa y original, aunque con alguna que otra influencia."

In his prologue to *Teatro de Vanguardia,* an anthology of plays written by the Arte Nuevo group, Alfredo Marqueríe lists the writers the group admired: "En algunas de estas obras se advierten influencias más o menos próximas de autores como Pirandello o Shaw, Wilder o Saroyan, Kayser o Rice, y también la sombra atormentada que pesa sobre las concepciones de un O'Neill o de un Sartre." [1]

Alfonso Sastre has stated that Pirandello influenced, in one way or another, all of the group; but that "en mí esa influencia no tiene mucho peso específico." [2] He has also mentioned that *Our Town* by Thornton Wilder was the most important point of departure for the Arte Nuevo group and that Wilder's *The Long Christmas Dinner* was also significant.

Therefore, in many of the plays which we will discuss here, the techniques associated with Pirandello will now appear filtered through Wilder's *Our Town*. Of course Wilder followed Pirandello and the techniques used in this play are certainly reminiscent of Pirandello's theater-within-the-theater trilogy. Wilder's central character is a stage manager who speaks directly to the audience, the play begins with the curtain up on an empty stage, and a few spectator-actors ask questions from the auditorium. But Pirandello's directors really give the impression of being directors, whereas the stage manager in *Our Town* is basically "an undisguised lecturer," as Groff calls him, who "tells his story with the aid of a series of dramatic 'slides.' " [3]

Alfonso Sastre has by far the greatest stature among the playwrights associated with the Arte Nuevo group. One of his most interesting experiments, *Ha sonado la muerte,* was carried out in collaboration with Medardo Fraile in 1946 and is a good example of the Wilder influence turned into something quite original.[4] The subtitle of *Ha sonado la muerte* is "Reportaje escénico en un acto." Henry Ridgwick tells the audience that he is a reporter for the *New York Herald* and that when the authors of this play discovered that he was going to pass through Madrid on his way home, they asked him to help them with the one-act play they had to write. "Tú podrías hilvanar cuatro cositas de las que te han pasado en la guerra; procura que sean un poco profundas y no te pongas tan patriótico que nos hables del Oeste, ni de pieles rojas. Nosotros pondremos a tu disposición unos buenos actores, y por último . . . firmaremos la obra." [5]

The prompter tells Henry that Bernard Hérault is waiting to see him, but Henry tells the prompter that he must first finish informing the audience. He relates that a bomb fell on Mrs. Hérault's home at seven-thirty one evening during the war, killing everyone in the house except the son Bernard, who happened to be away at the time. Earlier Henry has stated that the question of how death selects its victims as treated by Thornton Wilder in *The Bridge of San Luis Rey* has occurred to him as a theme.

When he first appears on the stage, Bernard thinks that he and Henry are in an empty theater. But then Henry tells him that they are actually performing and calls his attention to the spectators. Bernard remarks that his jokes are stupid and starts to leave: "¿Estás haciendo un drama escénico de mi drama vivido?" (p. 180), he inquires. But, by explaining to him how carefully he had prepared everything, Henry persuades Bernard to relive the last moments with his family. He adds, "acaso esta ficción, al hacerte soñar, se convierta en una realidad para ti" (p. 180).

At a signal from Henry the curtain goes up to reveal the living room in which Mrs. Hérault is seated. Bernard goes in and sits next to her and Henry retires to the front side of the stage to observe. Henry interrupts the action several times in order to question Bernard. At 7:27 the reporter embraces Bernard, thanks him, and tells him that he needs nothing more. After the bomb strikes, Henry introduces the actors to the spectators. Someone starts to applaud, but suddenly stops because Bernard has appeared. He says that this isn't his family, although he had begun to believe that it really was, and delivers a harangue against war and man's hate for man. Henry tells Bernard that they can speak no longer, the actors crowd around Bernard, and then Henry turns to the spectators and tells them that this has been a disagreeable incident, but he hopes that everyone is all right. He repeats his own name and says that he has finished his report.

This play shows a very interesting combination of levels of reality. The reporter is almost a lecturer and is extremely aware of the presence of the audience. While Bernard functions as an actor among actors in scenes from his life, he is very conscious of Henry's presence, but is careful to maintain the separation between fiction and life. At one point he wishes to reproach the reporter, but cannot step outside the frame of the play-within-the-play: "Bernard mira con insistencia a Henry, sin atreverse a hablarle, para no romper su realidad ficticia" (p. 183). But, in the end, he finds it impossible to accept the conversion of his experience into art. He becomes confused because he begins to think of the actors as being his real family when he replays scenes from his life with them. When he speaks after the play is supposedly over, he is no longer acting. The confrontation of two levels of reality when Bernard appears at the end of the play is a jolting experience for everyone concerned. The audience cannot applaud because it is impossible to applaud in front of the man whose family has apparently just been killed. Henry, extremely conscious that Bernard's outburst has destroyed the distance which should exist between art and life, tries to silence him, but the damage has already been done.[6]

On the whole, at the time when other writers of his group were quite daring in their application of techniques suggested to them by foreign writers, Sastre remained comparatively conservative. In *Cargamento de sueños,* a one-act play written in 1948, he limited himself to an attempt to activate the audience at the beginning of the play, when Man, the protagonist, looks disconsolately at the spectators before the action begins. According to the stage directions, his first utterance is clearly directed to the audience: "Bueno, vamos a ver. ¿A qué habéis venido aquí? (Sarcástico.) Me gustaría saberlo. (Con voz aburrida.) Resulta curioso pensar que ni vosotros mismos lo sabéis." [7] When Jeschoua enters, he inquires if Man has been speaking to someone, and Man, nervously looking at the audience, says that many people are looking at him. Although Jeschoua tells him that he is mistaken because they are alone, Man explains that he feels he is being observed by all of humanity. Of course this technique is very appropriate to this protest against formal conventions which Sastre wrote when he was twenty years old.

Later, Alfonso Sastre actually rejected an exaggerated form of audience-stage coalescence in his final version of *Prólogo patético*. He explains in an article that it took him six years to finish the play because of ideological and literary problems. He states that several experimental *cuadros* "cayeron sacrificados en el altar de la economía dramática sartriana—*Huis Clos, Morts sans sépulture*— y de la *Poética*, de Aristóteles, recién descubierta." [8] One of the scenes which he rejected involved Oscar's escape from prison. The main floor (*patio de butacas*) of the auditorium was to have been the exterior esplanade of the jail and two of the boxes were to have been sentry-boxes from which machine guns were being fired at Oscar, who was to have run toward the lobby while a searchlight beam explored the *patio*.

Ana Kleiber is Sastre's full-length play which resulted from the experiments made in the Arte Nuevo group, although he did not actually write it until after the experimental period, and the première did not take place until 1961 in Paris. In this play there is a strange mixture of levels of reality. Sastre, himself, is the central figure, although the plot, if it can be called that, involves the difficulties of the lovers, Ana and Alfred. The writer occupies many different positions in the play and passes from one level of reality to another. At the beginning of the play he is Sastre, the man who has written *Escuadra hacia la muerte*, and is being interviewed by two reporters. Then he becomes the author of the play in progress, which is based on his direct observation of the lovers' story. Since the play itself gives the impression of being a drama-in-the-making, because it combines narration and the acting of short scenes, has a fragmentary nature, and an irregular sequence of time, the whole thing could represent the process of creation as it occurs in the author's mind. The writer himself intervenes in the action and is often the confidant, that is, he is a character in his own play. He is also an actor, for at times he consciously acts out scenes, and at one point he even becomes a director. He often speaks directly to the audience, thus ignoring the fourth-wall convention.

The hotel clerk also passes from one plane of reality to another. At the beginning he plays the clerk, observes Ana's arrival, and later he is a witness when her body is discovered. He becomes the writer's collaborator, advising him at times how to present the events, and he becomes an actor when he plays a waiter in a café in one scene. He is also a stagehand, for throughout the play he assists the bellboy in arranging the settings.

Both protagonists of the story exist on two different levels of reality. The barrier is always maintained between Ana and the audience. When everyone around her is communicating with the public, she is unaware that she is anything other than a character in a traditional play. When she narrates, she is always talking to Alfred, whereas Alfred and the author speak directly to the audience. Ana is an actress, which permits a prompter, a producer, and an actor to take part in some of the scenes.

The writer takes Alfred into his confidence by telling him that perhaps some day he will try to tell Alfred's and Ana's story, and he even describes the first scene. Alfred functions as a critic, because he warns the playwright that if he writes the play it will be unsuccessful. Alfred, therefore, is associated with the actual formation of the play and participates more closely in the breakdown of theatrical illusion than does Ana.

Although the acknowledged influence of Thornton Wilder can definitely be seen in *Ana Kleiber,* Wilder is even more obviously present in *Un tic-tac de reloj* (1946) by José Gordon and Alfonso Paso. The author addresses the audience, telling about himself and then describing the protagonist, who appears and is introduced to the audience as the Young Man. The author was supposed to write a play based on the youth's ideas, but instead, the protagonist himself will now be in direct contact with the audience. He will speak from fifteen to twenty minutes, and the author, who reserves the right to interrupt the lecture, tells him that he may receive the help of actors or props.

The young man begins his address. He tells the story of Samuel and Marta who were young, attractive, and full of illusion, but then slipped into the monotony of routine and failed to fulfill their potential. Samuel and Marta are brought back from the dead to act out their story. "Spectators" ask questions and put forth objections, the author participates and when Marta and Samuel are speaking, the youth intervenes. He wants people to struggle, to do something in life, to escape from routine existence. He almost has to be dragged from the stage, and the author tells the audience at the end of the play that his parents had to commit the youth to an asylum.

In addition to the obvious influence of *Our Town, The Long Christmas Dinner* also influenced *Un tic-tac de reloj,* especially in the manner in which time is handled. At one point, as in *The Long Christmas Dinner,* the actors merely put on grey wigs, without leaving the stage to do so, in order to indicate the passage of time.

Some of the same devices which seem so appropriate in serious drama have been used by Alfonso Paso in a meaningless little farce entitled *3 Mujeres 3* (1948). The central character, who is again the author, tells about three women he has known. The author speaks to the audience about plays, playwrights, and actresses; and then short scenes are performed between him and three different women in whom he was interested. Stagehands change the scenery while the actors are reciting. A chorus comments throughout the play and at the end discusses the different possible endings before turning to the public to say that everything turned out well because the author married and had children. A line within the play shows Paso's attitude and in the process accurately assesses his own contribution: "Conozco una preciosa definición del baile. Baile, manera inmoral de hacer el idiota. Existe un modo más moral de hacerlo: es tratar de renovar el teatro español." [9]

José María Palacio has written what is surely the zaniest play to result from Spanish theater-within-the-theater experiments: *Tres variaciones sobre una frase de amor* (1946), subtitled "Fantasía para monomaniáticos." At the beginning, Autumn, Summer, and Winter, personified, are playing poker with days as the stake. Suddenly, Winter sees the audience: "¡Cuánta gente! ¡Santo Dios!" [10] Summer wonders what the people are doing there. They ask the spectators, but no one answers. They decide that they should introduce themselves, but they are interrupted by the arrival of Spring. She criticizes her fellow seasons for playing cards, but Winter cautions her not to put forth dangerous judgments, and he shows the audience to her. She says she doesn't see anything, and a spectator, who has come to the stage by this time, remarks that she should have her eyes tested. The spectator introduces himself: "Llámeme don Espectador Escéptico" (p. 305). He compliments Spring, but in his sentence he uses three words which the seasons later tell him bring bad luck: teeth, swans, and ducks. The spectator remarks that this is a stupid superstition. The seasons inform him that they will prove their assertion that there are historical examples of disasters which have been caused by the use of this dangerous combination of words. Autumn explains that he was in London in 1892 when he saw light at midnight in Oscar Wilde's home. Then the scene switches to the Wilde home where Oscar's wife, Constanza, is saying good night to Alfred, who is in love with her, when she sees Oscar and the critic Stevens Corner who are entering from the rear of the *patio de butacas*. After introductions, Alfred and Corner leave together, and as they go down the aisle of the theater Corner shouts "Ya seguiremos hablando de esas influencias, Oscar" (p. 309).

Later Constanza utters the three fatal words and then the curtain falls on the Wilde episode. The spectator remains unconvinced of the evil power of the words, so the seasons show him another example, which involves Napoleon, a Polish count, and the count's wife María who, after the count has uttered the three words, is very easily persuaded to favor Napoleon with her company in order to gain lenient treatment for her country.

Winter asks the spectator if he is convinced now. The spectator explains his abrupt "¡No!" by saying that if he were to say yes they would not be able to do the rest of the play. The remainder of the scene intermingles various levels of reality and time sequences in a fanciful way. Napoleon and the count enter, and Napoleon asks that Nero be brought to him, then orders him to convince the spectator. When Nero does not recite his first line immediately, the prompter gives him his cue. Nero asks the prompter who he is and then exclaims "¡Ah, también forma parte de todo este lío?" (p. 327). He then thanks the prompter and speaks his first line.

The scene turns to the epoch of the Roman Empire with the figures of Nero and his teacher Seneca who speaks with an Andalusian accent and wears a Cordoban hat. In an effort to make time meaningless Seneca teaches his pupil about the discovery of America. Nero says he is going to recite his poetry now because later the tragedy will prevent it, but he is stopped from saying more by Ernest (who had also been Oscar Wilde's servant). He gives Nero a message from "otro señor que está ahí dentro muy nervioso," (p. 333) a man who asked him to tell Nero not to reveal the end of the play. But if Nero wishes, he may say that the scene shows influence of Pedro Muñoz Seca, who would probably turn out to be the author of "Navidades en la Casa Bayard" (Thornton Wilder). Nero, in a conversation with Marco, says the fatal words, he accidentally kills Popea, Marco inadvertently takes the poison which Agripina had intended for Popea, Nero kills Agripina and then even orders poor Ernest to drink the remaining glass of poison. As Nero prepares to commit suicide by throwing himself on his own sword, the spectator shouts from the auditorium for him to wait and then rushes to the stage to tell him that he is supposed to say his dying words later when General Galba gains control of the government and comes to take him prisoner. Nero, addressing him as the Escéptico Espectador, tells him not to approach too closely because twenty centuries separate them. The spectator objects to being called "skeptic," because he now believes, and apologizes for uttering the three words. Nero asks when he said them, and the spectator answers that it was in the summer of 1939. Nero confirms that 1939 will be a tragic year and then tells the spectator to escape, for Galba is coming. Nero speaks his last words and falls on his sword.

Even the details of this play show the constant awareness of the art-life opposition. The stage directions, for example, are often whimsical reminders that this is not a conventional play. When Nero remains alone for a moment on the stage, the directions say that he may use the time to greet a friend in the audience. When Constanza is upset, Palacio remarks in a stage direction, "Fuera de sí, pero dentro de la escena" (p. 311).

The character, Oscar Wilde, seems to be concerned about the art-life relationship, as he tells Ernest, "Tengo una terrible duda relacionada contigo. No sé si he copiado de ti a los mayordomos de mis comedias o si eres tú quien les copias a ellos" (p. 312). Ernest tells him that he has no opinion because he does not understand Oscar Wilde's writings.

In sharp contrast to the foregoing are two plays Joaquín Calvo Sotelo wrote a few years later. Although he also wrote a play in 1947, *Plaza de Oriente,* under the influence of Wilder, his two important Pirandellian plays do not depend on twentieth-century technical innovations but rather can be compared to the plays which treat the psychological problems of a character who is unable to distinguish between reality and illusion or who finds himself clinging to an illusion which becomes more important than reality.

In *María Antonieta* (1952) a girl thinks she is the historical personage who has come back to life. The girl, whose real name is

Susan, never wavers in her belief that she is Marie Antoinette, and there is no doubt that she is insane. Jaime hopes to cure her, although he is informed that the best psychiatrists have pronounced her incurable. The cause of her insanity was a traumatic experience she had while being photographed dressed as Marie Antoinette: a fire broke out in which the photographer and several other people perished. Jaime prepares to cure her by creating an atmosphere in which Susan's insane conviction is reinforced. Marcela, Jaime's maid, pretends she is Marie Antoinette's lady-in-waiting, and Jaime becomes Hans, Marie Antoinette's lover, who tells her that he has also been brought back to life. He hopes to make her recognize reality by unmasking himself and Marcela; when they admit their true identity he hopes she will admit hers. Jaime arranges the scene in Versailles and persuades the uniformed museum guard to play the part of the officer demanding that they all tell him who they are. But this attempt to cure Susan fails. Jaime cannot endure her agitation when her identity is challenged, and, influenced by her obsession, he again takes up the role of her lover, Hans. He tells the others to leave, and calls her Marie Antoinette.

The girl's friends then plan a much more elaborate attempt to cure her. They redouble their efforts to surround her with people and things which confirm her insane idea that she is Marie Antoinette. They plan to make her relive the death scene, thinking that at the crucial moment she will admit her true identity in order to save her life. They hire actors to help them, and in order to obtain permission to erect a guillotine in the middle of a public square in Paris, they say that they are making a film. But when Jaime tries to persuade Susan to escape death on the guillotine by admitting that she is not Marie Antoinette, she refuses to do so. Her hair actually turns white as legend says the real Marie Antoinette's did on the eve of her execution. Susan resolutely climbs the stairs to the guillotine, and dies there, of a heart attack probably. Only in death does her true identity of Susan Wiedemann return to her.

María Antonieta quite probably owes something to Pirandello's *Enrico IV*. Just as in this play the character adopts the identity of a historical personage after donning the costume of that personage. Unlike Enrico, however, Susan never recognizes reality. Although it is mentioned that in the past she has had lucid periods, during the action of the play she constantly clings to the belief that she is Marie Antoinette.

When the characters surround Susan with things which confirm her insane idea, the effect is similar to that created for Don Quijote by the Duke and Duchess, although the motivation is different. Her friends desire to cure her and their willingness to go to any lengths to do so is akin to the attempts of Don Quijote's friends from La Mancha to restore his sanity. The end, when Susan can only regain her true identity in death, begs comparison with Don Quijote's disenchantment followed closely by death.[11]

Calvo Sotelo's *La ciudad sin Dios* (1957) is another account of the problems caused when men attempt to govern the uncontrollable manifestations of illusion. This play takes place in an imaginary country where Christianity, through long years of repression, is no longer part of people's lives. The Commissar asks Nicolai to help with an experiment to find out if religion is really dead. He plans for Nicolai to play the part of a prophet who will perform false miracles. Nicolai will improvise the role, based on instructions the Commissar will give him. "Los cómicos italianos del Renacimiento, si no me equivoco, trabajaban así." [12] After Nicolai has played the part awhile, it takes possession of him. When students mock him, he really loses consciousness of himself and acts as a real prophet of Jesus would: he humbly kneels and kisses the hand of one of his tormentors. When the Commissar compliments him for his acting, Nicolai is confused because he was not acting.

Nicolai's fame begins to grow, and therefore the Commissar plans to destroy this growing religion by having Nicolai accomplish false miracles which will be exposed. The inmates of a concentration camp, who are members of an amateur theatrical group, will play the roles of people who are miraculously cured of deafness and blindness, and Nicolai is also to effect a false resurrection. Nicolai informs the Commissar that he now believes, but, by using David and a girl as hostages, the Commissar forces him to carry out his agreement. Nicolai "cures" the blind girl and the deaf man, but when he prepares to resurrect the man he discovers that the man is really dead. He thinks that God has intervened, and he confesses before everyone that he had been effecting false cures and that now God has actually acted.

The Commissar realizes that the only way in which he may return the people to their condition of nonbelief is to declare Nicolai insane and confine him to an asylum. Nicolai's friend, David, understanding that Nicolai would prefer death, shoots him. At the end of the play we understand that fiction will triumph over truth because a crippled girl walks after having prayed at the site of Nicolai's death.

The persistence of certain Pirandellian themes in Spanish literature is certainly brought out by this play in which Calvo Sotelo
employed the same general idea which Lope de Vega used in *Lo
fingido verdadero*.[13] In both plays an actor who plays the role of a
Christian actually becomes one and is then willing to sacrifice himself rather than deny the truth of the illusion. The solution offered
at the end of Calvo Sotelo's play, that the damage done by the
protagonist be repaired by sending him to an asylum, has also been
used by Pirandello in *Il berretto a sonagli* and by Echegaray in
O locura o santidad.[14]

The playwrights discussed in this chapter have written everything from frivolous farce to serious drama using certain themes
and techniques suggested to them by Thornton Wilder, Luigi
Pirandello and other foreign writers. The experimental period in
which enthusiasm for these innovations was high did not last long,
but it yielded some very fine examples of plays in which life and
reality invade the realms of their dimensional opposites, theater and
illusion.

Notes
Selected Bibliography
Appendix

NOTES

PART I

Chapter 1. *Miguel de Cervantes*

1. Américo Castro, "Cervantes y Pirandello," *Santa Teresa y otros ensayos* (Santander: Historia Nueva, 1925), pp. 219–31.
2. Miguel de Cervantes Saavedra, *Don Quijote de la Mancha* (Madrid: Espasa-Calpe, 1958), 4:35. All subsequent quotations from this source will be to this edition and cited by volume and page numbers in the text.
3. Américo Castro, "Cervantes y Pirandello," p. 222.
4. *Ibid.*, p. 221.
5. Luigi Pirandello, *Saggi* (Verona: Mondadori, 1952), p. 105.
6. Miguel de Cervantes Saavedra, *Comedias y entremeses* (Madrid: Bernardo Rodríguez, 1915), 1:325.

Chapter 2. *From Lope de Vega to Galdós*

1. Lope Félix de Vega Carpio, *Obras escogidas* (Madrid: Aguilar, 1962), 3:188. All subsequent quotations from this source will be to this edition and volume and cited by page numbers in the text.
2. *El gran teatro del mundo* has often been mentioned by critics as a pre-Pirandellian play. See, for example, Angel Valbuena Prat, *Historia del teatro español* (Barcelona: Noguer, 1956), pp. 365–89. Valbuena Prat has the Pirandellian slant in mind, for he often points out Pirandellism in Spanish writers in his *Historia de la literatura española*.
3. Pedro Calderón de la Barca, *Autos sacramentales* (Madrid: Espasa-Calpe, 1957), 1:95. All subsequent quotations from this source will be to this edition and volume and cited by page numbers in the text.
4. Gerónimo Cáncer, Pedro Rosete, and Antonio Martínez, "El mejor representante, San Ginés" (Copy in the Biblioteca Nacional), p. 215.
5. Tirso de Molina, *Obras dramáticas completas* (Madrid: Aguilar, 1946), 1:1303.
6. Ventura de la Vega, *Obras escogidas* (Barcelona: Montaner y

Simón, 1894), p. 230. All subsequent quotations from Ventura de la Vega will be from this edition and cited by page numbers in the text.

7. For a complete discussion of possible sources see Ramón Esquer Torres, *El teatro de Tamayo y Baus* (Madrid: Consejo Superior de Investigaciones Científicas, 1965), pp. 197–212.

8. Manuel Tamayo y Baus, *Obras* (Madrid: Rivadeneyra, 1900), 4:171. All subsequent quotations from Tamayo y Baus will be from this edition and volume and cited by page numbers in the text.

9. See also Leon Livingstone, "Interior Duplication and the Problem of Form in the Modern Spanish Novel," *PMLA* 73 (1958): 393–406; Ricardo Gullón, *Galdós, Novelista moderno* (Madrid: Taurus, 1960), pp. 67–74; and J. Chicharro de León, "Pirandelismo en la literatura española," *Quaderni Ibero-Americani* (1954): 406–11.

10. Benito Pérez Galdós, *Obras completas* (Madrid: Aguilar, 1960), 4:1165. All subsequent quotations from *El amigo manso* will be from this volume and cited by page numbers in the text.

11. Robert H. Russell, "'El amigo manso': Galdós with a Mirror," *Modern Language Notes* 78 (1963): 161–68.

12. Galdós's earlier novel *La sombra* should be mentioned here, for Dr. Anselmo thinks that Paris has moved out of a painting and is courting his wife. The autonomous Paris appears to be a creation of Dr. Anselmo's imagination ("la personificación de una idea") who completely controls his life, and in this case there is considerable conflict between creator and creation.

13. Benito Pérez Galdós, *Obras completas* (Madrid: Aguilar, 1967), 5:1901. All subsequent quotations from Galdós's *Misericordia* will be from this volume and cited by page numbers in the text.

Chapter 3. *Ramón de la Cruz and the Género Chico*

1. Francis Fergusson, *The Idea of a Theater* (Garden City, N.Y.: Doubleday Anchor Books, 1953), p. 191.

2. Narciso Díaz de Escovar and Francisco de P. Lasso de la Vega, *Historia del teatro español* (Barcelona: Montaner y Simón, 1924), 1:296.

3. Emilio Cotarelo y Mori, *Colección de entremeses, loas, bailes, jácaras y mojigangas* (Madrid: Bailly/Bailliere, 1911), tome 1, vol. 1, p. xxi.

4. *Ibid.*, tome 1, vol. 2, p. 338.

5. Eugenio Asensio, *Itinerario del entremés desde Lope de Rueda a*

Quiñones de Benavente, con cinco entremeses inéditos de Quevedo (Madrid: Gredos, 1965), p. 61.

6. Hannah E. Bergman, *Luis Quiñones de Benavente y sus entremeses* (Madrid: Castalia, 1965), p. 34.

7. Emilio Cotarelo y Mori, *Colección de entremeses,* tome 1, vol. 2, p. 545.

8. The entire script is not available, and Cotarelo does not give the author's name.

9. Emilio Cotarelo y Mori, *Colección de entremeses,* tome 1, vol. 1, p. clx.

10. Cesco Vian, *Il teatro "Chico" spagnolo* (Milano: Cisalpino, 1957), p. 35. Cesco Vian also discusses other performances by Juan Rana in which the distance between the audience and the performers is obliterated.

11. Emilio Cotarelo y Mori, *Sainetes de Don Ramón de la Cruz* (Madrid: Bailly/Bailliere, 1928), 2:393. All subsequent quotations from Ramón de la Cruz will be from this edition and cited by volume and page numbers in the text, except where otherwise indicated.

12. Oscar Büdel, *Pirandello* (London: Bowes and Bowes, 1966), p. 61.

13. Emilio Cotarelo y Mori, *Don Ramón de la Cruz y sus obras* (Madrid: José Perales y Martínez, 1899), p. 542.

14. *Ibid.,* p. 231.

15. *Ibid.,* p. 232.

16. *Historia del teatro español* by Díaz de Escovar and Lasso de la Vega (see note 2 above) gives some very interesting examples of audience behavior in the eighteenth century.

17. Ramón de la Cruz wrote *El pueblo quejoso* in answer to those who criticized him for satirizing certain people. Francisco Mariano Nifo, for example, had written *La sátira castigada por los sainetes de moda* in which the characters complain about satires against them.

18. Emilio Cotarelo y Mori, *Sainetes de Don Ramón de la Cruz* (Madrid: Bailly/Bailliere, 1915), vol. 1, p. 256.

19. This *sainete* was written ten years before *Las resultas de las ferias* in which a different attitude is expressed.

20. Juan Ignacio González del Castillo, *Sainetes* (Cádiz, 1846), 3:92.

21. *Ibid.,* p. 94.

22. Serafín y Joaquín Alvarez Quintero, *Obras completas* (Madrid: Espasa-Calpe, 1925), 30:173.

23. The Alvarez Quintero brothers even wrote a satirical *Zarzuela* dealing with the theatrical world: *El estreno,* with music by Ruperto

Chapí. It has three acts: "Infierno," which involves the rehearsals, "Purgatorio," which is the première, and "Gloria," after they have survived the two previous stages.

Chapter 4. *José Echegaray*

1. These characters are not misanthropic, nor are they, like Ibsen's Brand, chiefly guided by religious motives.

2. José Echegaray, *Teatro escogido* (Madrid: Aguilar, 1959), p. 378. All subsequent quotations from Echegaray's plays will be from this edition and will be cited by page numbers in the text except where otherwise noted.

3. Domenico Vittorini, *The Drama of Luigi Pirandello* (New York: Dover, 1957), p. 189.

4. *Ibid.*, p. 198.

5. Luigi Pirandello, *Il berretto a sonagli, La giara, Il piacere dell'onestà* (Verona: A. Mondadori, 1958), p. 122.

6. *Ibid.*, p. 55.

7. *Ibid.*, pp. 56–57.

8. José Echegaray, *La realidad y el delirio* (Madrid: José Rodríguez, 1887), p. 54.

9. *Ibid.*, p. 72.

10. *Ibid.*, p. 89.

11. *Ibid.*, p. 18.

12. José Echegaray, *Un crítico incipiente* (Madrid: José Rodríguez, 1891), p. 87.

13. Luigi Pirandello, *Maschere nude* (Verona: A. Mondadori, 1967), 1:39.

14. Echegaray, *Un crítico incipiente*, p. 9.

15. *Ibid.*, p. 15.

16. Pirandello, *Maschere nude*, 1:45.

17. Augusto Martínez Olmedilla, *José Echegaray* (Madrid: Sáez, 1949), p. 10.

18. Echegaray, *Un crítico incipiente*, pp. 10–11.

Chapter 5. *Ramón Gómez de la Serna*

1. Critics commonly use Ramón's first name. Guillermo de Torre explains in his article "Ramón y Picasso": "(Ya comprenderéis, por lo demás, de qué Ramón se trata; de Ramón Gómez de la Serna, cuyos

apellidos se agazapan como humildes gozques a los pies del mayúsculo y dominante RAMON.)" Guillermo de Torre, prologue to Ramón Gómez de la Serna, *Obras completas* (Barcelona: Editorial A H R, 1957), 2:10.

2. As a matter of fact, Pirandello was also taking his first steps toward *Sei personaggi* around this time. *La tragedia d'un personaggio,* involving an autonomous character, was published in *Corriere della Sera* in 1911.

3. This is the title of Roger Shattuck's book which deals with the arts in France from 1885 to 1918 (New York: Harcourt, Brace, 1958).

4. For example: "y greguerías van diciendo todos los personajes que dialogan en el 'teatro en soledad.' Greguería sería, sin duda, ese drama que, pre-pirandellianamente, buscan sus personajes." Gonzalo Torrente Ballester, "Teatro de Ramón," *Insula* XVIII, cxcvi, 5. "Comenzó con un ensayo dramático, prepirandelliano, *Teatro en soledad,* en contacto con la bruma modernista." Angel Valbuena Prat, *Historia del teatro español* (Barcelona: Noguer, 1956), p. 598. Granjel quotes what Ramón and other critics have said about the subject, but adds nothing new. Luis S. Granjel, *Retrato de Ramón* (Madrid: Ediciones Guadarrama, 1963), pp. 162–63.

5. Gaspar Gómez de la Serna, *Ramón (Obra y vida)* (Madrid: Taurus, 1963), p. 56.

6. Ramón Gómez de la Serna, *Automoribundia* (Buenos Aires: Editorial Sudamericana, 1948), pp. 206–07.

7. Ramón Gómez de la Serna, *Obras completas* (Barcelona: Editorial A H R, 1956), 1:9.

8. For example, Joseph E. Gillet, "The Autonomous Character in Spanish and European Literature," *Hispanic Review* 24 (1956): 179–90; Jacqueline Chantraine de Van Praag, "España tierra de elección del pirandellismo," *Quaderni Ibero-Americani* 27 (1962): 218–22; and J. Chicharro de León, "Pirandelismo en la literatura española," *Quaderni Ibero-Americani* (April 1954):406–14.

9. Gonzalo Torrente Ballester, "Teatro de Ramón," *Insula* XVIII, cxcvi, 5. However, many of Ramón's plays, which he refers to collectively as "Teatro muerto," are available: Ramón Gómez de la Serna, *Obras selectas* (Madrid: Plenitud, 1947) contains *Los medios seres* and *Escaleras,* and his *Obras completas,* Vol. 1 (Barcelona: Editorial A H R, 1956) contains *El drama del palacio deshabitado, La utopía, Beatriz, La corona de hierro,* and *El lunático.*

10. The copy of *El teatro en soledad* which I have used in the preparation of this chapter belongs to the Biblioteca Nacional de Madrid. The "Ex-Libris" page is marked Ismael Smith, Paris, 1911. The pages are

numbered by hand and there are several printing errors, a few of which have been corrected by hand. I believe it is actually an offprint taken from the periodical *Prometeo* directed by Ramón's father. All subsequent quotations from *El teatro en soledad* will be from this edition and cited by page numbers in the text.

11. Luigi Pirandello, "Sei personaggi in cerca d'autore," *Maschere Nude* (Verona: Mondadori, 1962), 1:71.

12. Domenico Vittorini, *The Drama of Luigi Pirandello* (New York: Dover, 1957), p. 291.

13. See Oscar Büdel, "Contemporary Theater and Aesthetic Distance," *PMLA* 76 (1961): 277–91.

14. Ramón Gómez de la Serna, "Pirandello," *Obras selectas* (Madrid: Plenitud, 1947), p. 1115.

15. José Ortega y Gasset's *El tema de nuestro tiempo* expresses a parallel attitude.

16. Ramón Gómez de la Serna, "Ismos," *Obras completas* (Barcelona: Editorial A H R, 1957), 2:997. All quotations from *Ismos* have been taken from this edition and are cited by page numbers in the text.

17. Pirandello was also a talented painter.

18. Ramón has been quoted by José Camón Aznar, *Picasso y el cubismo* (Madrid: Espasa-Calpe, 1956), and John Golding, *Cubism: A History and an Analysis* (New York: G. Wittenborn, 1959).

19. He states that cubists thought "las verdades del intelecto son más fijas que las verdades aparentes de la vista" (p. 993).

20. Guillermo de Torre, *Historia de las literaturas de vanguardia* (Madrid: Guadarrama, 1965), p. 239.

21. See also Büdel, "Contemporary Theater and Aesthetic Distance." A parallel can also be drawn between this aspect and Picasso's habit of driving nails through the back of his paintings: "Picasso hammered nails through the back of his cubist paintings so that the points protruded through the finished surface. Their motives were not strictly aesthetic, but also destructive and playful." Shattuck, *The Banquet Years*, p. 255.

22. *The Banquet Years* by Roger Shattuck, especially the chapter entitled "The Art of Stillness," is directly pertinent to this chapter, as many of his statements about painting apply equally well to "Pirandellian" innovations in the theater. For example, he discusses the "art-about-art" trend which caused artists to paint paintings about painting. He also treats the breaking down of distinctions between art and reality: "We are ourselves incorporated into the structure of a work of art. Its very *form* importunes us to enter an expanded community of creation which

now includes artist and spectator, art and reality" (p. 256). He discusses the lack-of-frame concept in cubist art, an idea which has also been examined by José Camón Aznar, who called it "la calidad metapictórica," and which implies the destruction of barriers between art and the spectators or the disappearance of aesthetic distance. Camón Aznar refers to an anecdote about Picasso told by Ramón: he did not consider his paintings perfect unless a cap looked well perched on top of the frame.

23. In *Ismos* Ramón quotes the famous remark attributed to Picasso when he was told a painting was beautiful: "¿Hermoso? ¿Con el trabajo que me he tomado para que no lo sea?" (p. 998).

24. Rodolfo Cardona, *Ramón: A Study of Gómez de la Serna and His Works* (New York: Torres and Sons, 1957), p. 9.

25. *Ibid.*, p. 16.

26. In spite of the promising title, I did not consider Guillermo de Torre's article "Ramón y Picasso" to be very pertinent to the topic under discussion. He believes there is a common nucleus in their art; he compares their homes; he thinks that the *greguería* is similar to Picasso's art and states that both Picasso and Ramón are in search of something. In Ramón Gómez de la Serna, *Obras completas*, 2: 9–29.

27. Lander MacClintock, *The Age of Pirandello* (Bloomington: Indiana University Press, 1951), p. 296.

28. *Ibid.*

29. Gaspare Giudice, *Luigi Pirandello* (Turin: Unione Tipografico-Editrice Torinese, 1963), p. 348.

30. Wylie Sypher, *Rococo to Cubism in Art and Literature* (New York: Random House, 1960), p. 289. All quotations from Sypher are taken from this book and cited by page numbers in the text. The chapter of Sypher's book entitled "Cubist Drama," which I have used in the preparation of this chapter, is now available in the collection of critical essays entitled *Pirandello* and edited by Glauco Cambon (Englewood Cliffs: Prentice-Hall, 1967), pp. 67–71.

31. Büdel, in "Contemporary Theater and Aesthetic Distance," after commenting on the analytical approach of contemporary playwrights, goes on to say: "The spectator has been 'liberated' from any fixed viewpoint, as the cubists proudly used to claim" (p. 291).

Chapter 6. *Miguel de Unamuno*

1. Some examples are Frank Sedwick, "Unamuno and Pirandello Revisited," *Italica* 33 (1956): 40–51—Professor Sedwick also lists twenty-

six earlier comments; Luis Leal, "Unamuno and Pirandello," *Italica* 28 (1952):193–99; Rudolf Brummer, "Autor und Geschöpf bei Unamuno und Pirandello," *Wissenschaftliche Zeitschrift der Friedrich-Schiller Universität Jena* 1955–1956: 241–48; José María Monner Sans, "Unamuno, Pirandello y el personaje autónomo," *La torre* 9 (1961): 387–402; Jacqueline Chantraine de Van Praag, "España tierra de elección del pirandellismo," *Quaderni Ibero-Americani* (1962): 218–22; and Vincenzo de Tomasso, *Il pensiero e l'opera di Miguel de Unamuno* (Roma: Cappelli, 1967).

2. Quoted by Sedwick, "Unamuno and Pirandello Revisited," p. 41, from Unamuno's article entitled "Pirandello y yo," which appeared in *La Nación* (Buenos Aires) of 15 July, 1923.

3. See also Leon Livingstone, "The Novel as Self-Creation," *Unamuno, Creator and Creation* (Berkeley and Los Angeles: University of California Press, 1967), pp. 92–115.

4. Miguel de Unamuno, *Niebla* (Madrid: Espasa-Calpe, 1966), p. 102. All quotations from *Niebla* are taken from this edition and cited by page numbers in the text.

5. The following article is pertinent here: Carlos Blanco Aguinaga, "Unamuno's 'Niebla': Existence and the Game of Fiction," *Modern Language Notes* (1964): 188–205.

6. In *Cómo se hace una novela* Unamuno confirms the fact that when he uses the word *hypocrite* he is aware of the Greek meaning: "¡Hipócrita! Porque yo que soy, de profesión, un ganapán helenista—es una cátedra de griego la que el Directorio hizo la comedia de quitarme reservándomela—sé que hipócrita significa actor. ¿Hipócrita? ¡No! Mi papel es mi verdad y debo vivir mi verdad, que es mi vida." Miguel de Unamuno, *Cómo se hace una novela* (Buenos Aires: Editorial "Alba", 1927), p. 100.

7. Recently this aspect of "Pirandellism" seems to have reached its definitive form in the opera *Votre Faust* by Pousseur and Butor in which the spectators, by voting, actually control the outcome of the work.

8. See also Geoffrey Ribbans, "The Structure of Unamuno's 'Niebla' ", *Spanish Thought and Letters in the Twentieth Century,* ed. Germán Bleiberg and E. Inman Fox (Nashville: Vanderbilt University Press, 1966), pp. 395–406.

9. This is reminiscent of the prologue to *Tres novelas ejemplares* in which Unamuno discusses *The Autocrat of the Breakfast Table* by Oliver Wendell Holmes, where John and Thomas really represent six

people because they change so completely according to the point of view from which they are contemplated.

10. Luigi Pirandello, *Maschere Nude* (Verona: Mondadori, 1962), pp. 80–81. Subsequent quotations from *Sei personaggi* are taken from this edition and cited by page numbers in the text.

11. See also Livingstone, "The Novel as Self-Creation," p. 100, and Germán Bleiberg, "Vivencia y creación: en torno a una carta de Unamuno," *Mélanges à la mémoire de Charles De Koninck* (Quebec: Les Presses de l'Université Laval, 1968) in which Bleiberg quotes a letter written by Unamuno the day on which his first child was born: "Trabajo más que nunca y con más fruto que nunca en mi hijo espiritual. Mientras pugnaba por salir el uno laboraba yo mentalmente en la gestación del otro. ¡Quiera Dios que se amparen uno á otro y puedan protegerse como hermanos y enorgullecerse el de carne viva de ser hermano del de idea! ¡Pobrecillo! Los dos irán á rodar el mundo expuestos á las injurias de los hombres." This letter is dated 3 August 1892.

12. See also Blanco Aguinaga, "Unamuno's 'Niebla'."

13. In a letter to Galdós written in 1898 Unamuno said: "¡Si usted supiera cuántas veces recuerdo á su Amigo Manso! . . . No es que lo haya visto, lo he sentido dentro de mí." Quoted by H. Chonon Berkowitz, "Unamuno's Relations with Galdós," *Hispanic Review* 7 (1940): 322.

14. See also Armando F. Zubizarreta, *Unamuno en su nivola* (Madrid: Taurus, 1960), pp. 21–89.

15. Allen Lacey's comments are interesting: "Censorship and 'Cómo se hace una novela,'" *Hispanic Review* 34 (1966): 317–25.

16. Miguel de Unamuno, *Cómo se hace una novela* (Buenos Aires: Editorial "Alba," 1927), p. 55. All quotations from this novel are taken from this edition and cited by page numbers in the text.

17. See also Ricardo Gullón, "Don Sandalio o el juego de los esprejos," *Papeles de Son Armadans* 30 (1963) 299–325.

18. Miguel de Unamuno, *San Manuel Bueno, mártir y tres historias más* (Buenos Aires: Espasa-Calpe, 1951), p. 95. Subsequent quotations from *La novela de don Sandalio* are taken from this edition and cited by page numbers in the text.

19. Miguel de Unamuno, *San Manuel Bueno, mártir y tres historias más* (Buenos Aires: Espasa-Calpe, 1951), p. 39.

20. Cassou, in his preface to *Cómo se hace una novela* explains Unamuno's interest in politics: "Y así, para Unamuno hacer política es,

todavía, salvarse. Es defender su persona, afirmarla, hacerla entrar para siempre en la historia" (p. 25). Therefore, literature and politics, two apparently opposite callings, in Unamuno's view of life have the same purpose.

21. Miguel de Unamuno, *Teatro completo* (Madrid: Aguilar, 1959), p. 584. Subsequent quotations from Unamuno's plays will be to this edition and cited page numbers in the text.

22. See also Ricardo Gullón, "Imágenes de 'El otro,'" *Spanish Thought and Letters in the Twentieth Century* (Nashville: Vanderbilt University Press, 1966).

23. According to Giovanni Sinicropi in a lecture given at the State University of New York at Buffalo, Signora Ponza symbolizes Truth, therefore this play illustrates the impossibility of knowing the truth.

24. Miguel de Unamuno, *Teatro completo,* p. 185.

25. Zubizarreta, *Unamuno en su nivola,* p. 315.

PART 2

Chapter 7. *Azorín*

1. Azorín, "Prólogo sintomático," *Obras completas* (Madrid: Aguilar, 1948), 4:855. All quotations from Azorín's plays are taken from this volume unless otherwise indicated and cited by volume and page numbers in the text.

2. Among others who have associated the two names are the following: Domingo Pérez Minik, "Azorín o la evasión pura," *Debates sobre el teatro* (Santa Cruz de Tenerife: Goya, 1953); Guillermo Díaz-Plaja, "El teatro de Azorín," *El arte de quedarse solo y otros ensayos* (Barcelona: Juventud, 1936); *Enciclopedia dello Spettacolo* (Roma: Le Maschere, 1961), 8:169: "Un'eco del teatro pirandelliano è forse anche in *Angelina* (1930) di Azorín"; J. Chicharro de León, "Pirandelismo en la literatura española," *Quaderni Ibero-Americani* (April 1954): 406; and Angel Valbuena Prat, "La generación del 98 y el teatro," *Historia del teatro español* (Barcelona: Noguer, 1956), p. 596.

Lawrence Anthony LaJohn, *Azorín and the Spanish Stage* (New York: Hispanic Institute, 1961) is in general a useful reference book for Azorín's theater. However, he does not treat this important aspect of Azorin's plays, even though he discusses the three collections of articles and all the plays and does indicate that Valbuena Prat has pointed out "similarities between *Angelita* and the works of Unamuno and Pirandello" (p. 170).

Other interesting comparisons are made by E. Inman Fox, "La campaña teatral de Azorín (Experimentalismo, Evreinoff e 'Ifach')," *Cuadernos Hispanoamericanos* (October–November 1968):375–89.

3. Azorín's articles on the theater which appeared in leading newspapers have now been published in three collections which appear in the Aguilar edition of *Obras completas* under the following titles: "La farándula" (vol. 7), "Escena y sala" (vol. 8), and "Ante las candilejas" (vol. 9). Azorín, *Obras completas* (Madrid: Aguilar, 1962, 1963, 1963). All quotations from Azorín's articles are taken from these collections unless otherwise indicated and are cited by volume and page numbers in the text.

4. Azorín believes that Pirandello has not treated this problem merely as a literary device: "No es un capricho del dramaturgo todo este mundo espiritual. Descartad cuanto queráis de convención y artificio literario; siempre, a cada paso, en la vida cotidiana, os encontraréis con un conflicto íntimo, con una duda patética, con una dificultad dolorosa basada

en este tremendo, hondo, inmensamente trágico desequilibrio entre la personalidad nuestra y el mundo circundante. Y ese desequilibrio es lo que constituye todo el teatro de Luis Pirandello" (9:147).

5. Azorín, "Memorias inmemoriales," *Obras completas* (Madrid: Aguilar, 1963): 8:510.

6. Thomas Bishop, *Pirandello and the French Theater* (New York: New York University Press, 1960), p. 51.

7. Leon Livingstone has discussed the antiform characteristic of Azorín's novels, "The Pursuit of Form in the Novels of Azorín," *PMLA* (March 1962): 121.

8. "Ove la commedia è da fare, come nel primo [*Sei personaggi in cerca d'autore*], da recitare a soggetto, come nel terzo [*Questa sera si recita a soggetto*], il conflitto, non uguale, né simile, anzi precisamente opposto, impedisce che la commedia si faccia e che l'improvvisazione sia governata e regolata e giunga seguitamente a una conclusione; ove la commedia è fatta, come nel secondo [*Ciascuno a suo modo*], il conflitto ne manda a monte la rappresentazione." Luigi Pirandello, *Maschere Nude,* 1:51.

9. Several articles have been published about this aesthetic problem. The most interesting are Edward Bullough, " 'Psychical Distance' as a Factor in Art and an Aesthetic Principle," *British Journal of Psychology* 5 (June 1912), pp. 87–118, and Oscar Büdel, "Contemporary Theater and Aesthetic Distance," pp. 277–91.

10. As early as 1907 Azorín felt the true need of the audience to participate spiritually in the formation of the play: "Es, pues, el teatro una colaboración entre el autor y el público; si hay en la sociedad un sentimiento medio dominante, este sentimiento es el que ha de herir o tocar el autor para alcanzar el éxito" (7:1126). He refers not to a select audience, but to "el inmenso público de las calles y de las plazas." However, at that time he thought that innovations would be out of place in the theater, that experimental plays would not be theatrical or would be impossible to produce.

11. In "Dos autos sacramentales" (9:151) Azorín makes a similar comparison.

12. "Teatro, fuera del teatro," of course, refers to the theater-within-the-theater. Usually the term "teatro dentro del teatro" is used in Spanish.

13. Azorín, *Obras completas* (Madrid: Aguilar, 1948), 4:1034. Both Azorín and Pirandello owe much to Henri Bergson, and this would be an interesting topic to investigate.

14. See also Frederick S. Stimson, " 'Lo invisible': Azorín's Debt to Maeterlinck," *Hispanic Review* 26 (1958), pp. 64–70.

15. Bishop, *Pirandello and the French Theater,* p. 54.

16. Oscar Büdel, *Pirandello* (London: Bowes and Bowes, 1966), p. 96.

17. An excellent general study of the autonomous character is Joseph E. Gillet, "The Autonomous Character in Spanish and European Literature," *Hispanic Review* 24 (1956): 179–90.

18. Ramón Gómez de la Serna, *Obras selectas* (Madrid: Plenitud, 1947), p. 1185.

19. Azorín, *Obras completas,* 4:906. All quotations from Azorín's plays are taken from this edition and cited by volume and page numbers in the text except where otherwise indicated.

20. Azorín, "A Voleo" 'La Pardo Bazán,' *Obras completas,* 9:1395.

21. Américo Castro's article is pertinent here: "Cervantes y Pirandello," in *Santa Teresa y otros ensayos* (Santander, 1929).

22. Azorín, *Obras completas,* 5:471. All subsequent quotations from *Angelita* are from this volume and cited by volume and page numbers in the text.

23. Pre-Pirandellism has been studied in Galdós by J. Chicharro de León, "Pirandelismo en la literatura española" and by Jacqueline Chantraine de Van Praag, "España tierra de elección del pirandellismo," *Quaderni Ibero-Americani* 27 (1962): 218–22.

24. Américo Castro, "Cervantes y Pirandello."

25. Leon Livingstone, "The Pursuit of Form in the Novels of Azorín," p. 128.

26. Américo Castro, "Cervantes y Pirandello," p. 221.

27. See also Pedro Barreda " 'El libro de Levante': Prenovela gaseiforme," *Hispania* 52 (1969): 39–44.

28. José Martínez Cachero, *Las novelas de Azorín* (Madrid: Insula, 1960).

29. Azorín's desire to give theater something it had lost since the Middle Ages is underlined in *Angelita,* which he calls an *Auto sacramental.* In the prologue to this play he explains the "eterno símbolo" which his play has in common with the religious genre. He also stresses the participation of the entire town in religious plays: "Ya en ensayo; ya incrustada en la evolución de una ciudad. La vida de la ciudad, con sus hombres y sus mujeres, enredada, mezclada a estos hombres y a estas mujeres de la obra" (5:448). Büdel, "Contemporary Theater and Aesthetic Distance" discusses the common participation factor found in religious theater and contemporary theater.

Chapter 8. *Manuel and Antonio Machado*

1. Manuel y Antonio Machado, *Las adelfas y El hombre que murió en la guerra* (Buenos Aires: Austral, 1947), p. 40. All subsequent quotations from this source will be taken from this edition and cited by page numbers in the text.
2. Thomas Bishop, *Pirandello and the French Theater*, p. 51.
3. Frank Sedwick, "Unamuno and Pirandello Revisited," p. 41.

Chapter 9. *Federico García Lorca*

1. Angel del Río, "Lorca: Poet in New York," *New World Writing* no. 8 (New York: The New American Library, 1955), p. 183.
2. Eric Bentley, *The Playwright as Thinker* (Cleveland: Meridian, 1964), p. xvii.
3. Francis Fergusson, *The Idea of a Theater* (Garden City: Anchor, 1953), p. 206.
4. Edwin Honig, *García Lorca* (Norfolk: New Directions, 1963), p. 135.
5. Federico García Lorca, "Charla sobre teatro," *Obras completas* (Madrid: Aguilar, 1957), p. 35. All quotations from García Lorca's writings are taken from this edition and cited by page numbers in the text.
6. Professor Rafael Martínez Nadal's *El Público: Amor, teatro y caballos en la obra de Federico García Lorca* (Oxford: The Dolphin Book Co., 1970) reached me when my own book was already in press. This book provides information about the manuscript and many excerpts.
7. In an interview García Lorca said: "En estas comedias imposibles está mi verdadero propósito" (p. 1635). And Angel del Río states: "Sabemos que el mismo Lorca y los amigos que la conocen íntegra le concedían bastante importancia." "Federico García Lorca (1899–1936)," *Revista Hispánica Moderna:* New York, 4: 3 and 4 (July–October 1940): 240.
8. Jean-Louis Schonberg, *Federico García Lorca* (México: Compañía General de Ediciones, 1959), p. 299.
9. Probably based on the fact that he did criticize commercial theater in interviews; and that in *El retablillo de Don Cristóbal,* the poet, after he has lost his artistic integrity because he has been forced to tell the audience only what the director wished, is then scornfully paid by him.

10. Roberto Sánchez, *García Lorca—Estudio sobre su teatro* (Madrid: Ed. Jura, 1950), p. 49.

11. Alfredo de la Guardia, *García Lorca, persona y creación* (Buenos Aires: Schapire, 1961), p. 321.

12. *Ibid.*, p. 124.

13. Angel del Río, "Lorca's Theater," in *Lorca, A Collection of Critical Essays,* ed. Manuel Durán (Englewood Cliffs: Prentice-Hall, 1962), p. 144.

14. Edwin Honig, "Lorca to Date," *Tulane Drama Review* 7 (1962), p. 121.

15. *Ibid.*, p. 124.

16. María Teresa Babín, *El mundo poético de Federico García Lorca* (San Juan: Biblioteca de Autores, 1954), p. 15.

17. Pirandello, *Maschere Nude,* 1:51.

18. Although the major part of this analysis concerns only "Cuadro Quinto," I have used the title *El Público* because it is more characteristic of this section than it is of the less important portion "Reina Romana."

I have used the word "Pirandellism" throughout this chapter when I mean the many varieties of theater-within-the-theater techniques associated with Pirandello. This term, of course, can also be used to connote the ambiguity-of-personality theme which is also such an important part of Pirandello's work.

19. Pirandello, *Maschere Nude,* 1:51.

20. Edward Bullough, " 'Psychical Distance' as a Factor in Art and an Aesthetic Principle," 87–118. This has been reprinted: Edward Bullough, *Aesthetics* (London: Bowes & Bowes, 1957), pp. 91–130.

21. Büdel, "Contemporary Theater and Aesthetic Distance."

22. *A Modern Book of Esthetics,* ed. Melvin M. Rader (New York: H. Holt & Co., 1935). (Only the first four chapters of *La deshumanización del arte* appear here.)

23. P. A. Michelis, "Aesthetic Distance and the Charm of Contemporary Art," *The Journal of Aesthetics and Art Criticism* 18 (September 1959): 1–45.

24. Büdel, "Contemporary Theater and Aesthetic Distance," p. 277.

25. Although the date 1933 is often given, García Lorca's acquaintances seem to be in agreement that he was working on it during and immediately after his stay in New York City. During this time he stated: "El teatro nuevo, avanzado de formas y teoría es mi mayor preocupación. Nueva York es un sitio único para tomarle el pulso al nuevo arte teatral" (p. 1608).

26. Michelis states: "Bullough's theory, then, would keep contemplation close to the spectator's psychological experience, while the theory of Ortega y Gasset would liberate it from every emotional link with the object, by the greatest possible retreat from it, thus making of aesthetic contemplation an almost exclusively intellectual act" ("Aesthetic Distance and the Charm of Contemporary Art," p. 2). It is possible that this statement is not quite accurate. The two men were doing completely different things. Bullough, as a psychologist, is analyzing the factors which create the ideal aesthetic distance for maximum aesthetic enjoyment. Ortega y Gasset is describing the characteristics of the new art which he believes removes itself from the common man. The former, therefore, is presenting this complex problem and analyzing psychological reactions. The latter is describing what he thinks the new art is. Both realize that too great an aesthetic distance will prevent enjoyment of the work of art, although Ortega y Gasset maintains that a select minority possesses the unusual ability to enjoy dehumanized forms.

27. José Ortega y Gasset, *Obras completas* (Madrid: Revista de Occidente, 1947), 3: 377. All quotations from "La deshumanización del arte" are from this edition and cited by page numbers in the text.

28. Professor Büdel also discusses this mocking aspect of the contemporary theater. "Contemporary Theater and Aesthetic Distance," p. 291.

29. *Lorca*—Selected and Translated by J. L. Gili (Bungay, Suffolk: Penguin, 1960), p. xviii.

30. Richard Saez, "The Ritual Sacrifice in Lorca's 'Poet in New York,'" in *Lorca, A Collection of Critical Essays,* ed. Manuel Durán (Englewood Cliffs: Prentice-Hall, 1962), pp. 108–29. Although Saez does not mention *El Público* in this article, his analysis of the propitiatory-victim aspect of *Poet in New York* is also directly applicable to this play.

31. Gustavo Correa, "El simbolismo de la luna en García Lorca," *PMLA* (January, 1958): 1084.

32. Büdel, "Contemporary Theater and Aesthetic Distance," p. 284.

33. Guillermo Díaz-Plaja has also quoted a pertinent remark made by García Lorca in this connection: "Creo que los toros es la fiesta más culta que hay en el mundo. Es el drama puro, en el cual el español derrama sus mejores lágrimas y sus mejores bilis. Es el único sitio adonde se va con la seguridad de ver la muerte rodeada de la más deslumbradora belleza. ¿Qué sería de la primavera española, de nuestra sangre y de nuestra lengua si dejaran de sonar los clarines dramáticos de la corrida?" *Federico García Lorca* (Madrid: Austral, 1961), p. 62.

34. For more information about García Lorca's puppet plays consult

William I. Oliver, "Lorca: 'The Puppets and the Artist,'" *Tulane Drama Review* 7: 76–95.

35. Sánchez, *García Lorca*, p. 25.

36. According to Professor Germán Bleiberg, García Lorca was influenced by Cervantes through Manuel de Falla's *El retablo de Maese Pedro*.

37. See Vernon Chamberlin on the topic of green symbolism: "Symbolic Green: A Time-Honored Characterizing Device in Spanish Literature," *Hispania* 51 (1968): 29–37.

38. R. G. Knight, "Federico García Lorca's 'Así que pasen cinco años,'" *Bulletin of Hispanic Studies* 43 (1966): 32–46.

Chapter 10. *Alejandro Casona*

1. Charles H. Leighton, "Alejandro Casona's 'Pirandellism,'" *Symposium* 17 (1963): 202–14. In this article Leighton examines *Las tres perfectas casadas, La sirena varada* and mentions several other plays. He does not discuss *Los árboles mueren de pie,* however, which I think is quite important in this connection. Harold K. Moon, "Casona and Solipsism," *Alejandro Casona, Playwright* (Provo, Utah: Brigham Young University Press, 1970), which appeared after the completion of my manuscript, may also be consulted.

2. Alejandro Casona, *Obras completas* (Madrid: Aguilar, 1965), 1: 135. All quotations from Casona's plays are from this volume and cited by page numbers in the text unless otherwise indicated.

3. Alejandro Casona, *Las tres perfectas casadas* (Buenos Aires: Losada, 1941), p. 86.

Chapter 11. *Jacinto Grau*

1. The most important articles which treat *El señor de Pigmalión* are Domingo Pérez Minik, "Jacinto Grau o el retablo de las maravillas," *Debates sobre el teatro español contemporáneo* (Santa Cruz de Tenerife: Goya, 1953), pp. 143–59; Gerardo Rodríguez Salcedo, "Introducción al teatro de Jacinto Grau," *Papeles de Son Armadans,* 42 (1966): 13–42; and J. Chicharro de León, "Pirandelismo en la literatura española."

2. William Giuliano, one of the few scholars who have studied Grau, mentions this in the preface to his edition of *El señor de Pigmalión* (New York: Appleton-Century-Crofts, 1952), p. 13.

3. Rodríguez Salcedo, "Introducción al teatro de Jacinto Grau," points out the fact that modern critics have given the playwright very little attention. However, his excellence has been recognized by many. Giuliano, *El señor de Pigmalión,* p. 2 reports: "A large group of Spanish and Spanish American writers and professors has sent a petition to the Nobel Prize Committee requesting that Grau receive the next award for literature." Antonio Buero Vallejo's comment is especially interesting: "Un poco más de consideración pública y literaria habrían quizá hecho de él otro Pirandello. Los "Seis Personajes" se estrenaron en 1921; por las mismas fechas se imprime "El Señor de Pigmalión" y en 1923 estrena Charles Dullin en L'Atelier su versión francesa, dos meses antes del estreno parisiense de los "Seis Personajes". Paris, y más tarde Praga, aplaudieron con asombro a aquel español, que podía hombrearse con el grande y aún muy discutido italiano. Un dramaturgo que no desmentiría con su labor posterior la singular calidad de su teatro, algunos de cuyos títulos acogieron Bruselas y otras ciudades." *Argentores,* "Día del autor," Julio-Diciembre de 1963. See also John W. Kronik, "Art and Ideology in the Theater of Jacinto Grau," *Kentucky Romance Quarterly* 16 (1969):261–76.

I have been unable to find any discussion of the three plays which are included in this chapter. Of course these plays became available only recently; *Tabarín* and *Bibí Carabé* were published by Losada in 1959, and *Las gafas de don Telesforo* in 1954.

4. Luigi Pirandello, "La tragedia d'un personaggio," *Novelle per un anno* (Verona: Mondadori, 1964), 1:715–16.

5. "Chi nasce personaggio, chi ha la ventura di nascere personaggio vivo, può infischiarsi anche della morte. Non muore più! Morrà l'uomo, lo scrittore, strumento naturale della creazione; la creatura non muore più! E per vivere eterna, non ha mica bisogno di straordinarie doti o di compiere prodigi. Mi dica lei chi era Sancho Panza! Mi dica lei chi era don Abbondio! Eppure vivono eterni perché—vivi germi—ebbero la ventura di trovare una matrice feconda, una fantasia che li seppe allevare e nutrire per l'eternità." *Ibid.,* p. 717.

6. *Ibid.,* p. 714.

7. *Ibid.,* p. 718.

8. *Ibid.,* p. 715.

9. Jacinto Grau, "Las gafas de don Telesforo o un loco de buen capricho," *Teatro* (Buenos Aires: Losada, 1954), 1:101. Subsequent quotations from *Las gafas* will be to this volume and cited by page numbers in the text.

10. *La tragedia d'un personaggio* is not nearly so well known as

Pirandello's famous play, but if Grau did not know about the story before 1939 it was surely called to his attention then when Monner Sans published an essay in which he discusses both *El señor de Pigmalión* and *La tragedia d'un personaggio*. José María Monner Sans, "Algunos aspectos externos del nuevo teatro," *Panorama del nuevo teatro* (Buenos Aires: Imprenta López, 1939), pp. 67–88.

11. Telesforo is not speaking to the author here but to another man, and he is not referring to himself but to the products of his imagination. The idea, however, is exactly the same as the autonomous character's claim to being more real than the author, who is only a mortal. This is the aspect of Unamuno's Augusto Pérez which is closest to Pirandello's ideas.

12. Luigi Pirandello, "La tragedia d'un personaggio," p. 717.

13. Azorín, "Los seis personajes y el autor," *Obras completas* (Madrid: Aguilar, 1954), 9:44.

14. Jacinto Benavente, *Los intereses creados* (Buenos Aires: Austral, 1965), p. 68.

15. Miguel de Unamuno, *San Manuel Bueno*, p. 49.

16. For more about this important aspect of twentieth century theater see Edward Bullough, " 'Psychical Distance' as a Factor in Art and an Aesthetic Principle" and Oscar Büdel, "Contemporary Theater and Aesthetic Distance."

17. Jacinto Grau, "Tabarín," *Teatro* (Buenos Aires: Losada, 1959), 2:193. Further quotes from Grau's plays will be from this volume and cited by page numbers in the text.

18. Since Grau lived in Buenos Aires after the Spanish Civil War until his death in 1958, the Argentinian theatrical environment must not be overlooked in considering his plays because Pirandello and playwrights inspired by him were important there. See Erminio Giuseppe Neglia, *Pirandello y la dramática rioplatense* (Florence: Valmartina, 1970).

Chapter 12. *Juan Ignacio Luca de Tena*

1. "Un'eco del teatro pirandelliano è forse anche in *Angelina* (1930) di Azorín, in *La sirena varada* (1934) di A. Casona e, più chiaramente percettibile, in *Quién soy yo?*, *Yo soy Brandel* e *De lo pintado a lo vivo* di Luca de Tena." *Enciclopedia dello Spettacolo* (Roma: Le Maschere, 1961), 8:170.

2. "¿Ustedes se acuerdan de aquella famosa obra pirandeliana 'Seis

personajes en busca de un autor'? Pues al revés. Nuestro tercer acto se titula "UN PERSONAJE SE ESCAPA DE UN AUTOR." Juan Ignacio Luca de Tena, *Obras completas* (Barcelona: A H R, 1958), 1:1195–96. All subsequent quotations are taken from this edition and cited by page numbers in the text.

3. This theme is also found in Echegaray's *Un crítico incipiente*, when a young critic, who thinks that a play has been written by a well-known author, is firmly convinced of his ability to judge it without attending the première.

4. Performed in the Teatro Infanta Isabel, Madrid, fall 1968.

Chapter 13. *Pedro Salinas*

1. For example, Marta Morello-Frosch, "Teatro y crítica de Pedro Salinas," *Revista Hispánica Moderna* 26 (1960): 116–18; Mario Maurín, "Tema y variaciones en el teatro de Salinas," *Insula*, no. 104; and Rodríguez Richart, "Sobre el teatro de Salinas," *Boletín de la Biblioteca Menéndez y Pelayo*, 36: 397–427.

2. Hugo W. Cowes, *Relación Yo-Tú y trascendencia en la obra dramática de Pedro Salinas* (Buenos Aires: Universidad de Buenos Aires, 1965). Professor Cowes has noticed that a relationship exists between Pirandello and Salinas. Although the scope of his book does not include a thorough analysis of this aspect of Salinas's work, in a section entitled "Apéndice a *El Chantajista*" he discusses this and four other plays which mix theatrical representation and reality: *Hamlet*, Pirandello's *Ciascuno a suo modo*, Sartre's *Kean*, and Genet's *Les Bonnes*. He also compares and contrasts Pirandello and Salinas in several footnotes.

3. Dámaso Alonso gives a very interesting report of the première of *La fuente del Arcángel* which took place at the theater of Columbia University, and was presented by a dramatic group from the Spanish Department of Barnard College. "Con Pedro Salinas," *Clavileño*, (September–October 1951):17–18.

In addition, in the "Nota preliminar" to Salinas's *Teatro completo*, Juan Marichal reports that *Judit y el tirano* was done by the Compañía Cubana de Teatro Universitario. Pedro Salinas, *Teatro completo* (Madrid: Aguilar, 1957), p. 11. All quotations from Salinas's plays are taken from this volume and cited by page numbers in the text.

4. Furthermore, Azorín also stresses the relationship of man to country-side, as he creates his autonomous character: "El personaje central de la novela, determinado por esta atracción ineluctable de los cerritos. La

personalidad moral del protagonista que se va concretando, solidificando, definiendo. Personalidad prefigurada por este paisaje o elemento primario de un paisaje." Azorín, "El libro de Levante," *Obras completas,* 5:368.

5. André Lebois, "La révolte des personnages: de Cervantès et Calderon à Raymond Schwab," *Revue de Littérature Comparée* 23 (1949): 482–506.

6. The latest example which has come to my attention is the cover blurb of Georges Piroué's *Pirandello:* "Ainsi saisie dans sa totalité, se dessine la figure d'un écrivain qui, victime de nos temps bouleversés et percevant dans sa chair même toutes nos contradictions, a su donner corps à ses rêves pitoyables et exaltants, nous les faire tenir pour plus évidents que nos branlantes convictions. Tout comme Don Quichotte, son lointain frère solitaire." (Paris: Denoël, 1967).

7. Hugo Cowes, *Relación Yo-Tú,* p. 39.

8. All of these plays are published in the *Teatro completo* except "Los santos" which appears in *Cuadernos Americanos,* XIII, 3 (May–June 1954).

9. This play is also quite reminiscent of *Sombras de sueño* by Unamuno.

10. In his article entitled "Pirandello y yo" which appeared in *La Nación* of Buenos Aires in 1923.

11. See, for example, Salinas's *El poema:* "En esta luz del poema,/ todo,/ desde el más nocturno beso/ al cenetal esplendor,/ todo está mucho más claro."

12. Lander MacClintock, *The Age of Pirandello* (Bloomington: Indiana University Press, 1951), p. 175.

13. Cowes, *Relación Yo-Tú,* in discussing *La bella durmiente,* also remarks about this difference between Salinas and Pirandello: "El destino de Soledad parece ilustrar este texto de Ortega, que supone, por la decisiva afirmación de un yo permanente, e invariable, que pugna por realizarse, y se mantiene aun en el fracaso, indestructible, una clara refutación del caos pirandeliano." p. 142.

Chapter 14. *Other Contemporary Playwrights*

1. Alfredo Marquerie, "Prólogo," *Teatro de Vanguardia* (Madrid: Ediciones Permán, 1949), p. 10.

2. Alfonso Sastre in a letter to the author dated 25 November 1968.

3. Edward Groff, "Point of View in Modern Drama," *Modern Drama* (December 1959): 280.

4. Alfonso Sastre, as a critic, is also interested in influences. For example, in his discussion of one of Antonioni's films he speculates: "Yo preguntaría cuál es la influencia real de Cesare Pavese en la obra de Antonioni; pero también cuál es la deuda, si es que existe, que yo creo que sí, de Antonioni con dos ilustres dramaturgos: August Strindberg y Luigi Pirandello." Alfonso Sastre, *Anatomía del realismo* (Barcelona: Editorial Seix Barral, 1965), p. 101.

See also Alfonso Sastre, *Drama y sociedad* (Madrid: Taurus, 1956) in which many non-Spanish playwrights, including Pirandello, are discussed.

5. Alfonso Sastre y Medardo Fraile, "Ha sonado la muerte," *Teatro de Vanguardia* (Madrid: Ediciones Permán, 1949), pp. 176–77. All subsequent quotations from this play are from this edition and cited by page numbers in the text.

6. Sastre's own discussion of aesthetic distance in *Anatomía del realismo*, pp. 52–55, is quite enlightening.

7. Alfonso Sastre, *Teatro*, "Cargamento de sueños" (Madrid: Taurus, 1964), p. 149.

8. Alfonso Sastre, *Teatro*, "Teatro de vanguardia, regreso al realismo y experiencia épica" (Madrid: Taurus, 1964), p. 141.

9. Alfonso Paso, "3 Mujeres 3," *Teatro de vanguardia* (Madrid: Ediciones Permán, 1949), p. 107.

10. José María Palacio, "Tres variaciones sobre una frase de amor," *Teatro de vanguardia* (Madrid: Ediciones Permán, 1949), p. 302. All subsequent quotations from this play are from this edition and cited by page numbers in the text.

11. Enrique Jardiel Poncela's play *Eloísa está debajo de un almendro* also may be said to echo certain concepts in *Enrico IV*. In Jardiel Poncela's play a young woman dons a dress which belonged to her mother in order to elicit the confession of the person who murdered the mother, who turns out to be the mother's insane sister.

12. Joaquín Calvo Sotelo, *La ciudad sin Dios* (Madrid: Escelicer, 1964), p. 13.

13. A similar comparison can be made in French literature. In 1646 Jean Rotrou wrote *Saint Genest*, which, like Lope's *Lo fingido verdadero* (written sometime between 1604 and 1618), is based on the life of an actor who was converted while playing the role of a Christian martyr. Then, almost immediately after Pirandello had made his first impact, Henri Ghéon wrote *Le Comédien et la Grâce*, also concerning the martyrdom of Saint Genès. Bishop states: "It hardly seems accidental

that the author should have been led to this old play at this particular time." Thomas Bishop, *Pirandello and the French Theater*, p. 58.

14. Theodore S. Beardsley lists among many contemporary plays which he considers to have "illogical characters" (a number of which have also been discussed in this book) Carlos Llopis's *Por cualquier puerta del sol* which includes action in the balcony of the theater. "The Illogical Character in Contemporary Spanish Drama," *Hispania* 41 (1958): 445–48.

SELECTED BIBLIOGRAPHY

Alvarez Quintero, Serafín y Joaquín. *Obras completas*. Madrid: Espasa-Calpe, 1925.

Azorín. *Obras completas*. 9 vols. Madrid: Aguilar, 1948–63.

Barbina, Alfredo. *Bibliografia della critica pirandelliana 1889–1961*. Florence: Le Monnier, 1967.

Bentley, Eric. *The Playwright as Thinker*. Cleveland: Meridian, 1964.

Bishop, Thomas. *Pirandello and the French Theater*. New York University Press, 1960.

Büdel, Oscar. "Contemporary Theater and Aesthetic Distance," *PMLA* (1961): 277–91.

————. *Pirandello*. London: Bowes and Bowes, 1966.

Bullough, Edward. " 'Psychical Distance' as a Factor in Art and an Aesthetic Principle," *British Journal of Psychology* (1912): 87–118. This has been reprinted: Bullough, Edward. *Aesthetics*. London: Bowes and Bowes, 1957.

Calderón de la Barca, Pedro. *Autos sacramentales*. 2 vols. Madrid: Espasa-Calpe, 1957–58.

Casona, Alejandro. *Obras completas*. 2 vols. Madrid: Aguilar, 1965, 1966.

————. *Las tres perfectas casadas*. Buenos Aires: Losada, 1941.

Castro, Américo. "Cervantes y Pirandello," *Santa Teresa y otros ensayos*. Santander: Historia Nueva, 1925.

Cervantes Saavedra, Miguel de. *Comedias y entremeses*. 6 vols. Madrid: Rodolfo Schevill y Adolfo Bonilla, 1915–22.

————. *Don Quijote de la Mancha*. 8 vols. Madrid: Espasa-Calpe, 1956–58.

Chantraine de Van Praag, Jacqueline. "España tierra de elección del pirandellismo," *Quaderni Ibero-Americani* (1962): 218–22.

Chicharro de León, J. "Pirandelismo en la literatura española," *Quaderni Ibero-Americani* (1954): 406–14.

Cotarelo y Mori, Emilio. *Colección de entremeses, loas, bailes, jácaras y mojigangas.* 2 vols. Madrid: Bailly/Bailliere, 1911.

———. *Sainetes de Don Ramón de la Cruz.* 2 vols. Madrid: Bailly/Bailliere, 1915–28.

De Filippo, Luigi. "Pirandello in Spagna," *Nuova Antologia* (1964): 197–206.

Echegaray, José. *Teatro escogido.* Madrid: Aguilar, 1959.

———. *La realidad y el delirio.* Madrid: José Rodríguez, 1887.

———. *Un crítico incipiente.* Madrid: José Rodríguez, 1891.

Fergusson, Francis. *The Idea of a Theater.* Garden City: Anchor, 1953.

García Lorca, Federico. *Obras completas.* Madrid: Aguilar, 1957.

Gillet, Joseph E. "The Autonomous Character in Spanish and European Literature," *Hispanic Review* (1956): 179–90.

Giudice, Gaspare. *Luigi Pirandello.* Torino: Unione Tipografico-Editrice Torinese, 1963.

Gómez de la Serna, Ramón. *Obras completas.* 2 vols. Barcelona: Editorial A H R, 1956–57.

———. *Obras selectas.* Madrid: Plenitud, 1947.

———. *El teatro en soledad.* Paris: Ismael Smith, 1911.

González del Castillo, Juan Ignacio. *Sainetes.* 4 vols. Cádiz: Imprenta de la Revista médica, 1846.

Grau, Jacinto. *El señor de Pigmalión,* ed. William Giuliano. New York: Appleton-Century-Crofts, 1952.

———. *Teatro.* 2 vols. Buenos Aires: Losada, 1954–59.

Guglielmini, Homero M. *El teatro del disconformismo (Pirandello).* Buenos Aires: Artes Gráficas Bodoni, 1967.

Leal, Luis. "Función de los personajes españoles en 'Il fu Mattia Pascal,' " *Forum Italicum* (1967): 325–35.

———. "Unamuno and Pirandello," *Italica* (1952): 193–99.

Lebois, André. "La révolte des personnages: de Cervantès et Calderon a Raymond Schwab," *Revue de Littérature Comparée* 23 (1949): 482–506.

Livingstone, Leon. "Interior Duplication and the Problem of Form in the Modern Spanish Novel," *PMLA* (1958): 393–406.

Luca de Tena, Juan Ignacio. *Obras completas.* 2 vols. Barcelona: A H R, 1958.

MacClintock, Lander. *The Age of Pirandello.* Bloomington: Indiana University Press, 1951.

Machado, Manuel and Antonio. *Las adelfas y el hombre que murió en la guerra.* Buenos Aires: Austral, 1947.

Monner Sans, José María. "Unamuno, Pirandello y el personaje autónomo," *La Torre* (1961): 387–402.

Nelson, Robert J. *Play within a Play.* New Haven: Yale University Press, 1958.

Pérez Galdós, Benito. *Obras completas.* 6 vols. Madrid: Aguilar, 1960–63.

Pirandello, Luigi. *Maschere nude.* 2 vols. Verona: A. Mondadori, 1962.

———. *Saggi.* Verona: Mondadori, 1952.

Ragusa, Olga. "Pirandello's Don Quixote: A passage from L'umorismo," *Cesare Barbieri Courier* (1967): 13–15.

Salinas, Pedro. *Teatro completo.* Madrid: Aguilar, 1957.

Sastre, Alfonso. *Anatomía del realismo.* Barcelona: Seix Barral, 1965.

———. *Drama y sociedad.* Madrid: Taurus, 1956.

———. *Teatro.* Madrid: Taurus, 1964.

Sedwick, Frank. "Unamuno and Pirandello Revisited," *Italica* (1956): 40–51.

Shattuck, Roger. *The Banquet Years.* New York: Harcourt, Brace, 1958.

Sinicropi, Giovanni. "Arte e vita nelle opere di Luigi Pirandello," *Italica* (1961): 265–95.

Tamayo y Baus, Manuel. *Obras.* 4 vols. Madrid: Rivadeneyra, 1898–1900.

Téllez, Fray Gabriel (Tirso de Molina). *Obras dramáticas completas.* 3 vols. Madrid: Aguilar, 1946.

Unamuno, Miguel de. *Cómo se hace una novela.* Buenos Aires: Editorial "Alba", 1927.

———. *Niebla.* Madrid: Espasa-Calpe, 1966.

———. "Pirandello y yo," *La Nación* (Buenos Aires, 1923).

———. *San Manuel Bueno, mártir y tres historias más.* Buenos Aires: Espasa-Calpe, 1951.

———. *Teatro completo.* Madrid: Aguilar, 1959.

Valbuena Prat, Angel. *Historia del teatro español.* Barcelona: Noguer, 1956.

Vega, Ventura de la. *Obras escogidas.* Barcelona: Montaner y Simón, 1894.

Vega Carpio, Lope Félix de. *Obras escogidas.* 3 vols. Madrid: Aguilar, 1962.

Vittorini, Domenico. *The Drama of Luigi Pirandello.* New York: Dover, 1957.

APPENDIX

Part 1: *Spanish Books in Pirandello's Library*

A reading of Luigi Pirandello's writings reveals that he was acquainted with *La vida es sueño, El poema de mío Cid,* and especially *El Quijote,* because he used examples from the latter to illustrate his theory of "umorismo." Pirandello has also indicated his awareness of Spain by inserting in his plays such Spanish references as the broken Spanish-Italian of Madame Pace in *Sei personaggi in cerca d'autore,* the father's query "Chi era Sancho Panza?" in the same play, and a drunken shout "Volevamo onorare la Spagna" in *Il giuoco delle parti.* Luis Leal has pointed out the key roles held by Spanish characters in *Il fu Mattia Pascal* ("Función de los personajes españoles . . ." *Forum Italicum* December, 1967).

Also, according to Andrenio in *Pirandello y compañía,* when Pirandello spent several days in Barcelona he indicated familiarity with contemporary Spanish theater, mentioning specifically Benavente and the Quintero brothers. In addition, Bernardo Sanvisenti has written a convincing article which suggests that Pirandello's *novella, Una voce,* owed its original inspiration to Galdós's *Marianela.*

On a more personal level, Pirandello was certainly conscious of the Spanish-speaking world because his daughter was married to a Chilean, Manuel Aguirre.

A visit to Pirandello's library, housed in the home where he died, on Via Antonio Bosio 15 in Rome, which is now the location of the Istituto di Studi Pirandelliani e sul Teatro Italiano Contemporaneo, reveals that Spain was not neglected in Pirandello's collection of books. Pirandello certainly read many of these books which were located in the room which served as study, living room, and library (Pirandello is photographed at his typewriter in this room in Giudice's book on page 496). His children also used the library, therefore some of the books may have belonged to them. Also, many Spanish books are found there which were sent to the Sicilian by their authors, and some remain uncut. In any case, the list which follows is extremely interesting and suggests many possibilities for investigation. Professor Alfredo Barbina and Miss Alfonsa Lorello are occupied in preparing a catalogue of this collection which will be published by the Istituto.

In addition to the books listed below, there are two Spanish-Italian dictionaries, one of which may have been acquired in 1921, and a *Grammatica della Lingua Spagnola*.

Araguistain, Luis. *Remedios heroicos*. Madrid: Mundo Latino, 1923. The dedication reads: "Homenaje de admiración á Luigi Pirandello, Araguistain." (Uncut)

Araguistain, Luis. *El archipiélago maravilloso*. Madrid: Mundo Latino, 1923. (Uncut)

Bacci, Luigi. *L'Universalità del Don Chisciotte*. Conferenza commemorativa detta il 6/5/16.

Calderón de la Barca, Pedro. *Das laute Geheimnis*. Leipzig: 1920 or 1921. Dedicated to Fraulein Marta Abba, 25 October.

Campoamor, Ramón de. *Poesías escogidas*. Madrid: Biblioteca Universal, 1879.

Catáleg de la Colecció Cervàntica. Barcelona: Institut d'Estudis Catalans, 1916.

Cejador y Frauca, Julio. *La lengua de Cervantes,* Vols. I and II. Madrid: Jaime Ratés, 1905. (Uncut)

Cervantes, Miguel. *Don Quijote de la Mancha*. Paris: Librería de Cormon y Blanc, 1825. This four-volume edition of Cervantes's book had one and probably two owners before Pirandello acquired it. Therefore, although there are a number of marks in the margins, they cannot necessarily be attributed to Pirandello.

Cesareo, G. A. *Don Juan (frammento)*. Catania: Giannotta, 1893. I include this title because the subject is Spanish.

De Sagarra, Josep M. *Dijous Sant*. Barcelona: Salvador Bonavía, 1924.

De Sagarra, Josep M. *Fidelitat*. Barcelona: Salvador Bonavía, 1925.

Hernádez, José. *Martín Fierro*. Madrid: Talleres "Calpe", 1924. Dedication: "Al gran Pirandello, recuerdo de una argentina, la Biblia de nuestras Pampas. Raquel Zichis González. 15/9/933."

Levi, Ezio. *Lope de Vega e l'Italia*. Florence: Sansoni, 1935. Pirandello wrote the preface to this book, the last paragraph of which reads: "Al lume di questa intuizione estetica, per me certissima, e del resto sul fondamento di notizie di fatto copiosissime, possiamo affermare con sicura coscienza che l'esplosione massima del teatro in tutta Europa che è del Seicento, con Shakespeare in Inghilterra, con Lope de Vega e Calderón in Spagna, con Molière in Francia, è frutto di matrice italiana."

Mallea, Eduardo. *Nocturno europeo.* Buenos Aires: Sur, 1935. Dedication: "A Luigi Pirandello Homenaje de E. Mallea, Buenos Aires, febrero de 1936." (Uncut)

Martínez Sierra, Gregorio. *Canción de cuna, Primavera en otoño, Lirio entre espinas.* Madrid: Saturnino Collega, 1920. (Uncut)

Martínez Sierra, Gregorio. *El corazón ciego, Juventud, Divino Tesoro, Sólo para mujeres, El enamorado.* Madrid: Estrella, 1922. (*El enamorado* is uncut)

Martínez Sierra, Gregorio. *El reino de Dios, La adúltera penitente, Navidad.* Madrid: Estrella, 1922. (Uncut)

Monner Sans, José María. *El teatro de Pirandello.* Buenos Aires: López, 1936. Dedication: "Al Signor Luigi Pirandello, colla mia ammirazione, questo saggio argentino sul suo chiarissimo teatro. Monner Sans, Mayo de 1936." (Uncut)

Orcajo Acuña, Federico. *Teatro de hoy.* Buenos Aires, 1936. Dedication: "A Luigi Pirandello, homenaje de F. Orcajo Acuña, Montevideo, 5/7/936."

Poetas contemporáneos. Biblioteca Universal, Colección de los mejores autores. Uncut except first part of Echegaray's *La galerna.*

Quevedo, Francesco de. *Vita di Pitocco (El buscón)* Roma: Formiggini, 1917.

Rojas, Fernando de. *La Celestina,* Vols. I and II. Madrid: Clásicos castellanos, 1913.

Romances moriscos novelescos. Vol. II. Madrid: Campuzano, 1889.

Unamuno, Miguel de. *Commento al "Don Chisciotte,"* Lanciano: R. Carabba, 1913. The first volume is all cut. The second is uncut except for the last part which treats the death of Don Quijote.

Valle Inclán y Montenegro, Ramón del. *La novella dei lupi.* (A cura di A. De Stefani.) Milano: Piantanida Valcarenghi, 1923. Dedication: "A Luigi Pirandello questa mistica e violenta storia spagnola che gli dovrebbe piacere. Devotamente, Alessandro De Stefani, Milano, Maggio 1924."

In addition, there are to be found in Pirandello's library numerous Spanish translations of his own works. One of these books is especially interesting, because in the margins of Francisco Gómez Hidalgo's translation, *Vestir al desnudo,* on the first ten pages, there are marked in two shades of black pencil large crosses, question marks, and a few corrections. Some of these marks appear to have been made in anger upon reading a poor translation.

Part 2: *Other Relevant Spanish Works:*

1. In *El romancero gitano,* "Muerte de Antoñito el Camborio," García Lorca has created an effect in poetry similar to the impact caused by the autonomous character in novels and plays. When his cousins are killing him Antoñito shouts to his author:

> "¡Ay Federico García,
> llama a la Guardia Civil!"

The poem, with the exception of these two lines, is the narration of the murder of Antoñito, but this shout for help suggests that the author, somehow, is actually present but is a disengaged observer. Perhaps more likely, in the era of autonomous characters, Antoñito is speaking to his author who is in the process of writing the poem, and is suggesting a more advantageous dénouement for his story.

2. Valle-Inclán in his novel *Tirano Banderas* (1926) occasionally calls attention to the fictional nature of the story. For example, although the story is supposed to be realistic, the *Libro tercero* is entitled "Guiñol dramático" and begins: "¡Fué como truco de melodrama!" (*Obras completas,* Madrid: Rivadeneyra, 1944, 2:727). Paul Ilie, *The Surrealist Mode in Spanish Literature* (Ann Arbor: University of Michigan Press, 1968, pp. 131–51), says many important things about this aspect of the novel.

Also some of Valle-Inclán's plays could be considered of marginal interest because they combine *commedia dell'arte* and Cervantine characters and elements. *La farsa italiana de la enamorada del Rey* in the collection *Tablado de marionetas* is especially interesting from this point of view because Maese Lotario, a puppeteer in the tradition of Maese Pedro, is an important character. Also, Rubén Darío and the Marqués de Bradomín appear in *Luces de Bohemia.* García Lorca's short plays, written later, give the impression that he may have learned something from Valle-Inclán.

3. Mario Verdaguer in his short novel *El marido, la mujer y la sombra* (1927) writes about an autonomous character. The writer makes a paper man for his children, and when he holds it up so that the two children will not tear it by fighting over its possession, the shadow of the paper man cast on the wall becomes autonomous, and, much to the

annoyance of the writer, begins to occupy an important place in his life. Although the beginning of the book is quite original, the development of the situation seems rather weak. It is almost as if the writer has created a character and then doesn't quite know what to do with him.

4. Benítez de Castro's *La rebelión de los personajes* is a 1939 novel in which a combination of historical personages and fictional characters appear. Shakespeare is a central figure and the novel continues the autonomous-character tradition as found in Galdós, Unamuno, and Pirandello.

5. Soon after *Sei personaggi in cerca d'autore* was shown for the first time in Barcelona, Joaquín Montero, the actor who had played Ciampa in *Il Berretto a sonagli* presented a farce in one act entitled *Sis autors cerquen un personatge*. This occurred on the Spanish equivalent of April Fools' Day, 28 December 1923. Luigi De Filippo, who reports this in his article "Pirandello in Spagna" (*Nuova Antologia*, 1964), relates that he was unable to find the manuscript.

INDEX